CASES
in Management Accounting and Control Systems
Fourth Edition

BRANDT R. ALLEN
E. RICHARD BROWNLEE II
MARK E. HASKINS
LUANN J. LYNCH
Darden Graduate School of
Business Administration
University of Virginia

PEARSON
Prentice
Hall

Upper Saddle River, New Jersey 07458

Acquisitions Editor: Bill Larkin
Editor-in-Chief: Jeff Shelstad
Assistant Editor: Sam Goffinet
Media Project Manager: Caroline Kasterine
Executive Marketing Manager: Beth Toland
Marketing Assistant: Melissa Owens
Managing Editor: John Roberts
Manufacturing Buyer: Michelle Klein
Production Manager: Arnold Vila
Cover Design: JMG Graphics
Printer/Binder: Courier–Bookmart

Pearson Prentice Hall™ is a trademark of Pearson Education, Inc.
Pearson® is a registered trademark of Pearson plc
Prentice Hall® is a registered trademark of Pearson Education, Inc.

Pearson Education LTD.
Pearson Education Singapore, Pte. Ltd
Pearson Education, Canada, Ltd
Pearson Education–Japan
Pearson Education, Upper Saddle River, NJ

Pearson Education Australia PTY, Limited
Pearson Education North Asia Ltd
Pearson Educación de Mexico, S.A. de C.V.
Pearson Education Malaysia, Pte. Lt.

10 9 8 7 6 5 4 3 2 1
ISBN 0-13-570425-1

A HEARTFELT DEDICATION

We are honored to dedicate this Fourth Edition of <u>Cases in Management Accounting and Control Systems</u> to our friend and colleague, the late Dr. William Rotch. For over 35 years, Bill and his wife Jane served the Charlottesville community, the University of Virginia, and the Darden Graduate School of Business Administration with enthusiasm, dignity, and true dedication. As the Johnson and Higgins Professor of Business Administration at the Darden School, Bill taught courses in management accounting, management control systems, and strategic cost management. He also served as the Area Coordinator for Accounting; Chairman of the First-Year Program Committee; Director of the Tayloe Murphy International Business Studies Center; and Associate Dean for Academic Affairs. One of Bill's favorite activities outside of Darden was serving as Chairman of the Board of Trustees of World Learning, Inc. in Brattleboro, Vermont, whose School for International Training includes the William Rotch Learning Center, which consists of classrooms, a library, and a career development center.

Bill enjoyed all aspects of academia – from athletic events to entertaining students in his home. He was a rigorous scholar, a devoted teacher, and a superb casewriter. His interest in writing teaching cases led to the first edition of this casebook, published over 20 years ago. We are pleased to carry on the casewriting tradition he began through the publication of this fourth edition. *Bill, this one's for you.*

Brandt R. Allen
E. Richard Brownlee, II
Mark E. Haskins
Luann J. Lynch

CONTENTS

PART III: FUNDAMENTALS OF PRODUCT AND SERVICE COSTING

PART IV: MANAGEMENT CONTROL SYSTEMS: BASIC VARIANCE ANALYSIS

PART V: MANAGEMENT CONTROL SYSTEMS: PLANNING, BUDGETING, AND STRATEGIC PROFITABILITY ANALYSIS

PART VI: MANAGEMENT CONTROL SYSTEMS: PERFORMANCE MEASUREMENT AND INCENTIVE SYSTEMS

PREFACE

Managers need accurate, timely, and relevant information in order to understand what is really going on in their businesses. They can use this information as a basis for assessing the extent to which assets are protected, as a means for assessing performance, and as a basis on which to make numerous business decisions. A great deal of the information managers require is financial in nature, and a significant part of such financial information is accounting related. We view a well-designed management accounting and control system as being an essential component of a well-managed company. In fact, there are times when we think it can provide a competitive advantage.

Our primary objective in writing this casebook was to create a collection of teaching cases that are interesting, thought-provoking and relevant to contemporary business situations. In designing courses pertaining to management accounting and control systems, we take the perspective that the materials used and the topics covered should allow students to gain an appreciation for the extent to which management accounting and control information can facilitate both operating and strategic decisions. Our experience has been, however, that the managerial relevance of such information is frequently not at all obvious to students. One reason for this is the tendency for courses to place too much emphasis on the accounting and not enough emphasis on the management.

We advocate broadening and strengthening the management dimensions of management accounting and control courses, and doing so without sacrificing essential accounting content. One very effective way to accomplish this objective is to select topics and materials that demonstrate how costs, cost analysis, and planning and performance measurement can be useful to managers in making operating and strategic decisions. This was our intent in writing <u>Cases in Management Accounting and Control Systems, 4th edition</u>.

CASE ORGANIZATION

As shown below, we have organized this casebook into six parts. Part One contains some suggestions for ways to begin a management accounting and control course such that its managerial relevance becomes obvious to students right away. Parts Two through Six address a variety of management accounting and control topics, beginning with understanding costs and cost behaviors and ending with performance measurement and incentive systems.

Part I	Introduction to Management Accounting and Control
Part II	Understanding Costs and Cost Behaviors
Part III	Fundamentals of Product and Service Costing
Part IV	Management Control Systems: Basic Variance Analysis

In the remainder of this Preface, we discuss the purpose and content of each of the six parts in detail. At the end, we have included a note to students.

Part I: Introduction to Management Accounting and Control

We recommend two alternatives that we find particularly effective in introducing a management accounting and control course. *Breezy Boat Company* is a one-page case that can be used effectively on the first day of the course to stimulate students' thinking regarding how accounting information can facilitate management decision-making. Students are presented with a description of the Breezy Boat Company, and are asked to consider what management decisions might be facilitated by having good accounting information, the types of accounting information that might be helpful, and the process by which such data might be obtained.

Our second suggestion is the textbook novel Code Blue, which provides a two-day course introduction. Code Blue, 3rd edition, written by Richard McDermott and Kevin Stocks, is the story of a consultant who assumes the role of interim hospital administrator for a community hospital at a time when the hospital is struggling with major financial challenges brought about by a changing healthcare environment. The interim administrator is faced with the responsibility of returning the hospital to profitability and avoiding closure. The novel profiles the challenges he faces in designing and implementing a cost accounting system to facilitate hospital management's operating and strategic decisions, performance assessment, and financial management during this difficult time. While the textbook novel is not included in this casebook, we include in the instructor's manual a teaching plan for using the novel in the accounting classroom.

Whether one opts for the one-day introduction using *Breezy Boat Company* or the more extensive two-day approach using the textbook novel Code Blue, students gain a true appreciation for how management accounting data support management decision-making. Our experience has been that once students gain that appreciation, their learning is significantly enhanced and their interest and enthusiasm for the course content increases dramatically.

Part II: Understanding Costs and Cost Behaviors

The cases in Part II deal with the nature of costs and cost behaviors, cost-volume-profit analysis, relevant costs, opportunity costs, sunk costs, and breakeven analysis. Relevant costs are expected future costs that change as a result of the decision being considered or that differ among alternative courses of action. Relevant costs must meet two criteria: (1) they must be expected to occur in the future, and (2) they must differ among alternative courses of action. Two important costing concepts that are related to the notion of relevant costs are sunk costs and opportunity costs. Sunk costs are costs that have already been incurred. They cannot be changed regardless of the course of action selected. Therefore, they are irrelevant in choosing among alternative courses of action. Opportunity costs are the contribution to income that is foregone by not choosing an alternative use for a resource. Because opportunity costs pertain to the future, if they differ among alternative courses of action, they are relevant in choosing among those alternatives.

When making a decision, managers would draw the same conclusion if they use only relevant data as they would draw if they used all of the applicable available data. However, making decisions using only the relevant data streamlines the decision-making process. It allows decisions to be made even when managers don't have all of the company's financial information. In addition, it focuses management's attention on the information that matters rather than on information that is irrelevant to the decision.

Frequently, it is the behavior of various costs that help managers determine whether such costs are relevant to a decision. Why? Because variable costs change in total in proportion to changes in activity level, whereas fixed costs remain unchanged, in the short run, regardless of changes in activity level.

Understanding the concepts of relevant costs, sunk costs, opportunity costs, and cost behavior is crucial to making good management decisions. The cases in this section of the book illustrate the use of these concepts in a variety of decision contexts, including outsourcing, accepting special orders, determining product mix, setting prices, and optimizing the use of constrained resources. The *FinePrint Company (A), (B), and (C)* series provides an excellent basic introduction to the concepts of cost behavior and relevant costs in the context of a decision regarding whether or not to accept a special order, and in the context of an outsourcing decision. *Sparta Glass Products, Blackheath Manufacturing Company*, and *Monroe Clock Company (A)* demonstrate the use of cost behaviors and relevant costs in a pricing decision. *Graphics, Inc. (A)* considers a similar decision in the format of a "cost game" that students are asked to play. *Giberson's Glass Studio* considers the impact of constrained resources on costs relevant to a decision about product mix, and it raises the issue of the relevance of cost allocation in a business situation where almost all of the costs are fixed. *The Horizon Insurance Agency* pertains to an outsourcing decision. Finally, the remaining cases explore more generally the concepts of relevant costs and sunk costs in a services environment (*Greenlawn Commercial Package Business*, and *The Craddock Cup*) and in a manufacturing environment (*The Saw Blades at Leeds*).

Part III: Fundamentals of Product and Service Costing

The cases in Part III address issues associated with determining the cost of products and services, including overhead allocation, allocation of common costs, and activity-based costing.

The first case, *Lambeth Custom Cabinets (A)*, requires students to record transactions related to product costs in the raw materials inventory, work-in-process inventory, and finished goods inventory accounts. Students are asked to prepare an end-of-period balance sheet to represent the costs of the company's products in the inventory accounts. This case provides a bridge from financial accounting concepts to managerial accounting concepts related to product costs.

Some costs (such as certain material and labor costs) can be traced directly to products. These costs are called *direct costs*. Other costs (such as manufacturing supplies, maintenance costs, occupancy costs, and plant administration, among others) often cannot be traced directly to products. These costs are called *indirect costs,* and they often represent manufacturing *overhead costs*. To obtain the full cost of a product, companies must include all direct costs associated with their products and some amount of indirect costs. The distribution of indirect, or overhead, costs to a product, service, or other unit of output, is called *allocation*.

Traditionally, indirect or overhead costs were accumulated by department and distributed among products in proportion to each product's use of some easily determined resource, typically direct labor. *Shun Electronics Company, Monroe Clock Company (B),* and *Whale Printing Company* focus on determining product costs, including the process of distributing overhead costs among products.

In recent years, however, companies have paid considerable attention to the process of cost allocation. First, pooling costs by department may not promote accurate costing because different costs in any given department might be driven by different activities. Instead of departments, companies have tried grouping overhead costs by type of activity (such as set-up, purchasing, inspection, etc.) which may have clearer cause-and-effect relationships to product costs than do manufacturing departments. Second, direct labor may not be a good indicator of the indirect resources consumed by a product. Therefore, in place of direct labor, companies have begun to use a measure of activity associated with each group of overhead costs to allocate those overhead costs to products or services. For example, the number of production runs might be used to allocate set-up costs, costs of inspection, and other production-run related costs. This focus on activities in allocating overhead costs has become know as *activity-based costing. Narnia, Inc., Monroe Clock Company (B), Breeden Electronics (A), (B), and (C),* and *Zauner Ornaments* all deal with the differences in traditional and activity-based costing in distributing overhead costs in a manufacturing environment. *Finnegan's Garden* introduces the use of activity-based costing to determine service-level profitability. *Data Services at Armistead* illustrates the use of activity-based thinking in distributing costs among different lines of business in ways that support strategic decisions.

Finally, *Wendy's Chili: A Costing Conundrum* addresses the issue of joint costs and the challenge of costing by-products. Wendy's must determine the cost of a bowl of chili in assessing the profitability of each of its products. This task is particularly difficult because chili is made using a by-product of its hamburgers.

Parts IV, V, and VI: Management Control Systems

The primary objective of a company's management control system is to influence its employees to behave in ways that support the strategic objectives of the organization. Management control systems enhance the decision-making process by providing direction and evaluating performance to ensure goals are achieved. Typically, they are formal processes that companies use to implement strategy and effect change.

Control systems facilitate decisions regarding organizational direction and goals and the manner in which they should be achieved. Specifically, plans and budgets establish targets against which performance and progress in achieving goals can be measured. Control systems help measure performance and provide information that facilitates good decision-making. Performance measures should be designed to assess the achievement of a company's desired goals and objectives. If incentives are based on the performance measures, the motivational effects associated with these measures are intensified. In addition, performance measures should relate to the responsibilities of the individuals whose performance they are measuring. For example, if a sales manager's responsibility is to generate profitable business, but the incentive plan is based primarily on increasing sales, the sales manager may be encouraged to generate additional sales regardless of whether the additional business is profitable.

The cases pertaining to management control systems are divided into three sections: basic variance analysis; planning, budgeting, and strategic profitability analysis; and performance measurement and incentive systems.

Part IV: Management Control Systems: Basic Variance Analysis

A common but somewhat narrow view of control systems is one of providing a feedback loop regarding organizational performance. The cases in Part IV illustrate the use of basic variance analysis as a tool to analyze performance and provide feedback. For example, a production manager plans the use of resources to achieve an expected output, then monitors results to see if he or she needs to take corrective action. One of the most commonly used techniques for doing so is the use of variance analysis. We include three cases that can be used to illustrate this technique. *Wilmont Chemical Corporation* focuses on the computation of material and labor variances. *Hydrochem, Inc.* introduces the added complexity of overhead variances in addition to material and labor variances. Finally, *Gomez Electronics, Inc.* provides students with the opportunity to perform a comprehensive variance analysis and to use their analysis to decide whether the company should use a full costing system or a direct costing system for internal purposes.

Part V: Management Control Systems: Planning, Budgeting, and Strategic Profitability Analysis

The cases in Part V provide the opportunity for in-depth discussion of important issues pertaining to planning and budgeting (including flexible budgeting techniques), and to strategic profitability analysis.

With *Blackheath Manufacturing Company—Revisited*, students are asked to prepare a production budget and a budgeted income statement, balance sheet, and statement of cash flow using information regarding the company's product costs and sales forecasts. This case provides students with an excellent overview of the steps involved in the preparation of a budget.

Several cases in Part V address strategic profitability analysis, and they also require a reconciliation of actual to planned results in a way that highlights the impact of important strategic factors on the difference. These cases are *The Squeaky Horn* (music industry), *Charley's Family Steak House (A), (B), and (C)* (restaurant industry), *Bellaire Clinical Labs, Inc. (A) and (B)* (laboratory testing industry), *Distillers Delight in the U.K.* (beverage industry), and *EntertainmentNow.com* (entertainment industry).

The *Oriole Furniture (A)* case describes a typical annual budgeting process for a division within a company. Students are presented with a situation in which a division is falling well short of its budget during the year, and they are asked to consider actions the company might take mid-year to help ensure it reaches its budget by year-end. The case challenges students to consider the purpose of budgets and to discover that ultimately the budget must be linked to realistic plans and strategies or it becomes a meaningless exercise. Finally, the *Consumer Service Company (A)* case addresses ethical issues associated with negotiating a profit plan.

The cases in Part VI address issues associated with performance measurement and incentive systems. Several of these cases focus on the choice of performance measures. First, *Performance Measurement at Thomas J. Lipton* provides the opportunity to address the challenges surrounding the choice of performance measures in general, and the surrounding use of ROI as a performance measure in particular. This case requires students to compare and contrast the benefits related to the use of ROI and Residual Income as performance measures. It also requires students to develop an understanding of alternative measures of income and investment used in the calculation of each of these metrics. Second, *Valmont Industries, Inc.* presents students with the decision of whether or not to adopt EVA™[1] as part of a change in strategic focus. Third, *Maverick Lodging* provides students the opportunity to examine the design and implementation of a balanced scorecard by a hotel management company. Students must identify the pros and cons of both financial and nonfinancial performance measures, and they are asked to evaluate the company's overall balanced scorecard in light of the organization's strategic approach to the marketplace.

Two cases focus on some interesting issues surrounding transfer pricing decisions. Specifically, *Lynchburg Foundry: The Ductile Dilemma* deals with transfer pricing in a manufacturing environment within the context of the castings industry; *Xyberspace Consulting, Inc.* deals with pricing shared services within the context of a consulting firm.

Both the *Bay Industries* and *Mountain Lumber Company* cases address issues associated with incentive compensation. Bay Industries challenges students to distribute a bonus pool among division managers. They must grapple with performance measures, controllability of factors affecting performance measures, benchmarks against which to compare performance, and objective versus subjective performance assessment. *Mountain Lumber Company* asks students to evaluate a performance measurement and incentive plan for a lumber company. They must consider the complexity of the plan, the proportion of compensation that is incentive-based, the appropriateness of certain performance measures, and the shape of the reward function. This case can be used to introduce issues related to performance measurement and compensation, and it can also serve to address a comprehensive set of issues at the end of a module pertaining to performance measurement and incentive systems.

TO THE STUDENT

Analyzing cases is primarily a process of asking and answering questions. In studying cases, the art and skill of asking the right questions is often as important as being able to answer them. For some cases, the questions are obvious, but for most cases, there will be more questions to explore than may be apparent at first.

Some of the cases in this casebook have questions listed at the end of the case; other cases do not contain a list of questions. Moreover, your instructor may or may not provide questions for you. Your assignment may simply be to analyze the case, draw conclusions, and be prepared to present your recommendations. If so, you need to

---

[1]EVA™ is a trademark of Stern Stewart & Co., New York, New York.

develop your own list of questions. One set of answers may lead to another set of questions, and so on. The process is somewhat like that of peeling an onion to get at the heart of the matter. It sharpens your analytical abilities and sets management accounting and control in the context of real business issues that require thoughtful decisions. We hope you enjoy the learning journey you are about to begin.

Brandt R. Allen
E. Richard Brownlee, II
Mark E. Haskins
Luann J. Lynch

ACKNOWLEDGMENTS

The collection of cases in this book has been made possible by the collaborative efforts of many individuals. We would like to acknowledge those who have contributed to the production of the works herein.

First, this book would not have been possible without the contribution of the late Professor William Rotch. We include in the casebook several cases that he wrote. He also has had a profound influence on many of the cases included in the book.

Second, Professor Francis J. Spreng of McKendree College was the original author of the following cases:

Lambeth Custom Cabinets (A)
Blackheath Manufacturing Company
Blackheath Manufacturing Company – Revisited

Third, the following Darden Graduate Business School faculty wrote or participated in the writing of the following cases:

Sparta Glass Products	Professor Sherwood Frey
Data Services at Armistead	Professor John Colley
Consumer Service Company (A)	Professor Robert Sack
Valmont Industries, Inc.	Professor Kenneth Eades

Fourth, we are pleased to recognize the following students who wrote several of the cases under the supervision of one of the authors. Kristy Lilly and Liz Smith contributed to *The Craddock Cup, Finnegan's Garden, Zauner Ornaments, The Squeaky Horn*, and *EntertainmentNow.com*. Karen Whitney contributed to *Maverick Lodging*. Robert Galinsky assisted with *Xyberspace Consulting, Inc.* In addition, *Greenlawn Commercial Package Business* and *The Saw Blades at Leeds* are based on issues and ideas contained in an old IMEDE case, *Stardust Grinder Company*.

Fifth, we would also like to acknowledge the support provided by University of Virginia's Darden Graduate School of Business Administration. We appreciate the financial support for case development provided by the University of Virginia Darden School Foundation. We would like to thank Kristy Lilly and Liz Smith for helping with revisions of earlier versions of many of the cases included in the book. We also would like to recognize Debbie Quarles, Karen Harper, Kathy Shelton, Liz Tallon, and Marie Payne for assistance in preparing the materials for publication. All of these individuals were valuable members of the team.

In addition, many companies deserve thanks for their willingness to be documented and scrutinized in order to enrich the education of future business leaders.

Most of the cases have been used in class with degree students and/or executives. This use often has resulted in changes to increase clarity and to make the cases more effective in achieving their learning objectives. We are grateful to all of the individuals who contributed to the content of this book.

PART I

INTRODUCTION TO MANAGEMENT ACCOUNTING AND CONTROL

BREEZY BOAT COMPANY

Cost accounting concerns the procedure for recording, organizing, analyzing, and reporting costs. Consider the operation of the Breezy Boat Company as described below and decide what cost information would be useful to the managers of the company and how they should go about getting it.

The Breezy Boat Company is beginning to manufacture two models of boats, nine- and twelve-foot sail boats, and is planning to sell the boats through dealers in the South and Mid-Atlantic states. The manufacturing process consists of designing and contracting for the manufacture of a mold for each size, applying fiberglass to the mold, curing and finishing the hull, and mounting the purchased hardware. Boats can be produced at the rate of about eight a day on each mold (one shift) and a mold will make 2,000 - 4,000 boats before it wears out.

There are two manufacturing departments, each with a foreman. One is the molding department, which carries the boats through the finishing work in the hull; the other is the assembly department, which installs the hardware and packs the mast, sail, and fittings ready for shipment.

When the plant is running one shift, there are six people working in the molding department and four in the assembly department; one person runs the warehouse with attached receiving and shipping operations, and there are two people in the clean-up crew. The office staff consists of one engineer who works on product design and production methods, the president, the sales manager, a production manager, and four people handling clerical duties including billing, payroll, and payables.

Monthly factory payroll with the full complement enumerated is about $30,000 a month; other payroll comes to around $12,000 a month. Material, purchased parts, and amortized mold costs for 320 boats—one shift production for one month—is about $53,000. Overhead per month when operating at the one shift level is estimated to be $17,000, excluding payroll. Sales revenue from 320 boats would be around $115,000.

Using your imagination to picture the operations of the Breezy Boat Company, make your list of the decisions or activities for which you would want to have cost information. Then try to outline a method by which this cost information could be obtained, disregarding for the moment the cost of operating your information gathering system.

PART II

UNDERSTANDING COSTS AND COST BEHAVIORS

FINEPRINT COMPANY (A)

John Johnson hung up the phone and began to contemplate the offer he had just received. Abbie Jenkins, a friend of Johnson's and the owner of a small company in nearby Keswick, Virginia, had just called to see if Johnson's printing company, FinePrint Company, could accommodate a special printing order next month.

COMPANY BACKGROUND

Johnson's company, FinePrint Company, printed elaborate high-quality color brochures in its facility located in Charlottesville, Virginia. It primarily served other businesses in the central Virginia area, although it did have some clients in southwest Virginia and as far east as the Chesapeake Bay region of the state. Monthly production at its Charlottesville facility was running at around full capacity of 150,000 brochures per month. John Johnson owned and managed the company. He employed one sales representative and one printing press operator, although he frequently relied on temporary labor to help in the printing process as needed to accommodate any changes in printing volume. John felt that many of his costs were fixed, but that some costs varied with the number of brochures he printed and sold. **Exhibit 1** contains information related to FinePrint's monthly operating costs for the company's current activity level of 150,000 brochures per month.

The company typically priced its printing services at an average of $17 per 100 brochures printed. Historically, Johnson had encountered little variation in pricing from job to job, although occasionally, special situations did arise. He wondered how he should handle those special situations. He didn't have a "rule of thumb" he could apply, but he wished he could find one.

THE SPECIAL ORDER

In her phone call, Abbie Jenkins indicated that she needed a special job printed next month. She needed 25,000 brochures related to a new product for distribution at three trade shows she was attending. When John quoted Abbie the usual price of $17 per 100 brochures, Abbie sighed. "John, I know that FinePrint does a high-quality job, but I'm short on funds right now because I have spent so much on getting this new product up and running. I can't go any higher than $10 per 100 brochures on this job. If you can't do it for that, I'll have to go to someone else. I'm sure the brochures won't look as nice, but that's all I've got to spend."

John was enthused about the potential business, but when he inquired about whether Abbie would have future printing needs that FinePrint could help with, Abbie expressed doubt. "We just don't do much of this type of stuff. This is the first material we've had printed like this in years, and we're only doing it because we're trying to get this new product off the ground. I suspect this will be the last for a long while."

John knew he didn't have the capacity at the moment to handle the special order. And, $10 per 100 brochures sounded low. John replied, "Let me look into this. I'm not sure we can do it for $10, but I'll be glad to think about it. I'll give you a call back in a couple of days." John realized that with this order he wouldn't have to pay his sales representative the typical sales commission of $1 per 100 brochures, but that $1 savings wouldn't begin to make up for the lower price.

Exhibit 1

FINEPRINT COMPANY (A)

Summary of Monthly Operating Costs

	Monthly costs at 150,000 volume
Manufacturing costs:	
Direct material – variable	$ 6,000
Direct labor – variable	1,500
Direct labor – fixed	3,000
Manufacturing overhead – variable	1,500
Manufacturing overhead – fixed	3,375
Total manufacturing costs	$15,375
Non-manufacturing costs:	
Sales – variable	1,500
Sales – fixed	1,875
Corporate – fixed	3,750
Total non-manufacturing costs	$ 7,125
Total costs	$22,500

FINEPRINT COMPANY (B)

John Johnson listened intently as Ernest Bradley, sitting across the table in Johnson's office, outlined his proposal. Ernest Bradley, the owner of a local one-room printing operation in Charlottesville, Virginia called SmallPrint Shop, had stopped by to see if Johnson's printing company, FinePrint Company, could use some help printing color brochures over the next few months.

COMPANY BACKGROUND

Johnson's company, FinePrint Company, printed elaborate high-quality color brochures in its facility located in Charlottesville, Virginia. It primarily served other businesses in the central Virginia area, although it did have some clients in southwest Virginia and as far east as the Chesapeake Bay region of the state. Monthly production at its Charlottesville facility was running at around full capacity of 150,000 brochures per month. John Johnson owned and managed the company. He employed one sales representative and one printing press operator, although he frequently relied on temporary labor to help in the printing process as needed to accommodate any changes in printing volume. John felt that many of his costs were fixed, but that some costs varied with the number of brochures he printed and sold. **Exhibit 1** contains information related to FinePrint's monthly operating costs for the company's current activity level of 150,000 brochures per month.

THE OUTSOURCING OPPORTUNITY

Ernest Bradley owned a local one-room printing operation called SmallPrint Shop. His largest customer had just informed him that it was going out of business and would no longer need his printing services. Most of SmallPrint's customers were small companies needing basic printing services in small quantities. But several of his customers, including his largest customer, used his services for both basic printing services and more elaborate work, including color brochures. Ernest had a long-standing relationship with the customer's owner and had purchased the small printing press he used for color brochures partially to serve this customer's needs. He wasn't sure how he was going to get enough business to make up for this loss, especially since he primarily was known for his basic printing services rather than printing elaborate brochures.

Ernest decided to stop by to talk with John Johnson, owner of FinePrint Company. "I've had some bad luck. My largest customer just informed me that it is closing its doors. I've been doing their color printing work for several years, and their closing leaves me with a lot of idle capacity. I wonder if you have any extra brochure printing I can help with. I'd be happy to do it really cheaply, just to keep my press going. I would go as low as $8 per 100 brochures. And I could handle 30,000 brochures for you next month."

John thought that $8 per 100 brochures sounded like a good deal. He wasn't sure that even he could print that cheaply. And he knew that SmallPrint did a good job. He had used them before. They did high quality work, and were dependable.

Exhibit 1

FINEPRINT COMPANY (B)

Summary of Monthly Operating Costs

	Monthly costs at 150,000 volume
Manufacturing costs:	
Direct material – variable	$ 6,000
Direct labor – variable	1,500
Direct labor – fixed	3,000
Manufacturing overhead – variable	1,500
Manufacturing overhead – fixed	3,375
Total manufacturing costs	$15,375
Non-manufacturing costs:	
Sales – variable	1,500
Sales – fixed	1,875
Corporate – fixed	3,750
Total non-manufacturing costs	$ 7,125
Total costs	$22,500

FINEPRINT COMPANY (C)

John Johnson thought about both offers he had received last week. First, he had to turn down Abbie Jenkins' special request for 25,000 brochures at $10 per 100 brochures. FinePrint just didn't have the capacity to produce 25,000 brochures at such a low price, especially since it didn't seem to have the potential to generate any future business beyond the special order. After some analysis, Johnson had realized that if he had the capacity to handle the 25,000 brochures, it would be a profitable order for FinePrint because a $10 price was greater than FinePrint's variable costs of printing the brochures. But, since the company was operating at full capacity, he just couldn't afford to drop his regular business to handle Abbie's request. Next, he had to turn down Ernest Bradley's offer to handle printing 30,000 brochures for FinePrint for $8 per 100 brochures. After considering that offer, Johnson had realized that FinePrint's variable costs of printing the brochures were even lower than the $8 per 100 brochures that Bradley was offering. So it really didn't make sense for FinePrint to outsource any printing to Bradley's company, SmallPrint Shop.

John wondered if he should call Ernest Bradley and let him know that Abbie Jenkins had a special printing request that he might be interested in. Then, when it occurred to him that Abbie was offering to pay $10 per 100 brochures, and Ernest was offering to print them for $8 per 100 brochures, Johnson thought, "Why shouldn't FinePrint be the one to get the $2 difference?" If he could outsource 25,000 brochures to SmallPrint, then he could print the 25,000 brochures that Abbie wanted.

John decided to spend some time that evening to determine if that would be profitable for FinePrint. He hoped that Abbie hadn't found someone else to do her special order. He also hoped that Ernest hadn't found another printing company that was interested in his help.

SPARTA GLASS PRODUCTS

In early August 2002, Christina Matthews, the product manager for nonglare glass at Sparta Glass Products (SGP), met with Robert Alexander, the controller of the Specialty Glass Division, to review the product's performance and prepare a pricing recommendation for the coming quarter. Once approved by the division president, the price would be announced and, as was customary in this segment of the glass industry, adhered to for at least 90 days.

INDUSTRY AND COMPANY BACKGROUND

The flat-glass industry was a $10-billion industry worldwide, of which $2.7 billion was generated in the United States. Approximately 57 percent of domestic production was for the construction industry, 25 percent for the automotive industry, and the remaining 18 percent for specialty products ranging from the mundane, like mirrors, to a wide variety of high-tech applications. Among the many technical applications of specialty glasses were solar panels, laminated and tempered safety glasses, heat- and bullet-resistant glasses, electrical and insulating glasses, photo-technical and photo-sensitive glasses, aerospace glass, and cookware. Nonglare glass was a fairly simple specialty product designed to reduce the glare of reflected light. It was used primarily to frame and protect artwork.

With 2001 sales of $345 million, SGP was a midsized, regional glass company serving several niche markets in the southeastern United States. The Specialty Glass Division was one of four divisions, each of which was operated as a profit center. For a number of reasons, SGP enjoyed a dominant market position for nonglare glass in its region: (1) SGP was known for its fast, reliable service, and was willing to deliver glass on short notice at no extra charge in any of a variety of cut-to-order sizes, including the industry-standard delivery size (48-by-96-inch sheets) and all the standard picture-frame sizes; (2) SGP provided an exceptionally high-quality nonglare glass with little light loss and virtually no blemishes; (3) SGP operated its own fleet of delivery vehicles so that delivery times were well managed and shipping charges were kept low; and (4) SGP's salaried sales staff was widely acknowledged for its helpful, courteous service and customer orientation.

The production of nonglare glass, like many other coated-glass products, began with flat glass, the output of one of SGP's other divisions. For such derivative products, company policy was for downstream products to be bought within the company at a market-based price that was adjusted on a quarterly basis. The flat glass was treated by the Specialty Glass Division with a patented coating that provided the desired optical characteristics. This process required specialized equipment that was usable only in the production of nonglare glass. The finished, treated glass was then cut to order, packaged, and shipped.

The business outlook for nonglare glass had been flat for the past several years, but was expected to return to historical growth rates as the economy came out of its slump. Last September, in response to increased corporate pressure to improve margins, Matthews and Alexander increased the price of nonglare glass by slightly less than 10 percent, from $2.15 to $2.36 per square foot. This pricing decision was one of many made during the past year in anticipation of the company's considerable capital requirements to fund a recently approved long-term expansion and modernization program. At the time of the price increase, Matthews and Alexander hoped that competitors would follow SGP's lead and increase their prices as well.

Unfortunately, SGP's competitors held the line on the price of nonglare glass, and Matthews believed that SGP's significant loss of market share in the last nine months was due solely to SGP's price change, as little else had changed in the industry during that period. To document the decline, Matthews prepared **Exhibit 1**, which presents the sales-volume and price-history data for nonglare glass in SGP's market region for the past eight quarters. Looking ahead, Matthews believed that a reasonable forecast of total regional volume for the fourth quarter of 2002 (usually the best quarter of the year) was 920,000 square feet. On the one hand, Matthews believed that if SGP were to return to the $2.15 price, it could regain a major portion of its original market share with sales of 275,000 square feet. On the other hand, if competitors' prices were not met, she feared a further decline. Nonetheless, because of SGP's outstanding reputation in the crafts marketplace, she reasoned that a sufficient number of customers would stay with SGP and prevent sales from falling below 150,000 square feet, even at the current price of $2.36 per square foot.

While reflecting on the upcoming meeting with Matthews, Alexander realized that price would be the major topic of discussion, so he had his staff prepare a schedule of expected costs to produce nonglare glass over a wide range of production levels. This schedule is presented in **Exhibit 2**.

THE MEETING

During their meeting, Matthews and Alexander together reviewed the historical sales levels and pricing data as well as the anticipated-cost schedule. They began by discussing the cost schedule. Matthews noticed that unit costs grew with increasing volumes, but Alexander said that the increasing unit costs were simply the result of the company's cost-allocation system. Next, Alexander asked whether there was any possibility that competitors might reduce their prices below $2.15 per square foot if SGP returned to that price. Matthews replied that she was confident no competitor would do so because all were facing the same general economic conditions resulting from the long recession and several were in particularly tight financial straits. They then discussed whether the pricing decision for nonglare glass would have any repercussions on other Specialty Glass products; both were convinced it would not. Finally, they explored the implications of SGP's returning to the industry price of $2.15 per square foot. Matthews believed recapturing lost market share was essential in order for SGP to maintain its dominant role in the nonglare-glass niche. Alexander, however, was concerned that, at $2.15, the product would show a loss, an outcome that would not be welcomed by senior management.

Exhibit 1

SPARTA GLASS PRODUCTS

Sales-Volume and Price History of Nonglare Glass

		Sales Volume (000 square feet)		Price ($ per square foot)	
Year	Quarter	SGP	Competitors	SGP	Competitors
2000	3	241	443	2.05	2.05
2000	4	313	592	2.05	2.05
2001	1	204	381	2.15	2.15
2001	2	269	513	2.15	2.15
2001	3	251	456	2.15	2.15
2001	4	238	672	2.36	2.15
2002	1	139	474	2.36	2.15
2002	2	162	642	2.36	2.15

Exhibit 2

SPARTA GLASS PRODUCTS

Nonglare Glass:
Estimated Cost per Square Foot at Various Production Volumes

Production volume (000 sq. ft.)	150	175	200	225	250	275	300	325
Direct material	$0.56	$0.56	$0.56	$0.56	$0.56	$0.56	$0.56	$0.56
Direct labor	0.32	0.31	0.30	0.32	0.34	0.36	0.37	0.38
Depreciation	0.27	0.23	0.21	0.18	0.16	0.15	0.14	0.13
Variable manufacturing overhead[1]	0.10	0.09	0.09	0.10	0.10	0.11	0.11	0.11
Fixed manufacturing overhead[2]	0.18	0.17	0.17	0.18	0.19	0.20	0.20	0.21
Shipping	0.11	0.11	0.11	0.11	0.11	0.11	0.11	0.11
Manufacturing cost	$1.54	$1.47	$1.44	$1.45	$1.46	$1.49	$1.49	$1.50
Corporate overhead[3]	0.11	0.11	0.11	0.11	0.12	0.13	0.13	0.13
Selling & general administration[4]	0.69	0.67	0.64	0.65	0.66	0.67	0.67	0.67
Total cost	$2.34	$2.25	$2.19	$2.21	$2.24	$2.29	$2.29	$2.30

[1]Consists of energy and miscellaneous supplies. Allocated as 30 percent of direct labor.

[2]Consists of supervision, insurance, quality assurance. Allocated as 55 percent of direct labor.

[3]Consists of purchasing, security, and data processing. Allocated as 35 percent of direct labor.

[4]Consists of sales-force compensation and corporate administrative support. Allocated as 45 percent of manufacturing cost.

BLACKHEATH MANUFACTURING COMPANY

Blackheath Manufacturing produced a single product called the Great Heath. During the past three weeks, Lee High, the new cost accountant, had observed that production efficiency and input prices were constant but that output varied considerably. These three weeks were thought of as typical by the sales representative, who said that they could be taken as average. Production costs were accumulated and accounted for under seven different groups listed below:

	Units of Output	Direct Materials	Direct Labor	Indirect Labor	Indirect Materials	Electricity	Factory Insurance	Other Overhead
Week 1	400	$300	$550	$180	$300	$115	$125	$310
Week 2	500	375	625	200	300	125	125	360
Week 3	600	450	750	220	300	135	125	410

Lee High thought that this would be an ideal time to do some cost analysis on the Great Heath. Based on the data for three weeks' production costs, he felt it would be possible to identify fixed costs, variable costs, and semivariable costs. Furthermore, Lee wanted to develop some equations which might be useful for managerial decision making. From such equations, it seemed that breakeven volume could be generated. Since production was usually based on orders actually received and since products were shipped immediately upon completion, inventories of work-in-process and finished goods were practically nonexistent. When talking to the sales representative, Lee discovered that on typical orders the selling price of Great Heath was $7.00. During lunch one day, Lee was told by the president that office expenses, including certain selling items, were fixed at $781 per week.

Lee High decided to begin his analysis with income statements for the three weeks:

	Week 1	Week 2	Week 3
Sales	$2,800	$3,500	$4,200
Cost of goods sold	1,830	2,110	2,390
Gross Margin	970	1,390	1,810
Less: other expenses	1,061	1,131	1,201
Net Income	$ (91)	$ 259	$ 609

From these statements, Lee realized that selling more added to profit. He also realized that cost of goods sold per unit seemed to fall as output rose:

---

when sales were 400, then cost of goods sold per unit was $4.57
when sales were 500, then cost of goods sold per unit was $4.22
when sales were 600, then cost of goods sold per unit was $3.98. `

Lee wasn't sure why cost of goods sold per unit should fall, because, after all, the efficiency and input prices had remained the same. He reasoned that there was something odd about the data and decided it would be good to work with some average. Since the three weeks for which Lee had data were thought to be typical, he decided that some "standardize cost information" based on sales of 500 units per week would be very helpful. He derived the following chart:

Useful Data on Great Heath

Average variable cost per unit produced	$2.80
Average fixed cost per unit produced	1.42
	4.22
Average fixed administrative and selling cost per unit	1.56
Commission per unit sold	.70
	6.48
Added amount for rounding error and some "funny" results in data	.12
	$6.60

The following should be kept in mind when selling Great Heath:

1. It costs us $6.60 to deliver a unit of Great Heath, so we make only 40 cents per unit at $7.00 selling price.

2. Decision rule #1 (for sales representative on the road): Never sell Great Heath for less than $6.60 plus a profit margin because at $6.60 we just break even.

3. Decision rule #2 (for direct office sales on which no commission is paid): Never sell Great Heath for less than $5.90 plus a profit margin because at $5.90 we just break even.

Lee was very pleased with his chart, particularly the part about different decision rules. When the chart was finished, Lee passed it on to Mr. Charlton Blackheath, who was the owner, president and chief decision maker at Blackheath Manufacturing. Charlton, who was skeptical of "scientific analysis," studied Lee High's chart and underlying data. That night Charlton said to his lawyer, with whom he was having dinner, "I finally have found the kind of practical fast-track analyst I need. This kid, Lee High, has just developed a set of decision rules that will solve all my pricing and profit problems."

The next day Charlton Blackheath sent a memo to the sales representative and others who were involved in pricing Great Heath. Among other things the memo stated, "Everyone should study Mr. High's chart, especially the decision rules he has generated through complex cost accounting procedures. From now on, all pricing decisions will follow these rules, and under no condition will we price at less than 10 percent above our delivery cost. Therefore, the lowest prices that can be quoted by the sales representative and office force are $7.26/unit and $6.49/unit, respectively. This new policy means the sales representative had better stop taking orders at $7.00 per unit."

When he read the memo, Lee was both pleased and bit disturbed. In the first place, he didn't expect Mr. Blackheath to take his chart so seriously; in the second place, he knew intuitively that any price higher than $7.00 per unit for Great Heath was too high. Lee explained his position to Mr. Blackheath, who in turn informed the sales representative that orders at $7.00 would be OK but nothing less would be accepted.

After this revision in policy, Lee felt better, Blackheath went on vacation, the sales representative was confused, and the members of the office force, who could take orders by phone, were pleased with their new role.

During the next week, the following four sales prospects were available to Blackheath Manufacturing for Great Heath.

1. The sales representative sold 450 units at $7.00 per unit.

2. The sales representative turned down a request from an irregular customer for 50 units at $6.50 per unit because of the $7.00 rule.

3. One telephone order was accepted for $6.50 per unit for 80 units, but another was rejected at $5.75 per unit for 50 units because of the $6.49 rule.

4. Ms. Adelaide Ladywell, a nineteen-year-old file clerk, received a phone call from Maze Woolwich when no one else was in the office. Maze said that he had seen Lee High's data on costs, and since Blackheath could produce more economically than Woolwich, he wanted to order 100 units at $5.50. Furthermore, Maze explained that since he was going out of business, this would be his only order. Adelaide said that $6.50 was the minimum price, but Maze responded that that was just Blackheath double-talk. Ms. Ladywell looked over the data and realized that on a special order like this, $5.50 would be a good price, considering that otherwise Maze Woolwich would produce the 100 units himself. She accepted the order and anticipated a promotion when Mr. Blackheath returned.

At the end of the week, Lee High prepared the following sales-cost report for Mr. Blackheath.

Source	_# of Units_	_Price/Unit_	_Cost/Unit_	_Profit/Unit_
Orders We Accepted				
From sales representative	450	$7.00	$6.60	$.40
Office manager	80	6.50	5.90	.60
Adelaide Ladywell	100	5.50	5.90	(.40)
Orders We Rejected				
From sales representative	50	6.50	6.60	(.10)
Office manager	50	5.75	5.90	(.15)

After Mr. Blackheath looked over the report, he did two things:

1. He called in the sales representative and explained that it would be better for the company to sell 350 units at $8.00/unit than the 450 at $7.00/unit. He went on to say that at $8.00/unit, he would pay a commission of 15% instead of 10%. His reasoning was as follows:

$8.00	Revenue	$7.00	Revenue
	Cost per unit per Lee's		Cost per unit per Lee's
5.90	chart	5.90	chart
2.10	Contribution	1.10	Contribution
1.20	Commission	.70	Commission
$ .90	Clear profit per unit	$ .40	Clear profit per unit
	350 units times .90 per unit equals $315 profit per week		450 units times .40 per unit equals $180 profit per week

The sales representative was instructed to sell at $8.00 and guaranteed at least a commission of 15 percent on the sales of 350 units.

2. Blackheath fired Adelaide Ladywell over the Maze Woolwich mess. He said, "No one is going to cause me to lose 40 cents per unit."

REQUIRED

What do you think about the whole situation? Develop a proper set of decision rules.

GRAPHICS, INC. (A)

You are the owner of Graphics, Inc., a local printing company which competes against three other similar companies. Business is obtained by successfully bidding (low bid wins) on jobs offered to all the local printers. Your print shop consists of several departments and the press department, with its one big machine, is where most of your costs are. This department is where the key resource resides and it is also the "bottleneck" for production scheduling.

Your company normally expects to run a 40-hour week. A second shift is not possible but overtime of up to two hours a day is possible for the press and the four press workers. To maintain worker satisfaction, however, company policy is not to run overtime in two consecutive weeks. Company policy is also not to lay off workers in slack times. Overtime pay for the press workers is 150% of normal wages.

Exhibit 1 shows a normal weekly budget for operating costs. Paper is not shown because on some work the customer supplies the paper and on the remaining jobs you simply charge customers your cost for the paper used on their jobs.

GETTING TO WORK

It is the last week of January and it is time to bid on the jobs being offered for the first part of next month. There is a sizeable amount of stress induced by having to fully utilize your company's resources through a sealed bid process on jobs made available to you and your direct competitors. There is the thrill though, of winning profitably priced jobs that keep the press department humming at full capacity. To date, you have been very adept at striking the right balance between low, but profitable, bids that have kept the company busy. Each new round of bids, however, is always a challenge with smarter, more aggressive moves by your competitors.

The first round of jobs to be bid on have already been made public and are shown in **Exhibit 2**. (Blank bid sheets are provided at the end of the case.) You are confident that at least three more rounds of jobs (there could be more) will be forthcoming and you expect to be a bidder in each of those rounds. It is unclear, however, how many or how big those subsequent jobs will be. (For purposes of this case, the first two rounds of jobs offered to the industry will be made during this last week of January so that the jobs won can be scheduled for production as early as Monday of the first week of February. The third and fourth rounds of bidding will take place as if on Friday of the second week in February where the earliest those jobs can be scheduled is Monday of week three.)

All the first round jobs have due dates ten workdays from February's first Monday. You know that late deliveries carry penalties for each day late. The job listings show estimated machine hours in the press department. The press can run only one job at a time. Because of expensive setup costs, it is not worthwhile switching to another job before the one currently being worked on is finished.

REPORTING PROGRESS AND RESULTS

In preparing for the upcoming flurry of bids, you want to get the company's management team together to develop a bidding strategy. Over the years you have found such a pre-bid meeting useful in getting everyone focused on the task at hand and for refining prior winning strategies and for debriefing and learning from prior loosing strategies. The questions to be discussed are always the same but no less important each time the team meets. For sure, you expect to discuss such questions as: Should we bid on all jobs offered or only a subset? Should we bid with a uniform profit margin on each job or should we vary it across bids? What percent of the hours we bid on should we plan to actually win? At what level of capacity do we want to operate the press department? Do we understand our current cost structure which we believe is similar to that of our competitors?

Once a strategy is agreed on, you have always "tested" it by preparing a budgeted, four-round (i.e., four-week) income statement—after all, a strategy that results in financial losses is not a very good strategy. (Note: Your instructor may ask you to turn in a half-page strategy statement and a budgeted four-week income statement before, or with, your first round bids.) In addition, after round two jobs have been awarded, you plan to take the time to prepare: (1) a production schedule for the jobs you have won; and (2) an interim, two-week income statement. (**Exhibit 3** presents a sample production schedule filled in as if Jobs 1-1, 1-5, 1-10, and 1-12, from the first round of bidding, had been won. Note that Job 1-12 was not finished at the end of week one and the schedule shows that 5 hours of work-in-process was completed on it and 15 hours of work remain for it to be completed. The first job worked on in week two has to then be 1-12.) Based on the circumstances reflected in these two interim reports, you may find it informative to prepare a short memo for the team summarizing the revisions (if any) to the initial bidding strategy. (Note: Your instructor may ask for all three documents at this point and prior to the offering of round three jobs.)

At the end of the fourth week in February, after round-four jobs have been awarded, a final production schedule will have to be prepared in order to tally the February results. This production schedule will need to reflect all jobs won even if it requires scheduling work beyond week four in February. In addition, a final, four-week February income statement will also have to be prepared using the completed-contract method of accounting (i.e., no revenue is recognized until a job is completely finished; costs assignable to partially finished jobs must be capitalized and recorded in the balance sheet work-in-process inventory account and therefore are not included as an expense on the four-week income statement). If, as of the end of the fourth week, the production schedule shows any jobs won not being delivered on time (even for those jobs scheduled in weeks five and beyond), the appropriate late penalty fee must be booked on the four-week income statement. The penalty fee equals $300 per job, per day where any fraction of a day counts as an entire day. Finally, a report must be prepared that analyzes the final financial results in terms of: (a) variance from the original budget, (b) effectiveness of the bidding strategy, and (c) challenges/opportunities presented by your competitors over the course of the bidding rounds.

SEQUENCE OF ACTIVITIES

At a minimum, and in preparation for your management team meeting, you have reviewed your company's current cost structure and given some thought to a bidding strategy that you think might be successful. (Your instructor may have additional requests of you prior to the start of the game.)

Just as you start to the door to head to the meeting, your cell phone rings. You pause, wondering if there is time to take the call. You unsnap the phone from your belt, flip it open, and hear the owner of Precision Printing (PP) on the other end. PP is a large printing company located 250 miles south of you in a large metropolitan area. The owner has been enticing you for months to sell Graphics, Inc. to him. He makes his brief pitch again and you tell him you will call back next week.

As you sit down in your familiar seat at the window-end of the conference room table, getting out of the rat race sounds pretty appealing. You have this odd, blended feeling. Yes, the opportunity to sell is tempting and you think, *If I can land some really profitable jobs during this round of bids that fully occupy our capacity for the next several weeks, I bet PP will increase their offer another 10-15%.* As your team begins to stream into the conference room, your mind races with post-sell-to-PP possibilities and the competitive juices begin to flow.

Exhibit 1

GRAPHICS, INC. (A)

Press Department Budget Per Week

Item

Labor hours per week on the press: 160 (4 workers staff the press department)
Machine hours available per week: 40
(Maximum overtime at time-and-a-half wages for the press workers is 10 machine hours or 40 labor hours.)

Dollar Budget

Press workers	$2,400
Supplies*	1,000
Machine operating and maintenance*	1,400
Machine depreciation**	1,000
All other manufacturing expenses**	1,400
Administrative and selling expenses**	800
	$8,000

*These items were expected to vary with machine hours.
**These items were expected to remain unchanged with normal variations in volume.

Exhibit 2

GRAPHICS, INC. (A)

Jobs Offered for Bidding-Round #1

Job No.	Day Job is Due*	Estimated Machine Hours for the Job
1-1	10	5
1-2	10	5
1-3	10	5
1-4	10	10
1-5	10	10
1-6	10	10
1-7	10	15
1-8	10	15
1-9	10	15
1-10	10	20
1-11	10	20
1-12	10	20
1-13	10	20
1-14	10	30
		200

*In this and future lists of jobs offered for bidding, the day a job is due is computed from the start of the competition (i.e., the first day of the month).

Note: Customers may discard or ask for rebid on any bid which, in their judgment, is too high or too low.

Bids should be in terms of the total dollars for a job and they should be submitted on the blank forms at the end of the case.

Exhibit 3

GRAPHICS, INC. (A)

Illustrative Production Schedule

Game _____
Team _____

WEEK 1
Days 1-5

Job	Hours	Cumul. Hours
1-1	5	5
1-5	10	15
1-10	20	35
1-12	5	40

Jobs partially completed:

Job	Hours completed	Hours to finish
1-12	5	15

Hours of Overtime Used
(Maximum: 10 machine hours)

WEEK 2
Days 6-10

Job	Hours	Cumul. Hours
1-12	15	15

Jobs partially completed:

Job	Hours completed	Hours to finish

Hours of Overtime Used
(Can be used only if no overtime used in prior week)

WEEK 3
Days 11-15

Job	Hours	Cumul. Hours

Jobs partially completed:

Job	Hours completed	Hours to finish

Hours of Overtime Used
(Can be used only if no overtime used in prior week)

Late Delivery

Job	Day Due	Days Late

WEEK 4
Days 16-20

Job	Hours	Cumul. Hours

Jobs partially completed:

Job	Hours completed	Hours to finish

Hours of Overtime Used
(Can be used only if no overtime used in prior week)

Late Delivery

Job	Day Due	Days Late

WEEK 5
Days 21-25

Job	Hours	Cumul. Hours

Job partially completed:

Job	Hours completed	Hours to finish

Hours of Overtime Used
(Can be used only if no overtime used in prior week)

Late Delivery

Job	Day Due	Days Late

GRAPHICS, INC. (A)

Bidding Sheet

Game _____

Round No. _____

Team _____

Job No.	_Amount Bid_
1	
2	
3	
4	
5	
6	
7	
8	
9	
10	
11	
12	
13	
14	
15	
16	

Bid in total dollars for each job bid on

GRAPHICS, INC. (A)

Bidding Sheet

Game _____

Round No. _____

Team _____

Job No.	Amount Bid
1	
2	
3	
4	
5	
6	
7	
8	
9	
10	
11	
12	
13	
14	
15	
16	

Bid in total dollars for each job bid on

GRAPHICS, INC. (A)

Bidding Sheet

Game _____

Round No. _____

Team _____

Job No.	_Amount Bid_
1	
2	
3	
4	
5	
6	
7	
8	
9	
10	
11	
12	
13	
14	
15	
16	

Bid in total dollars for each job bid on

GRAPHICS, INC. (A)

Budgeted Four-Week Income Statement

Game _____

Team _____

Budget at _____ *Machine Hrs.*

Sales
Cost of goods sold:
   Labor
   Overtime
   Supplies
   Machine operation & maintenance
   Depreciation
   Other manufacturing
     Total cost of goods manufactured
   Less work in process (if any) end week 4
   Total cost of goods sold

Gross margin

Administrative & selling
Late charges

Profit or (Loss)

GRAPHICS, INC. (A)

Interim Two-Week Income Statement

Using estimated costs per week and actual sales and machine hours

Game _____

Team _____

Budget at _____ *Machine Hrs.*

Sales
Cost of goods sold:
    Labor
    Overtime
    Supplies
    Machine operation & maintenance
    Depreciation
    Other manufacturing
    Total cost of goods manufactured
    Less work in process (if any) end week 2
    Total cost of goods sold

Gross margin

Administrative & selling
Late charges

Profit or (Loss)

This form is to be filled out after two rounds of bidding have been completed and scheduled.

GRAPHICS, INC. (A)

Final Four-Week Income Statement Report

Game _____

Team _____

	Budget at _____ Machine hrs.	Actual at _____ Machine hrs.	Variance From Budget	Explanation
Sales				
Cost of goods sold:				
Labor				
Overtime				
Supplies				
Machine operation & maintenance				
Depreciation				
Other manufacturing				
Total cost of goods manufactured				
Less work in process (if any) end week 4				
Total cost of goods sold				
Gross margin				
Administrative & selling				
Late charges				
Profit or (Loss)				

GRAPHICS, INC. (A)

Production Schedule

Game _____
Team _____

WEEK 1
Days 1-5

Job	Hours	Cumul. Hours

Jobs partially completed:

Job	Hours completed	Hours to finish

Hours of Overtime Used
(Maximum: 10 machine hours)

WEEK 2
Days 6-10

Job	Hours	Cumul. Hours

Jobs partially completed:

Job	Hours completed	Hours to finish

Hours of Overtime Used
(Can be used only if no overtime used in prior week)

WEEK 3
Days 11-15

Job	Hours	Cumul. Hours

Jobs partially completed:

Job	Hours completed	Hours to finish

Hours of Overtime Used
(Can be used only if no overtime used in prior week)

Late Delivery

Job	Day Due	Days Late

WEEK 4
Days 16-20

Job	Hours	Cumul. Hours

Jobs partially completed:

Job	Hours completed	Hours to finish

Hours of Overtime Used
(Can be used only if no overtime used in prior week)

Late Delivery

Job	Day Due	Days Late

WEEK 5
Days 21-25

Job	Hours	Cumul. Hours

Jobs partially completed:

Job	Hours completed	Hours to finish

Hours of Overtime Used
(Can be used only if no overtime used in prior week)

Late Delivery

Job	Day Due	Days Late

GRAPHICS, INC. (A)

Production Schedule

Game _____

Team _____

WEEK 1
Days 1-5

Job	Hours	Cumul. Hours

Jobs partially completed:

Job	Hours completed	Hours to finish

Hours of Overtime Used
(Maximum: 10 machine hours)

WEEK 2
Days 6-10

Job	Hours	Cumul. Hours

Jobs partially completed:

Job	Hours completed	Hours to finish

Hours of Overtime Used
(Can be used only if no overtime used in prior week)

WEEK 3
Days 11-15

Job	Hours	Cumul. Hours

Jobs partially completed:

Job	Hours completed	Hours to finish

Hours of Overtime Used
(Can be used only if no overtime used in prior week)

Late Delivery

Job	Day Due	Days Late

WEEK 4
Days 16-20

Job	Hours	Cumul. Hours

Jobs partially completed:

Job	Hours completed	Hours to finish

Hours of Overtime Used
(Can be used only if no overtime used in prior week)

Late Delivery

Job	Day Due	Days Late

WEEK 5
Days 21-25

Job	Hours	Cumul. Hours

Jobs partially completed:

Job	Hours completed	Hours to finish

Hours of Overtime Used
(Can be used only if no overtime used in prior week)

Late Delivery

Job	Day Due	Days Late

GIBERSON'S GLASS STUDIO

When Felicia Coates, a first-year MBA student at the University of Virginia's Darden Graduate Business School, first visited Giberson's Glass Studio in April 2003, she found the business files in disarray and the proprietor wondering how much longer he could stay in business. Records of production and data on product costs were nonexistent, and the only financial records were a checkbook, unreconciled bank statements, and several tax returns. Edward Engelhardt Giberson, the proprietor, was a skilled glassblower who had recently moved his studio from Charlotte, North Carolina, to Charlottesville, Virginia. Giberson's wife had always taken care of the books and other records, but the bookkeeping had been neglected since their divorce the previous year. Even though his glass work sold well during his first year in Charlottesville, Giberson was quickly draining his limited financial resources. He did not expect a big salary, but estimated that he would need a minimum of $25,000 a year in wages and benefits. Notwithstanding his lack of organized financial information, he knew that something needed to change if he were to avoid bankruptcy. In desperation, he contacted the student consulting group at the Darden School, and Felicia Coates volunteered to assist Mr. Giberson.

PRODUCTION PROCESS

Giberson produced fine, hand-blown glassware in the form of tumblers, paperweights, patterned glasses, and vases. In a refurbished shed behind the McGuffey Art Center in historic downtown Charlottesville, Giberson fashioned hand-blown items from molten glass gathered on a long metal blowpipe. Using his own breath to shape the object, Giberson formed each vessel by a process analogous to blowing honey on the end of a straw. Once the bottom was formed, a metal punty was attached, and the vessel was broken from the pipe. After reheating, the lip was trimmed, fire-polished, and formed. When the object was broken off from the punty, the characteristic "punty mark" was left. The glass was first annealed (a slowed process of cooling) for several hours in an oven to relieve the stress and was later ground, sanded, and polished before shipping.

CHARGING

Production began each week by melting a 200-pound batch of glass in the furnace. Each batch contained about 80 percent new raw materials and chemicals and no more than 20 percent cullet, which was clear scrap glass from the previous week. Giberson carefully monitored the proportion of the ingredients in each batch, including the amount of cullet used, because he believed that any deviation from the desired mix and batch size resulted in an inferior quality of glass. Therefore, although he usually had to dispose of a considerable amount of good unused glass at the end of each week, he was reluctant to reduce the quantity of the batch below 200 pounds. **Table 1** shows the typical recipe for a batch.

Table 1
Materials for a Batch

Batch Mix	Cost/Unit	Cost/Batch
100 lbs. sand	$35/ton	$1.75
38 lbs. soda	$110/700 lbs	5.97
9 lbs. potassium	$105/200 lbs.	4.72
3 lbs. borax	$.50/lb	1.50
14 lbs. lime	$5.50/50 lbs.	1.54
2 lbs. flourispar	$.47/lb	.94
3 lbs. zinc oxide	$1.40/lb	4.20
169 lbs.		$20.62

Additional Ingredients

20 grams antimony	$5.20/lb.	$.23
40 grams arsenic	$6.50/lb.	.57
		$ .80
	Total	$21.42

Cullet: 31 lbs.

Melting required an entire day, because the materials had to be put in the furnace gradually; the day after was lost to fining, a process that allowed the gas bubbles to escape from the molten batch. Typically, Giberson charged the furnace on Sunday, fined on Monday, and blew glass Tuesday through Saturday. Because the furnace ran continuously and daily oven use was known during the weeks that glass was being blown, total gas used (one of his biggest cost items) was a predictable $1,000 per month.

BLOWING

Lighting the glory hole[1] to bring it up from room temperature to 2,300° F, which took about two hours, was the procedure that began the daily production. Meanwhile, Giberson increased the furnace temperature to get the molten glass up to 1,800° F. About 40 minutes before glassblowing began, he turned on the annealing ovens so that they would be at 850° F when everything else was ready. As the furnace and ovens were heating, Giberson did miscellaneous chores, including grinding and polishing the previous day's production, office work, and general maintenance.

---

[1] Area from which molten glass is gathered.

Giberson usually blew paperweights first, because they were solid and needed more time to relieve stress. He spent approximately two hours on these pieces and on vases. After lunch, he began to make glasses. He worked approximately four hours in the afternoon, making a total of six hours' worth of glassblowing on a typical day. Finished items varied as to their content of glass, as shown in **Table 2**. At week's end, unused glass became cullet or was scrapped. On average, about 50 pounds of unused glass was "dirty scrap" that could not be recycled as cullet. Disposal costs were insignificant, although public concerns over the community landfill and other environmental issues were expected to make glass disposal more difficult and more expensive.

Table 2
Glass Content

Item	Weight/Piece
Patterned glasses	.5 lb.
Paperweights	.9 lb.
Wrapped tumblers	.5 lb.
Vases	.6 lb.

During the forty weeks a year when he blew glass, Giberson worked in his studio almost every day. He did, however, spend considerable time speaking to visitors and friends who dropped by to watch him work. Giberson typically spent some time on Sundays and Mondays doing miscellaneous chores and catching up on grinding, sanding, and polishing that had not been completed during the previous week.

FINISHING AND SHIPPING

Solid glass pieces had to be ground, sanded, and polished before shipping. For one solid piece of glass, 40 percent of the finishing time was spent on the initial grinding, 15 percent on the second grinding, 20 percent on the first sanding, 10 percent on the second sanding, 5 percent on third sanding, and 10 percent on the polishing. Total finishing time averaged 15 minutes per piece. Hollowware pieces required only polishing, with an average of three minutes per piece for glasses and five minutes for vases. The finishing procedure was referred to as "cold time," as contrasted with blowing, which was known as "hot time."

Orders were packed and shipped several times each week as needed. Packaging involved wrapping, boxing, and labeling. It took about 15 minutes to pack a case of twelve glasses, and Giberson used part-time labor for packing, shipping, and general shop cleaning.

QUALITY CONTROL

During the production runs, firsts, seconds, clean scrap, and dirty scrap were produced. Firsts were those objects that met the artist's criteria for a quality piece of art glass. Seconds had some minor flaw, such as a lesser glass quality (too many small bubbles) or a bad break from the punty rod. Some clean scrap became cullet, and the excess was discarded; dirty scrap was always discarded. Seconds required the same hot and cold time as firsts. Only firsts were packed for shipment. Seconds were sold only at the studio, and their number varied with the item being produced. Rarely were items of such inferior quality that they could not at least be sold as seconds.

PRODUCTION TIME

By closely watching the business over a six week period, Felicia estimated that Giberson spent the times shown in **Table 3** for each type of object blown. (Also shown in **Table 3** is the typical production rate for a week.) Thus, wrapped tumblers were his biggest volume item: On average, they took 15 minutes to blow and another 3 minutes to "finish." Giberson did all of the blowing and finishing by himself, although he mentioned to Felicia that he was considering hiring additional part-time labor to do some or all of the finishing.

Table 3
Production Times and Weekly Output

| | Production Time | | Average Weekly Production | |
Item	Hot Time	Cold Time	Firsts	Seconds
Patterned glasses	15 min.	3 min.	18	1
Paperweights	15 min.	15 min.	10	0
Wrapped tumblers	15 min.	3 min.	30	2
Vases	25 min.	5 min.	7	1

Giberson worked a rigorous schedule from September through early June. During the summer, he spent about ten weeks traveling to trade shows where he exhibited his work, and he spent the remaining two weeks of the year vacationing in the mountains.

SALES

Giberson sold firsts directly from his studio in response to customer orders received by phone, by mail, or though the internet. He also received orders at trade shows. The individual prices are shown in **Table 4**. Sales were slightly seasonal, and Giberson almost always had at least a two-week backlog. Seconds, that were available to customers who visited his small studio, sold for the same price as firsts.

Table 4
Per Unit Price List[2]

Item	Price
Patterned glasses	$9.00
Paperweights	$15.00
Wrapped tumblers	$8.00
Vases	$25.00

OPERATING COSTS

In addition to the costs for raw materials and gas, Giberson's business incurred various operating costs (see **Exhibit 1**). With the exception of expenditures for office supplies, hand tools, manufacturing supplies, and part-time labor, operating costs were incurred every month regardless of whether production occurred. Some of the ongoing costs were not incurred evenly throughout the year, and the amounts shown therefore represent monthly averages.

ASSETS AND LIABILITIES

Felicia produced a rough balance sheet for the business as of its inception on September 1, 2002 (see **Exhibit 2**). The most crucial facilities (i.e., the furnace and ovens) had a life span of only two years. The equipment and gas tanks were expected to last eight years and the truck five years. Giberson's truck payments were $205 a month for 36 months beginning in September 2002.

KEY ISSUES AND CONCERNS

The most critical issue facing Mr. Giberson was his rapidly deteriorating financial position. He had only a few thousand dollars of personal savings left, and he doubted that either the banks or his former wife would be receptive to providing additional financing. His need for additional resources was, of course, directly related to the lack of profitability of his business. It was clear to Giberson that he needed to make some significant changes in the way he did things, but he didn't know what to change or how to change. He was also troubled that he didn't know what each of his products cost or which items were most profitable. He knew his prices were too low, but he didn't know how to think about a new pricing strategy. On a more positive note, he had been receiving numerous requests from his existing customers to produce unique, made-to-order products they had designed. To date, he had not fulfilled any of these requests, primarily because he didn't know how to calculate their costs or how to price them. He was, however, quite interested in expanding his product portfolio. He was quickly running out of time and was open to whatever recommendations Felicia might have.

---

[2]These amounts do not include shipping charges. Orders were prepaid and included an estimated shipping charge.

Exhibit 1

GIBERSON'S GLASS STUDIO

Average Monthly Operating Costs

Office supplies	$ 25.00
Hand tools and manufacturing supplies	150.00
Part-time labor (at $5.00/hour)	100.00
Professional services	50.00
Advertising and promotion	20.00
Contributions	15.00
Dues and subscriptions	35.00
Travel and entertainment	75.00
Insurance	90.00
Taxes and licenses	45.00
Repairs and maintenance	25.00
Rent	175.00
Utilities and telephone	60.00
Miscellaneous	50.00
	$915.00

Exhibit 2

GIBERSON'S GLASS STUDIO

Balance Sheet
September 1, 2002

Assets			Liabilities and Equity		
Cash	$	100	Accounts payable	$	125
Inventory:			Truck loan		6,000
Supplies		75			
Raw materials		50	Total liabilities		$6,125
Prepaid insurance		200	Owner's equity		11,375
Prepaid rent		175			
Furnace and ovens		5,000			
Equipment		3,000			
Gas tanks		400			
Truck		8,500			
Total		$17,500	Total		$17,500

THE HORIZON INSURANCE AGENCY

Horizon Insurance (HI) was a full-service, regional insurance agency located in Albuquerque, New Mexico. To date, HI had done all of its own printing and publishing of promotional brochures, newsletters, informational pamphlets, and required regulatory reports.

Ms. Wolfe, the business manager of the agency, had for some time thought that the firm might save money and get equally good service by contracting the publishing work to any one of the three or four specialty firms operating in the greater Albuquerque area. After several inquiries, she approached a firm specializing in such work, G-Art Inc., and asked for a quotation. At the same time, she asked Mr. Myer, her controller, to prepare an up-to-date statement of the cost of operating Horizon's publishing department.

Within a few days, the quotation from G-Art Inc. arrived. The firm was prepared to provide all the required publications work for $410,000 a year, the contract to run for a guaranteed term of four years with annual renewals thereafter. If the estimated number or assumed mix of publications changed in any given year beyond the baseline planning estimates, the contract price would be adjusted accordingly.

Wolfe compared G-Art's quote with the internal cost figures prepared by Myer.

Annual Cost of Operating HI's Publications Department: Mr. Myer's Figures

Materials		$ 40,000
Labor		290,000
Department overhead:		
Manager's salary	$ 48,000	
Allocated cost of office space	10,000	
Depreciation of equipment	32,500	
Other expenses (travel, education, etc.)	25,000	
		115,500
		445,500
Share of company administrative overhead		30,000
Total cost of department for year		$475,500

Wolfe's initial conclusion was to close Horizon's publications department and immediately sign the contract offered by G-Art. However, she felt it prudent to give the manager of the department, Mr. Richards, an opportunity to question this tentative conclusion. She called him in and put the facts before him, at the same time making it clear that Richards' own employment with the agency was not in jeopardy because even if his department were closed, there was a search currently underway for a manager to fill an open position to which he could be moved without loss of pay.

Richards agreed to review the data and to think the matter over. The next morning, when they met again, he raised a number of considerations that he felt ought to be borne in mind before his department was closed:

> For instance what will you do with the customized graphic design and printing equipment? It cost $260,000 four years ago, but you'd be lucky if you got $80,000 for it now, even though we had planned on using it for another four years at least. And then there is the sizeable supply of print materials that includes a lot of specialized ink, specialty card stock, paper, envelopes, etc. We bought all that a year ago when we were pretty flush with cash. At that time it cost us about $125,000 and at the rate we are using it now, it will last us another four years. We used up about one-fifth of it last year. As best as I can tell, Myer's figure of $40,000 for materials includes about $25,000 for these customized supplies and $15,000 for generic supplies we use on a regular basis. If we were to buy these supplies today it would probably cost us 110 percent of what we paid. But, if we try to sell it, we would probably get only 60 percent of what we paid for it.

Wolfe thought that Myer ought to be present during this discussion. She called him in and put Richards's points to him. Myer said:

> I don't much like all this conjecture. I think my figures are pretty conclusive. Besides, if we are going to have all this talk about 'what will happen if', don't forget the problem of space we're faced with. We're paying $12,000 a year in outside office space. If we close Richards' department, we could use the freed-up space as office space and not need to rent it on the outside.

Wolfe replied:

> That's a good point, though I must say I'm a bit worried about the people if we close the publications department. I don't think we can find room for any of them elsewhere in the firm. I could see whether G-Art can take any of them, but some of them are getting on in years. There's Walters and Hines, for example. They've been with us since they left school 40 years ago, and I think their contract requires us to give them a total severance payoff of about $60,000 each, payable in equal amounts over four years.

Richards showed some relief at this. "But I still don't like Myer's figures," he said. "What about the $30,000 for general administrative overhead. You surely don't expect to fire anyone in the corporate office if I'm closed, do you?"

"Probably not," said Myer, "but someone has to pay for those costs. We can't ignore them when we look at an individual department, because if we do that with each department in turn, we will convince ourselves that accountants, lawyers, vice presidents, and the like don't have to be paid for. And they do, believe me."

"Well, I think we've thrashed this out pretty fully," said Wolfe. I've told G-Art that I'd let them know my decision within a week. I'll let you know what I decide to do before I write to them."

REQUIRED

1. Assuming no additional financial information can be readily obtained, what action should be taken? To the extent necessary, support your decision by completing the attached worksheet (**Exhibit 1**).

2. What, if any, additional financial information do you think is necessary for a sound decision?

3. What, if any, additional non-financial information do you think is necessary for a sound decision?

Exhibit 1

HORIZON INSURANCE AGENCY

Worksheet

	Myer's Figures	Total Cost Inside	Total Cost with G-Art, Contract	Savings (Higher Cost) Contracting outside
Material: generic supplies	$15,000			
custom supplies	25,000			
Labor: wages	290,000			
severance				
Overhead: manager's salary	48,000			
office (internal)	10,000			
office rental				
equip. depreciation	32,500			
other	25,000			
Share of G & A	30,000			
Total	$ 475,500			

G-Art Contract	$410,000			
Net difference	$ 65,500			

GREENLAWN COMMERCIAL PACKAGE BUSINESS

Memorial Day found Amy Carter in her office putting the final touches on her plan for transforming Greenlawn Inc.'s Commercial Package Division. Her New Era project would be a hat trick for the division: she would recommend replacing most of the company's fertilizers and pesticides with a new generation of products that were easier to apply, lower cost, and more environmentally friendly. Headquartered in Bethesda, Maryland, Greenlawn was the largest lawn-care and landscape-services company in the United States. Daughter of Greenlawn's chairman and CEO, Avery Carter, Amy Carter had been with the firm just over one year. A graduate of Ohio State University's College of Food, Agricultural, and Environmental Sciences, she had become the division's "thought leader" when it came to biological engineering and the environment. As New Era was also her first big proposal, she hoped she had not forgotten anything important.

HISTORY

Greenlawn began in 1971 as Chemcare, a division of a large science and technology company headquartered in Michigan. A spinout in 1989 followed by rapid growth in the 1990s had expanded its business from residential-lawn-care products and services into the commercial-landscape industry. By mid-2002, the company also provided total lawn and landscaping services, including mowing, edging and trimming, irrigation installation and maintenance, and landscape design. Greenlawn was the industry's technology leader, developing environmentally responsible pesticide and fertilizer spraying and delivery systems such as contained-spray applicators and dual-line spray guns. Specially built, compartmentalized, computer-controlled trucks with the bright Greenlawn logo were a common sight in residential neighborhoods and in industrial parks. Greenlawn even maintained the White House Rose Garden.

COMMERCIAL PACKAGES

Greenlawn's most profitable business was its commercial accounts. A typical office building, hospital, or apartment complex had lawns and landscaping that required fertilization and insect protection. The typical commercial package provided five applications or visits per season. Budgets for 2002 had been prepared assuming an average treatment price of $400/visit. A pay-in-advance, five-visit annual contract with a 10 percent price reduction was available, but few clients chose this option. Most clients hoped they could skip an application from time to time. Although no two regions were the same, an average commercial region with 5,000 clients would generate about $10 million in revenue (see **Table 1**). Budgets at the regional level did not include corporate costs.

Table 1

Budget: Average Regional Commercial Package Business

Activity drivers for average region:	
Commercial package clients	5,000
Average applications/client/season	5
Capacity/truck (applications/season)*	410
Trucks required/region	61
Revenues	$10,000,000
Direct Costs:	
Lease expenses on trucks	793,000
Service technicians	2,415,600
Fertilizers, pesticides, etc	3,111,000
Fuel, insurance and other operating costs	683,200
Total direct Costs	7,002,800
Contribution on direct costs	2,997,200
Marketing, sales and promotional expenses**	1,100,000
Regional administrative costs	645,000
Contribution	$ 1,252,200

*Note: Assumes a properly scheduled truck can average 12 applications a week over the 34
week season. If not well scheduled the application rate falls to about 10.

**Note: Allocated to regions on the basis of budgeted revenues.

The Commercial Package Division tried to set prices affording a 43 percent margin over direct costs. One of the biggest costs was the fleet of custom-built application vehicles: Greenlawn-designed, compartmentalized, storage basins and power dispensers mounted on standard truck bodies. Trucks for commercial applications were larger than those for residential service, and were equipped with dual-line sprayers that could dispense either fertilizers or pesticides. A remote controller permitted the service technician to change the pesticide without returning to the service vehicle. A new commercial service vehicle cost about $55,000.[1]

Greenlawn service technicians were specially trained and licensed professionals who were employed only during the season (typically, eight months).

Fertilizers and pesticides were the firm's largest operating expense. Purchases were made from a number of different wholesalers and, in some cases, directly from the

---

[1]Almost all its vehicles were leased, typically on six-year, noncancelable contracts that transferred ownership to Greenlawn at the end of the lease. Average annual lease costs were $13,000. Because the Commercial Package Division was newly organized following a series of acquisitions, most vehicles were quite new. The average remaining lease life for the commercial fleet was four years.

---

manufacturers. Prices varied considerably from year to year, and it was not unusual for Greenlawn to forward-buy at discounted prices.

A NEW ERA

Amy Carter stated, "2002 is the beginning of a new era for the firm." Commercial-pesticide prices were dropping dramatically because of many factors: products coming off patent, better science as to their application, new products, and new suppliers.[2] Fertilizer costs were also dropping, primarily because Greenlawn had perfected a safe and odorless process for substituting liquefied organic nitrogen for urea-ammonium nitrate. With the company purchasing new applicators and providing additional training, Carter expected to realize a 56 percent reduction in these costs. She also expected to save 22 percent on labor because the technicians would need less training and less experience.

Some aspects of the program would be more costly. Fuel and other direct operating costs would jump 32 percent, and new vehicles with new superstructures and applicators would be required, although the average lease cost for the new vehicles would be slightly less, averaging $12,000 a year.[3] Carter observed, "Perhaps the best part of all of this change is what it will mean environmentally. We'll produce the same results for our clients while using far less organophosphates, fertilizers, and other chemicals. We all win. And the typical client will only need three treatments a season."

---

[2]These products included Dithane, Dimethoate, DACONIL 2787®, and Permethrin.

[3]It was not clear what would become of the old vehicles. The teardown cost of the superstructure was about equal to what the truck chassis might bring by itself.

THE SAW BLADES AT LEEDS

Toward the end of 2002, managers at the Leeds Works, Imperial Optronics PLC, met to decide how to respond to a competitor's launch of a cutting tool that could replace the carbide-steel blades used worldwide in Imperial's eyeglass-processing equipment. The composite-based blades appeared to last much longer and cost less than Imperial's carbide ones. By itself, this one decision would have only a modest impact on the group's financials, but the Parts Division at Imperial was far more profitable than its original-equipment divisions, so the blade issue could eventually have a significant impact on the full range of replacement parts produced by Leeds.

Imperial was the global leader in dry-cut lens-processing equipment. When glass was the only material for making eyeglasses, the most effective way to edge or glaze a lens was with a diamond wheel and flood coolant. As glass was replaced by plastic, polycarbonates, and Trivex, Imperial's dry-lens equipment became the preferred approach because plastic materials would gum up diamond-wheeled edgers. Optometrists and eyeglass labs throughout the world used Imperial edgers, tracers, and finishers. Blades were an important consumable in this equipment. They could be quickly replaced, and lasted about two months in average use. Blades produced at Leeds were also sold as replacement parts for Leeds' competitor's lens-processing equipment.

Barry Sullivan was the division executive at Leeds. His instincts, after 10 years as head of Sales, were to rush a composite blade to market as soon as possible, especially in France, where the composites had first been introduced; however, Sullivan had only recently become the head of the Leeds Works, and he now had other points of view to consider. The head of Operations warned that stocks of finished blades and carbide steel were at £1,930,000 and that the large inventories of steel had been necessary because Leeds was the only customer for that particular alloy. Carbide-lens saws were the only use that Leeds had for the special steel. The head of Marketing cautioned that a composite product, even on a rush basis, would not reach the marketplace for six months. The new head of Sales warned that a composite blade might be needed only in the French market for some time as their competitor lacked the manufacturing and marketing capability to expand quickly, but in France it was needed immediately. He was concerned that, as the composite blades appeared to last four times longer than the carbide blades, they would quickly destroy the attractiveness of the carbide blades in France.

Even the comptroller had a warning. She said that group headquarters in London would expect Sullivan to act in the best interests of the group, not merely his division. The blade issue was likely to become a benchmark for other parts decisions facing Leeds and Imperial. Substitute spares were constantly being introduced by European, American, and Asian firms, particularly those in China.

Sullivan had accumulated other data pertaining to the blade issue:

Special-carbide-steel inventory was £345,000.

- Carbide-blade sales averaged 10,000 a week, including blades sold for replacement, new equipment, and competitors' machines.

- Leeds would have 140,000 finished carbide blades available when a plastic replacement would first be shippable.

- During the Holiday months, Leeds would not operate at capacity. Following labor agreements, the company employed excess labor at 70 percent of the regular wage on various make-work projects. This labor was available to produce carbide blades, should that become necessary.

A key issue would be pricing. The new plastic blade had been priced at least equal to and, in some cases, higher than the Leeds blades, even though the manufacturing cost of the plastic product was expected to be much lower. If both products continued to be sold at the current carbide-blade price of £5, he concluded that the extra profit on the plastic blade would easily cover the cost of the steel inventory, were it to be no longer required. To prove his point, Sullivan produced the manufacturing-cost data shown below:

	Expected Cost of Composite	Current Carbide Costs
Material	0.06	1.15
Direct labor	0.23	0.70
Overhead:	--	--
Divisional*	0.48	1.48
Group allocation	0.21	0.63
Total cost	0.98	3.96

*Overhead was allocated on the basis of direct-labor dollars. It was estimated that the variable overhead costs included here were largely fringe benefits related to direct labor, and amounted to 40% of the divisional amounts.

MONROE CLOCK COMPANY (A)

As Jim Monroe, president of Monroe Clock Company, stared at the numbers compiled his controller, Tom Grant, and his sales manager, Frank Tyler, the look on his face was one of confusion. "The more I look at this the more it looks like we really don't know how much this new household timer is going to cost. We need to get a better handle on the costs of this thing or we will never be able to decide how to price it."

THE COMPANY

Monroe Clock Company was started by Jim Monroe, the company's president, in 1985. In 1998, Monroe had sold out to Piedmont Appliance Corporation, but he remained with the company as Monroe Clock's president. Originally, Monroe Clock made decorative electric clocks, but by 1992 Jim had decided he was much better at making the works than the decorations. So the company shifted to making accurate, durable, but inexpensive electric timing mechanisms. The company now made only three basic models, differing in size and strength. Slight modifications were made to fit each customer's needs. Sales had grown to over $50 million, and the timing mechanisms were made entirely for producers of timed electrical appliances. About half of Monroe's output went to Piedmont Appliance and about half to other companies.

THE NEW HOUSEHOLD TIMING DEVICE

It all started because sometime over the 2000 Labor Day weekend, Jim Monroe's house was burgled while he and his family were enjoying the last days of their summer vacation. Thereafter, though he knew he was closing the proverbial barn door after the cow had gone, Jim did a number of things to try to prevent a repetition. Besides improving locks, he bought two timers that could be set to turn on house lights in the evening.

That is what gave him the idea to make a better timing mechanism for household use, one that had two features that he thought made his timer superior to those currently on the market. The Monroe timer had two options: a 48-hour cycle (so that lights would not turn on and off at the same time each day), or two different 24-hour cycles, so that one timer could operate two lights, each on a different 24-hour cycle. The design of these features was quite simple. There were two different 24-hour cycles, and for the 48-hour option, the timer switched back and forth.

Jim's sales manager, Frank Tyler, was not sure how important or valuable these options would be to the potential customer. Furthermore, this complete product would have to be sold through wholesalers and manufacturers' representatives, which were new to Monroe Clock. The company's sales force usually sold to a relatively small number of industrial customers. Price, he thought, would be an important factor since other timers were on the market.

PRICING THE NEW HOUSEHOLD TIMING DEVICE

Jim asked his controller, Tom Grant, to put some cost figures together. Tom presented the table shown in **Exhibit 1**. The basic timing mechanism, Model A2B, was Monroe's highest volume product, which showed a cost of $4.40. To make the timer that Jim had designed would cost about $11.60. No more machining would be required, but a little fabrication work and a number of wiring and assembly operations would be necessary.

Tom had checked on available capacity before computing his costs. As it happened, adequate space for the timer's assembly had just become available because the company had shifted from having one warehouse for finished goods at the plant, to two warehouses, one in Pennsylvania and the other in Texas. Making the warehouse into an assembly area would require some tables, lighting, and small tools but no major capital expenditure. About $20,000 ought to cover it, Tom thought.

Jim asked Tom to show his figures to Frank. On seeing the $11.60 production cost, Frank did the following rough calculation using normal mark-ups to see what this cost might indicate for a retail selling price.

$11.60	Total manufacturing cost
1.74	Selling, General and Administration (15% of cost)
13.34	
1.34	Profit (10% of cost)
14.68	
14.68	Wholesale, Retail and Distribution (50% of Selling Price)
$28.76	

"Holy smokes," said Frank to himself, "we'll never sell any at that price." He knew that the similar Sears model was selling at $19.98, and others were not more than a dollar or two away from that.

He studied the controller's numbers. "Tom," he said, "isn't most of this overhead fixed? You have used a plant-wide rate for as long as I can remember, and that seems to have worked OK. But if we are just adding on a little fancy assembly stuff to sell more timing mechanisms, that isn't really going to increase our overhead, is it?"

"Well, yes and no," said Tom. "Any one increment in volume won't necessarily increase overhead by 300 percent of the direct labor for that increment, but somewhere along the line, overhead is going to increase." To explain what overhead consisted of, Tom showed Frank the schedule shown in **Exhibit 2**.

Frank asked Tom a few questions about the list of overhead costs and then computed his own figures, shown as the right hand column in **Exhibit 2**. He concluded that only about $2.00 of the $7.30 of overhead costs was really variable, so he thought $5.30 should be considered fixed and not relevant to this decision. In that case, he thought the cost and selling price figures should look like this:

$11.60	Total manufacturing cost as first computed for the new timer
5.30	Fixed manufacturing costs
6.30	Variable costs for the new timer
1.00	Plus about 15% SG&A
7.30	
.70	Plus profit at about 10% of cost
8.00	Factory price
8.00	Plus wholesale and retail costs (50% of Selling Price)
$16.00	Estimated retail selling price

At a factory price of $8.00, Frank figured they could sell 50,000 timers. He figured there should be a $50,000 advertising budget that would be spent regardless of sales volume. He figured the $1.00 per unit for general administrative and selling expense would just cover the advertising cost and could be allocated to advertising, since other SG&A costs would be fixed.

When Frank showed his proposal to Jim, the latter flatly disagreed with the idea of cutting overhead. "You start doing that," he said, "and pretty soon you've got lots of volume and no profit. You can't just wave your calculator like a wand over the numbers and have a product actually cost less. Furthermore, I think you haven't figured in the value of the product options. There's not another timer like this on the market. I think we can put a factory price of $14.70 on it, and customers will be eager to buy it at $29.40."

Tom, who had heard most of the discussion, said he thought the $14.70 factory price was a much better idea. "Look," he said to Frank, "if your breakdown of fixed and variable costs is right—and I think it is probably OK for the short run—then we'll only need to sell some smaller number of units at $14.70 to be as well off as we would be with your plan."

"Well," said Jim, "That may be right, but the more I look at this the more it seems to me that a little knowledge is a dangerous thing here. I don't think we really know how much the new timer is going to cost either in the short run or the long run."

Exhibit 1

MONROE CLOCK COMPANY (A)

Estimated Cost of New Timer

Basic mechanism A2B	Purchased Parts	Direct Labor	Expend. Supplies	Overhead at 300% of D.L.	Total
Purchased parts	$ 1.334				
Fabrication		$ 0.364	$ 0.022		
Machining		0.152	0.026		
Assembly		0.230	0.034		
Total A2B	1.334	0.746	0.082	$ 2.238	$ 4.400
Additions to make new timer					
Purchased parts	0.356				
Fabrication		0.036	0.002		
Machining		--	--		
Assembly		1.650	0.098		
Total additions	0.356	1.686	0.100	5.058	7.200
Total New Timer	$ 1.690	$ 2.432	$ 0.182	$ 7.296	$ 11.600

Note:

Fabrication work was punching out shapes, stamping to form pieces, and drilling holes, using both automatic and hand operated machines.

The machining operations used lathes, milling machines, and grinders to make the gears, plates, holes, etc. with proper tolerances. Many of these used automatic feed mechanisms.

Exhibit 2

MONROE CLOCK COMPANY (A)

The Overhead Schedule Tom Showed Frank
Overhead Components as Percent of Direct Labor

Overhead item	% of Direct Labor	Frank's Estimate of Variable Amount
Supplementary compensation for direct labor (Social Security, holidays, insurance, etc.)	35%	35%
Supervision (including supplemental compensation)	15%	15%
Indirect labor (including supplemental compensation)	30%	30%
Machine maintenance	55%	0%
Machine depreciation	40%	0%
Manufacturing engineering	35%	0%
Plant administration (including supplemental compensation)	40%	0%
Electricity	10%	2%
Occupancy cost	40%	0%
Total as percent of direct labor	300%	82%

(Explanation: This says, for example, that total supervision cost for all departments for the year was expected to be 15% of the total direct labor cost for the year.)

Frank's computation

Total direct labor per timer = $2.44 (Shown as $2.432 in **Exhibit 1**)

82% of $2.44 = about $2.00

Therefore, incremental overhead per timer made would be $2.00.

THE CRADDOCK CUP

Jose Rivaldo shuffled through the papers on his desk and sighed. As the general manager of the Craddock Youth Soccer League (CYSL), Rivaldo was committed to providing high-quality soccer activities to boys and girls in the area. In addition to managing regular CYSL operations, Rivaldo was heavily involved in putting on a regional soccer tournament, the Craddock Cup, which brought approximately 32 premier high-school soccer teams from throughout the region each May.

This year's tournament, like its predecessors, had been considered a great success by players, their families, and the local community. The weather had been beautiful, the referees had been fair, and the local hotels and restaurants had profited from the influx of people. Nevertheless, Rivaldo knew that the Craddock Cup was in trouble. Tournament expenses continued to rise, while corporate sponsorships remained difficult to obtain. CYSL had founded the Craddock Cup, in part, to fund a field-acquisition program for the league, with the expectation that the tournament would generate at least $6,000 annually toward that goal. Unfortunately, with tournament profits averaging a loss of almost $4,000 a year, CYSL's board of directors was beginning to express frustration with the lack of profits generated by the Craddock Cup. Rivaldo knew the Craddock Cup was in danger of being canceled and that he risked losing his job with CYSL if he did not devise a plan to increase tournament profits. He decided to review the organization and expenses of the Craddock Cup to see if there was a way to increase the Cup's profits and continue the tournament.

BACKGROUND

The Craddock Cup was widely regarded as the premier tournament for high-school soccer players in the region. The tournament consisted of a boys' high-school bracket and a girls' high-school bracket, each with 16 teams. Through a series of rounds and consolation rounds, the rankings of all the teams, from 1 to 16, were determined, with each team playing four games throughout the course of the tournament. See **Exhibit 1** for the current year's Boys' High School Division results and bracket structure.

Funding for the tournament came from team registration fees, corporate sponsorships, T-shirt sales, concession sales, and participation fees for soccer clinics held during the tournament for younger siblings of tournament participants. Each team paid a $295 registration fee to enter the tournament.

During the past few years, the Craddock Cup had evolved into a showcase event for talented high-school players. On average, about 25 college scouts attended the tournament each year for recruiting purposes. The Craddock Cup encouraged recruiters' attendance by paying for their hotel rooms and by publishing a "face book" that included a photograph and profile of each player 16 years of age or older. The presence of the scouts also enabled the tournament to attract the region's best high-school teams.

PROFIT STATEMENT ESTIMATES

Rivaldo looked at the profit estimate for next year's Craddock Cup (**Exhibit 2**). He planned to use this information as the basis for his recommendations to the CYSL board. He used the following data in compiling the profit statement:

1. CYSL purchased tournament T-shirts for $6 a shirt, and sold them for $15 each. Historically, the tournament sold 10 shirts per team.

2. The Craddock Cup expended the equivalent of $15 for food and beverages per player to stock the concession stands. These concessions were sold at a 100 percent markup.

3. The tournament hosted two soccer clinics (one on each day of the tournament) for younger siblings of tournament participants. The participation fee was $10 per child per day; it cost CYSL $6 per child per day. The previous year, 216 children had participated in the soccer clinics each day.

4. Corporate contributions averaged $14,000 a year. Despite Rivaldo's best efforts, he had been unable to secure additional corporate sponsorships for the tournament.

5. CYSL was required to pay $1,500 every year to register the Craddock Cup with the state Youth Soccer League, and also had to pay a $4 insurance premium per player. On average, each team fielded 18 players.

6. CYSL rented 10 soccer fields from the city for 40 weeks a year for a total fee of $48,000. Although the Craddock Cup used the fields for only two days a year, Rivaldo allocated one week's rent to the Craddock Cup. In addition to the two days of tournament play, CYSL spent two days preparing the fields for the tournament and two days cleaning up after the tournament.

7. Each team played four games during the course of the tournament, and each soccer field accommodated four games a day. Currently, the Craddock Cup required the use of eight soccer fields. Additional fields could be rented from local schools at a cost of $150 per day per field, while two goals for each additional field were rented at a cost of $60 a day.

8. Two soccer balls were purchased for each field at a cost of $27 per ball.

9. Three referees were hired for each game at a cost of $100 a game ($25 each for two linesmen and $50 for the head referee).

10. Trophies were provided for the winning team in each bracket. On average, each trophy cost $25.

11. The Craddock Cup defrayed approximately $80 a night in hotel costs for each college scout attending the tournament. The scouts generally stayed for two nights.

12. Face books were published at a cost of $6 a book. The Craddock Cup published extra face books and sent them to colleges that requested a face book but did not

send a representative to the tournament. The previous year, the tournament had published 75 face books.

13. Marketing and advertising costs had been $2,200 the previous year.

14. Currently, CYSL employed Rivaldo full-time at $42,000 a year and three part-time workers at $12,000 a year each. Rivaldo worked on both the Craddock Cup and regular CYSL operations. He spent approximately 15 percent of his time on the Craddock Cup. One of the part-time employees, Renee Jansten, worked solely on the Craddock Cup, while the other two part-time employees did not work on the Craddock Cup at all. Currently, office rent and utilities were allocated to the Craddock Cup based on the time Rivaldo spent working on the Craddock Cup, as follows:

	CYSL Cost	% Allocated	Allocated to Craddock Cup
Rivaldo's salary	$ 42,000	15%	$ 6,300
Jansten's salary	12,000	100%	12,000
Rent, utilities	18,000	15%	2,700
Total	$ 72,000		$ 21,000

Rivaldo thought about the overhead expenses allocated to the Craddock Cup and wondered whether the allocation was accurate or even whether overhead should be allocated to the Craddock Cup at all. If the tournament were discontinued, CYSL would still incur field-rental expenses for 40 weeks. Furthermore, CYSL would still have the same salary expenses for Rivaldo and two of the other employees, though Jansten's position would be eliminated. Rivaldo wondered what the tournament's true operating profit really was, as a portion of the tournament's costs was allocated from CYSL.

THE FUTURE OF THE CRADDOCK CUP

Looking at the profit data, Rivaldo thought about what changes, if any, could be made before next year's tournament to improve profitability and convince CYSL's board to continue hosting the event. One easy way to raise additional revenue would be to increase the size of the tournament by adding two middle-school brackets, one for boys and one for girls. This move would increase the number of participating teams from 32 to 64. Because most of the high-school teams had a corresponding middle-school team, Rivaldo thought he could easily double the size of the tournament with little effort. Rivaldo knew the Craddock area had enough fields, equipment, hotels, and referees to support a tournament with 64 teams. Above this number, Rivaldo estimated that the costs for additional fields, rented goals, and referees would increase significantly.

The CYSL board had also asked Rivaldo to determine the profit impact of increasing the marketing and advertising expenses. The board was hoping that a big advertising push would increase the visibility and prestige of the tournament. Rivaldo thought that by spending an additional $1,000 on marketing and advertising, he might attract about 15 more college recruiters to the tournament. This action would require CYSL to increase the number of published face books to 95. Rivaldo thought that this strategy might allow CYSL to charge a higher registration fee for the tournament.

In preparing for his meeting with the board, Rivaldo decided that he needed to review the overhead-expense allocations and determine the impact of adding 32 teams to the Craddock Cup. Finally, Rivaldo planned to calculate the financial impact of increasing the tournament's advertising budget by $1,000 and to determine how much the registration fees for 64 teams would have to be raised in order to fund this initiative.

REQUIRED

1. In determining whether to keep or drop the Craddock Cup, review the overhead-expense allocations currently made from CYSL to the Craddock Cup to see if they should be revised or eliminated.

2. Calculate the expected financial impact of adding 32 more teams to the tournament schedule.

3. Calculate the breakeven increase in registration fees per team for 64 teams given a $1,000 increase in advertising expense, 15 more college recruiters, and 20 additional face books.

Exhibit 1

THE CRADDOCK CUP

This Year's Boys' High School Division Tournament Results

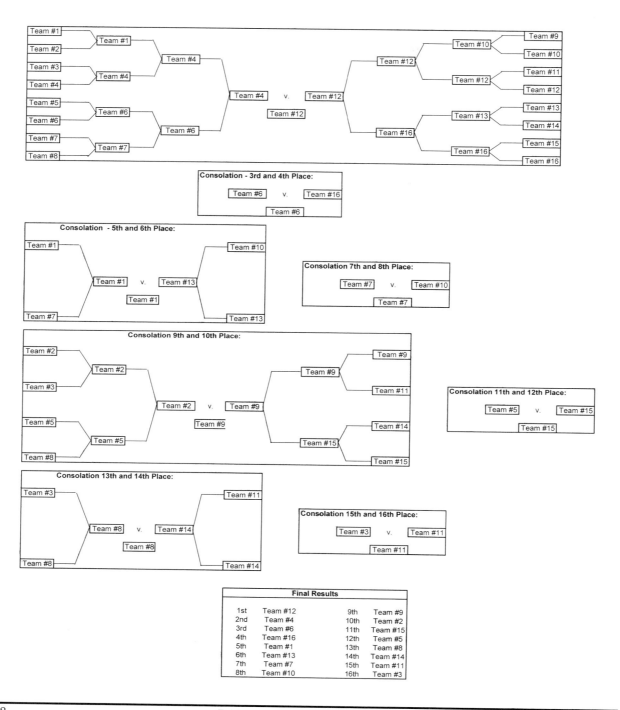

Final Results			
1st	Team #12	9th	Team #9
2nd	Team #4	10th	Team #2
3rd	Team #6	11th	Team #15
4th	Team #16	12th	Team #5
5th	Team #1	13th	Team #8
6th	Team #13	14th	Team #14
7th	Team #7	15th	Team #11
8th	Team #10	16th	Team #3

Exhibit 2

THE CRADDOCK CUP

Profit Statement

	Current Size
Registration fees	$ 9,440
T-shirts	4,800
Concessions	17,280
Soccer clinic	4,320
Contributions	14,000
Total revenue	49,840
T-shirts	1,920
Concessions	8,640
Soccer clinic	2,592
Player insurance	2,304
Registration with state YSL	1,500
City field rental	1,200
Soccer balls	432
Referees	6,400
Trophies	900
Hotels	4,000
Face books	450
Marketing and advertising	2,200
CYSL salaries	18,300
CYSL rent	2,700
Total expenses	53,538
Profit (loss)	$ (3,698)

PART III

FUNDAMENTALS OF PRODUCT AND SERVICE COSTING

LAMBETH CUSTOM CABINETS (A)

Jack Lambeth, a master cabinet maker, owns and operates a shop where he sells custom-made cabinets. At the beginning of September, his business had no outstanding debt and the following amounts were on his books:

1. Raw materials inventory, $2,150.

2. Supplies inventory, $620.

3. Work-in-process inventory, $5,650.

Job	Materials	Labor	Overhead (50% of Labor)	
A-3	$ 750	$1100	$ 550	
A-4	900	650	325	
A-5	325	700	350	
Total	$1,975	$2,450	$1,225	$5,650

4. All other assets as of September 1 were $16,890.

During the month, Lambeth's woodworking crew finished jobs A-3, A-4, and A-6 but did not finish A-5. Job A-7 was started but not finished during September. Overhead costs (pertaining primarily to equipment and shop depreciation, cleaning supplies, and insurance) are applied to every job at the end of the month unless the job is finished during the month, in which case overhead is applied when the job is finished.

During September, the following direct materials and direct labor costs were incurred:

Job	Direct Materials	Direct Labor
A-3	$ 280	$ 750
A-4	350	1300
A-5	180	550
A-6	375	490
A-7	590	370
	$1,175	$3,460

Other financial factors of importance pertaining to September were:

a. $1,675 of raw materials were purchased during the month.

b. Supplies of $580 were purchased while $490 were used and thus transferred to the manufacturing overhead account.

c. Total increases to the labor general ledger account were $5,460. (Apparently there was $2,000 indirect labor charged.)

d. General and administrative expenses for the month were $3,420.

e. Collections received from customers on jobs A-3, A-4, and A-6 amounted to $6,125, $8,600, and $1,750, respectively, for a total of $16,475.

f. At the end of the month, Lambeth Custom Cabinets had no outstanding debts.

While Jack was reviewing the September data he became very concerned about the manufacturing overhead variance (MOV). Since Jack never wanted to lay off an employee, the MOV was always large in months when business was slow. (Jack assigned unoccupied workers to general clean-up and repair work and charged their wages to indirect labor.) Of course, Lambeth realized why the MOV was so large. What he was worried about, however, was Mrs. Carter.

Mrs. Carter, a neighbor, had stopped in the shop one day in early September to get a price on some cabinets she wanted built. Jack's son, Jack Jr., spoke with her. Jack Jr. was working in the shop while on summer vacation between his first and second year of graduate business school. Jack Jr. studied the plans that Mrs. Carter had and estimated the cost to build her cabinets at $1,625. His job estimation sheet showed:

Lumber	$590
Finishing materials	75
Direct labor cost	640
Overhead	320
	$1,625

When Jack Jr. quoted a price of $1,900 ($1,625 cost $275 profit) to Mrs. Carter, she said that she could get the same thing built by Walworth Custom Kitchens for $1,500. Furthermore, she informed Jack Jr. that, "I would throw the dumb economics books away before I would pay a penny more than $1,500 for book cabinets to store them."

Jack Jr. simply told her that his best price would be $1,900. He explained all about labor, materials, profit, overhead, and competitive capitalism. In addition, he told Mrs. Carter that Walworth couldn't make money on a $1,500 price and if Walworth was really willing to build the shelves for $1,500 she would be stealing from Mr. Walworth!

Mrs. Carter, was very angry when she left. Jack Jr. later told his father the whole story and laughed as he said, "Heck, we can't build stuff that costs $1,625 and sell it at a price of $1,600, let alone $1,500, can we?" At that time Lambeth didn't think much about the incident but he began to wonder whether Jack Jr. had learned anything at graduate business school. Lambeth became especially concerned when he saw Bob Walworth, who said, "Mrs. Carter saved me last month." It seems that Walworth had just delivered

Mrs. Carter's new cabinets for which she paid $1,500. Jack Lambeth wondered who was right – Jack Jr. or Walworth?

REQUIRED

1. Show in a series of ledger accounts the transactions for September (you may use the T accounts below).

2. In the greatest detail possible, prepare balance sheets as of September 1 and September 30 and an income statement for September. (Do not concern yourself with taxes.)

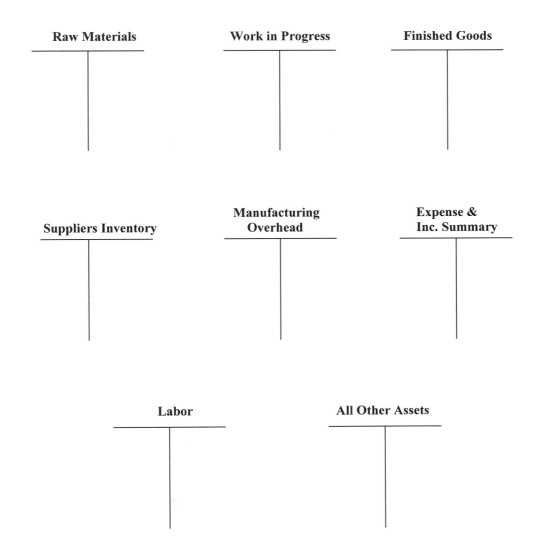

SHUN ELECTRONICS COMPANY

"Manjit," said Chan Choong Tho, Controller of the Shun Electronics Company's KL Radio Division, "I understand how you arrived at these new cost figures, but I'm not sure how we should present them to our colleagues. May Hwang is not going to be happy when she sees higher costs on four of our six radios, and she may not understand the cost principles involved. I don't know about Azraf—he's apt to say the costs are just estimates and we should stay with the present system."

Chan Choong Tho was speaking to Manjit Singh, his new assistant controller. May Hwang was the division's sales manager and Azraf Tahir was the Division Manager. Six weeks earlier Chan had given Manjit the task of examining the division's cost accounting system to see if the product costs it produced were reasonably accurate. Manjit had reconstituted the basic cost data in a way that he thought might be more accurate and was reviewing the results with his boss.

The Shun Electronics Company was a medium-sized, family-owned firm in the Malaysian electronics industry. The company had two operating divisions. The KB Monitor Division manufactured computer monitors that were primarily sold to off-brand computer companies. The KL Radio Division made two basic radios—a shelf model and a portable model. Each of the two models were available in three versions: one version was for use in a bathroom shower (a popular option especially in the American market); another had a 1950's-style metal cabinet; and the third version had a wooden cabinet. All six radios were distributed primarily through high-end catalog retailers.

THE PRODUCTION PROCESS

Radio production was carried out in three departments, two of which were organized into three sections. The Assembly department assembled the basic chassis using parts purchased from outside the company. In this department, Section 1 was where the various electronic components were staged for production and assembled into functioning, modular units. In Section 2, the modular units were tested and any electronic problems were rectified. In Section 3, the modular units were mounted on a basic chassis and tested again before being passed on to the Fabrication department.

In the Fabrication department, the radios took one of three routes. Those intended for in-the-shower use went to Section 1 where they were sprayed and treated to protect them against moisture. Before leaving Section 1, the sprayed modular units were encased in a colorful plastic cabinet the division bought from a vendor. Those radios destined to receive a 1950's-type metal cabinet went to Section 2. In that section the cabinets were cut from sheet metal, punched, bent to shape, and painted. The metal cabinet was then mounted on the chassis. In Section 3, Shun's distinctive wooden cabinets were crafted, finished and fitted to the chassis.

In the Finished Goods department, all radios were given a final testing and adjustment in one area and packed for storage or shipment in another area.

The Assembly and Fabrication departments were run by foremen. Reporting to them were section leaders for each of the sections. The Finished Goods department had no foreman or section leaders and only part of its efforts were devoted to the KL Radio Division. The test area was under the supervision of a quality control engineer who was part of the company's engineering department. The packing area was run by a supervisor.

THE PRODUCT COSTING SYSTEM

The KL Radio Division used a standard cost system in which a standard product cost was computed for each of the six radios. **Exhibit 1** shows a condensed version of the six standard cost sheets based on the most recent year's budget expectations. Budgeted direct material and direct labor costs per radio were based on standard quantities and hours and expected material costs and labor rates. Actual costs were collected periodically by the departments for comparison with the standard cost of work completed in the department.

A standard overhead cost allocation rate was applied to direct labor plus direct materials in the Assembly department, and on direct labor alone in the other two departments. The percentage used for the overhead rate was derived from the expected relationship between budgeted direct labor, direct material, and overhead costs, all at an assumed normal production volume. For example, in the Assembly department, budgeted overhead equaled 50 percent of budgeted direct labor and direct material costs combined. The standard overhead charge for each radio was therefore 50 percent of the standard direct labor and direct material costs for that radio.

Overhead cost allocation rates usually had to be revised annually, but the standards for direct labor and direct material costs were changed only when prices, production methods, or product designs changed significantly. The standard costs were used in the division for a number of purposes. They had some bearing on pricing, particularly in bidding on larger orders. The standard cost figures were also used in a variety of longer-run functions such as in determining changes in the product offerings, make or buy decisions, financial planning, and corporate management's evaluation of divisional performance.

The cost system produced monthly labor, material, and overhead variances which were checked by Azraf Tahir to see if any were significantly out of line. Though he kept in close touch with what was going on in the plant, a variance would occasionally show a deviation over time that was not easy to spot in daily observations.

EXAMINATION BY MANJIT SINGH

Early in his investigation of the cost system, Manjit Singh began to consider the existing definition of cost centers. He wondered if the total product costs would be different if the aggregation of costs was in more detail than just at the departmental level. Specifically, he wondered if better information could be obtained by using eight cost centers: the six sections in the Assembly and Fabrication departments and the two areas in the Finished Goods department.

Direct labor and direct material costs were easy to assign to the smaller cost centers since that was the way the standard cost sheets were already computed. In order to identify the overhead costs incurred within the sections, however, he asked the department foremen for estimates of the resource costs incurred in each of their various sections for such items as indirect labor, equipment repair, and supplies. In addition, an examination of recent invoices helped him verify some of the details the foremen submitted. **Exhibit 2** shows the existing departmental overhead budget and the results of Manjit Singh's further distribution of those amounts to the six sections and two areas.

With this more detailed identification of costs, and based on dropping direct material costs as part of the allocation based used in the Assembly department, Manjit recalculated the standard cost sheets to see if product costs changed. **Exhibit 3** shows the results of these calculations. Of the six types of radios sold, four showed a higher factory cost and two a lower cost. Since he was not sure what his next step should be, he consulted his boss Chan Choong Tho who, after studying the figures, made the response which appears at the beginning of the case.

Exhibit 1

SHUN ELECTRONICS COMPANY

KL Radio Division Standard Cost Sheets
(cost per radio in ringgit (M$))

Assembly department	Portable Model	Shelf Model
Units Budgeted	4,000	3,000
Direct material	M$ 8.00	M$12.00
Direct labor Section 1	1.00	4.00
Direct labor Section 2	2.00	3.00
Direct labor Section 3	1.00	5.00
Total direct labor and direct materials	M$12.00	M$24.00
Overhead at 50% direct labor and direct material	M$ 6.00	M$12.00
Total Assembly department	M$18.00	M$36.00

Fabrication department

	PS*	PM	PW	SS	SM	SW
Units Budgeted	1,000	2,000	1,000	500	1,500	1,000
Direct material	M$5.00	M$2.00	M$4.00	M$6.00	M$3.00	M$8.00
Direct labor	3.00	2.50	2.00	5.00	5.00	2.00
Overhead at 200% of direct labor	6.00	5.00	4.00	10.00	10.00	4.00
Total Fabrication department	M$14.00	M$ 9.50	M$10.00	M$21.00	M$18.00	M$14.00

Finished Goods department

	Portable	Shelf
Direct material (packing)	M$ 1.00	M$ 1.50
Area 1: test direct labor	.50	1.00
Area 2: packing direct labor	.25	.25
Total direct labor	.75	1.25
Overhead 100% of direct labor	.75	1.25
Total Finished Goods department	M$ 2.50	M$ 4.00

	PS*	PM	PW	SS	SM	SW
Total Direct Factory Cost	M$34.50	M$30.00	M$30.50	M$61.00	M$58.00	M$54.00

*PS=portable/shower   PM=portable/metal   PW=portable/wood
SS=shelf/shower   SM=shelf/metal   SW=shelf/wood

Exhibit 2

SHUN ELECTRONICS COMPANY

KL Radio Division Overhead Cost Distributions

		Manjit Singh's Distribution		
Assembly department	Present Budget	Section 1	Section 2	Section 3
Foreman	M$ 6,000	M$ 2,000	M$ 2,000	M$ 2,000
Section leaders	15,000	5,000	5,000	5,000
Indirect labor	12,000	3,500	3,000	5,500
Equipment repair	2,250	500	750	1,000
Supplies	1,250	500	250	500
Occupancy and electricity	5,000	2,000	1,000	2,000
Depreciation on equipment	5,500	500	2,000	3,000
Storage and handling of material	10,000	10,000		
Miscellaneous	3,000	1,000	1,000	1,000
	M$60,000	M$25,000	M$15,000	M$20,000

		Section 1	Section 2	Section 3
Fabrication department				
Foreman	M$ 6,000	M$ 2,000	M$ 2,000	M$ 2,000
3 Section leaders	15,000	5,000	5,000	5,000
Indirect labor	4,000	1,500	1,500	1,000
Equipment repair	3,750	1,000	2,000	750
Supplies	2,500	2,000	250	250
Occupancy & Electricity	3,000	1,000	1,250	750
Depreciation on equipment	4,750	1,500	2,000	1,250
Storage and handling of material	2,000	1,000	500	500
Miscellaneous	3,000	1,000	1,000	1,000
	M$44,000	M$16,000	M$15,500	M$12,500

		Area 1	Area 2
Finished Goods department			
Equipment repair	M$ 500	M$ 500	---
Supplies	1,750	250	M$ 1,500
Occupancy & Electricity	1,750	750	1,000
Depreciation	2,250	2,000	250
Miscellaneous	500	250	250
Total	M$ 6,750*	M$ 3,750	M$ 3,000

*This was the KL Radio Division's share of the Finished Goods department's total overhead budget.

Exhibit 3

SHUN ELECTRONICS COMPANY

KL Radio Division Standard Costs Using Redistributed Overhead Costs

	Portable Model	Shelf Model
Units Budgeted	4,000	3,000

Assembly department

	Portable Model	Shelf Model
Direct material	M$ 8.00	M$12.00
Direct labor Section 1	1.00	4.00
Overhead Section 1:		
156% direct labor	1.56	6.24
Direct labor Section 2	2.00	3.00
Overhead Section 2:		
88% direct labor	1.76	2.64
Direct labor Section 3	1.00	5.00
Overhead Section 3:		
105% direct labor	1.05	5.25
Total Assembly department	M$16.37	M$38.13

Fabrication department	PS*	PM	PW	SS	SM	SW
Units Budgeted	1,000	2,000	1,000	500	1,500	1,000
Direct material	M$5.00	M$2.00	M$4.00	M$6.00	M$3.00	M$8.00
Direct labor	3.00	2.50	2.00	5.00	5.00	2.00
Overhead						
Section 1: 291% direct labor	8.73			14.50		
Section 2: 124% direct labor		3.10			6.20	
Section 3: 313% direct labor			6.25			6.25
Total Fabrication department	M$16.73	M$ 7.60	M$12.25	M$25.50	M$14.20	M$16.25

Finished Goods department

	Portable Model	Shelf Model
Direct material	M$ 1.00	M$ 1.50
Direct labor Area 1	.50	1.00
Overhead Area 1: 75% direct labor	.37	.75
Direct labor Area 2	.25	.25
Overhead Area 2: 172% direct labor	.43	.43
Total Finished Goods department	M$ 2.55	M$ 3.93

	PS	PM	PW	SS	SM	SW
Total Direct Factory Cost	M$35.65	M$26.52	M$31.17	M$67.56	M$56.26	M$58.31

*PS=portable/shower   PM=portable/metal   PW=portable/wood
  SS=shelf/shower   SM=shelf/metal   SW=shelf/wood

Exhibit 3 (continued)

SHUN ELECTRONICS COMPANY

Explanatory Notes

The overhead totals for each section and area shown in **Exhibit 2** were allocated to the radios going through the sections and areas on the basis of direct labor dollars. For example, the M$25,000 overhead allocated to Section 1 in the Assembly department was 156% of the M$16,000 budgeted direct labor costs for the department (4,000 units times M$1.00 plus 3,000 units times M$4.00 equals M$16,000). The overhead to be charged to each unit was therefore 156% of the standard direct labor cost. Other sections and departments were handled in like manner.

Direct labor alone was used by Manjit as a base for allocation in the Assembly department since he thought inclusion of direct material costs in the overhead allocation process introduced a slight distortion. If direct labor alone had been used in the division's present system, the cost of a portable model radio in the Assembly department would come out M$1.38 lower, and the shelf model radio M$1.85 higher. This would have resulted in total direct factory costs as follows:

PS	PM	PW	SS	SM	SW
M$33.12	M$28.62	M$29.12	M$62.85	M$59.85	M$55.85

WHALE PRINTING COMPANY

It was Monday morning, and Victor Hussey, president of Whale Printing Company, was considering whether to take on a job at what seemed to him to be a marginal price. A half hour earlier, Katharine Salter, president of Salter Associates, had called to say she needed 10,000 copies of an advertising brochure by Friday noon. She gave Hussey the specifications and said there had been so many delays in getting the copy ready that her regular printer did not have capacity that week. She said he had previously agreed to do the work for $700, and Hussey could have the job at the same price. She needed an answer within an hour.

Hussey's job estimator had converted the specifications to times for the main operations and produced the estimated cost shown in **Exhibit 1**. Material costs were computed and charged separately. **Exhibits 2** and **3** show an abbreviated version of the annual budget plan and the overhead rate computation.

Three people worked in the lithography department, in which copy was converted to plates for the press. Hussey knew that in this week's job schedule were two big jobs to do for regular customers who often prepared copy rather poorly, requiring the lithography people to spend extra time solving problems. Though he had done business with Salter only twice in the previous year, each time the copy had been quite well prepared. Thus, as he saw it, the lithography department would probably have the capacity to handle Salter's job, but problems with the two big jobs could change that. As an unwritten policy, Hussey did not like to ask the lithography people to work overtime unless a real emergency arose.

If he took it, the job would run on one of the three smaller presses. Whale also had a large press that was faster, had more capability, and was more complex to set up. On this Monday, the small presses were not fully scheduled for the week.

The other two departments (cut and bind, and package and ship) probably had capacity because it was easier to run them overtime if necessary.

In a normal week, the presses would run three shifts around the clock for five days, the lithography department one shift, and the other departments one shift with occasional overtime.

Hussey noted that business had been reasonably good of late. However, this coming week showed higher than normal unused capacity on the small presses, though like this Salter job, work for those presses often came in at the last minute.

Exhibit 1

WHALE PRINTING COMPANY
Cost Estimate for Salter Job
(In dollars except for Direct Labor Hours)

Department	Direct Labor Hours	Direct Labor	Supplies	Overhead Rate	Overhead	Total
Lithography	2	$ 30	$40	$30 per DLH	$ 60	$130
Press	4	80	15	80 per DLH	320	415
Cut and Bind	4	60	20	20 per DLH	80	160
Package and Ship	1	15	5	15 per DLH	15	45
	11	$185	$90		$475	$750
Administration and Selling						$ 90
Total						$840

Notes:

Overhead related to plant operations, and the overhead rate was in dollars per direct labor hour. The overhead rate was set at the beginning of each year and was based on the relationship between the budgeted overhead assigned to the department and the budgeted direct labor hours for the department.

The largest items in the overhead cost pool were

- Employee benefits
- Depreciation on building and equipment
- Departmental supervision and plant administration
- Maintenance and engineering, including the computerized control on the large machine
- Utilities

Corporate administration and selling expense amounted to about 10 percent of sales.

Exhibit 2

WHALE PRINTING COMPANY

Hussey's Budget Plan for the Year

Sales	$ 4,000,000
Cost of Sales:	
Direct Labor	700,000
Supplies	400,000
Overhead	2,200,000
Total	$ 3,300,000
Admin. and Selling	400,000
Total Expense	$ 3,700,000
Profit	$ 300,000

Exhibit 3

WHALE PRINTING COMPANY

Overhead Rate Computation

Department	Overhead Budget	Direct Labor Hours Budget	Rate
Lithography	$ 180,000	6,000	$ 30 per hr
Press	1,920,000	24,000	80 per hr
Cut and bind	80,000	4,000	20 per hr
Package and ship	30,000	2,000	15 per hr
Total	$2,210,000		

FINNEGAN'S GARDENS

Patrick Finnegan sat back in his office chair and frowned. In front of him lay the latest income statement for Finnegan's Gardens, the landscaping business he had run since purchasing The Garden Center from Mary Jane Bowers more than four years ago. In general, Finnegan did not spend too much time reviewing his company's financial data. As long as profits continued to rise, Finnegan considered finances to be the responsibility of his accountant, Sue Bennett. Recently, however, he had become more focused on the financial results of Finnegan's Gardens. Finnegan had four children nearing college age, and he knew his family would be incurring substantial higher-education costs over the next several years. Finnegan wanted to grow his business, but did not know which of the company's three service lines presented the most lucrative opportunity.

BACKGROUND

After earning a college degree in landscape architecture, Finnegan spent a summer touring the renowned gardens of Great Britain. Inspired, he returned to his hometown and purchased The Garden Center from Mary Jane Bowers. Finnegan expanded the existing nursery, discontinued retail operations, and transformed the company into a full-service landscaping business. Over time, Finnegan's Gardens gained a solid reputation locally, and demand for the company's services continued to grow. Finnegan took great pride in providing a full spectrum of landscaping and maintenance services to both commercial and residential customers.

SERVICES PROVIDED

Finnegan's Gardens offered three main landscaping services to clients in and around the local area. Finnegan and one other full-time designer provided landscape-design services, which brought in revenue of $180,000 during the past year. In addition, 10 part-time employees installed plant and irrigation systems for Finnegan's design clients and other customers, generating $820,000 in revenue for the company over the past year. Finnegan's Gardens also provided such landscape-maintenance services as lawn mowing, mulching, and pruning on a scheduled basis. During the past year, revenue from this segment totaled $280,000, and Finnegan employed eight part-time workers to handle the existing clientele. The company's one-time design and installation clients often became long-term-maintenance customers.

FINNEGAN'S ANALYSIS

Finnegan looked again at the company's most recent statement of earnings (**Exhibit 1**). Although the firm was clearly making a profit margin of approximately 12

---

percent overall, Finnegan was unsure if all three services were equally profitable, information he needed in order to decide which service(s) he should try to expand. He concluded it was about time he paid attention to the company's accounting data, and decided to call Sue Bennett with some additional questions. Based on their discussion, Finnegan learned the following information:

1. In addition to Finnegan's $85,000 annual salary, the other garden designer earned $62,000 a year. During the past year, an average of 80 percent of the designer's time was spent on design, the rest on general supervision and administration.

2. Plant and sod costs were 45 percent of installation revenues for the year and 15 percent of maintenance revenues.

3. Each installation employee worked an average of 1,500 hours a year at a rate of $15 an hour. Each maintenance employee worked an average of 1,200 hours a year at a rate of $12 an hour.

4. Miscellaneous materials and other supplies averaged 3 percent of revenues for all three service lines.

Following his discussion with Bennett, Finnegan sat down and prepared a statement of earnings for each of the company's service lines (**Exhibit 2**). Finnegan knew that an accurate allocation of the shared costs of depreciation, rent, and support personnel was critical to determining the service-line profits for his company, but he did not know how to go about allocating those expenses. Therefore, he put those costs in a column labeled "Administration," and called Bennett for help.

"I've seen it done several ways," Bennett told Finnegan in response to his questions about overhead allocation. "Sometimes, shared costs for service businesses are allocated based on the number of full-time equivalent employees (FTEs) in each service line. Other times, overhead costs are allocated based on direct-labor dollars, direct-labor dollars plus direct-materials cost, or another metric of your choosing. In addition, you might want to consider which of your three service lines actually use each of the overhead departments."

Together, Finnegan and Bennett determined the number of FTEs for each service line, and how each line used the shared resources of the company during the past year (**Exhibit 3**). He also considered the effects on the shared resources if he decided to grow revenues by approximately 10 percent for each of the service lines. He knew that he was currently at full capacity with his existing trucks, and would need to purchase a new truck to expand any of the service lines. A new truck would cost approximately $25,000, and would be used for at least five years. In addition, if he expanded either the installation or maintenance line, he would have to rent additional nursery space at a cost of $10,000 a year. He thought that most of the other costs would remain approximately the same regardless of the service line he chose to expand. Finnegan looked forward to completing his analysis as soon as possible, and hoped he would not have to concentrate on the financial data for Finnegan's Gardens too much longer.

REQUIRED

1. Using information given in the case, allocate the company's shared costs to each service line four different ways: based on FTEs, direct-labor costs, direct labor and direct materials, and the specific usage information given to Finnegan by Bennett.

2. Calculate the profit percentage for each service line under each overhead-allocation method.

3. Which service line is the most financially attractive? Does the fact that design and installation clients often use Finnegan's Gardens for maintenance services change your answer?

4. Assume volume and revenues for each service line could grow by 10 percent. Which service line should Finnegan expand? Is your answer congruent with your answer to question 3? Why or why not?

Exhibit 1

FINNEGAN'S GARDENS

Statement of Earnings

		Total
Total revenue	$	1,280,000
Plants, sod		411,000
Direct labor		487,200
Other materials, supplies		38,400
Payroll and reception		49,000
Purchasing, accounts payable		31,000
Vehicle depreciation		28,000
Equipment depreciation		18,750
IT systems depreciation		14,000
Office rent and utilities		30,000
Nursery rent, utilities and maintenance		25,000
Total expenses		1,132,350
Net profit	$	147,650
Profit margin		12%

Exhibit 2

FINNEGAN'S GARDENS

Earnings Statement by Service Line

		Total		Design	Installation		Maintenance	Administration
Total revenue	$	1,280,000	$	180,000 $	820,000	$	280,000	-
Plants, sod		411,000		-	369,000		42,000	-
Direct labor		369,600		117,600(a)	225,000		115,200 $	29,400
Other materials, supplies		38,400		5,400	24,600		8,400	-
Payroll and reception		49,000		-	-		-	49,000
Purchasing, accounts payable		31,000		-	-		-	31,000
Vehicle depreciation		28,000		-	-		-	28,000
Equipment depreciation		18,750		-	-		-	18,750
IT systems depreciation		14,000		-	-		-	14,000
Office rent and utilities		30,000		-	-		-	30,000
Nursery rent, utilities and maintenance		25,000		-	-		-	25,000
Total expenses		1,014,750		5,400	618,600		165,600	225,150
Net profit (loss)	$	265,250	$	174,600 $	201,400	$	114,400 $	(225,150)
Profit margin		21%		97%	25%		41%	

a) 80 percent of two designers' salaries

Exhibit 3

FINNEGAN'S GARDENS

Departmental Usage of Shared Resources

	Office Square Feet	Nursery Square Feet	Vehicle Usage	Equipment Usage	IT Systems Usage	FTEs	Purchase Orders
Design	360	-	10%	0%	60%	2.0	20
Installation	65	5,000	45%	90%	5%	7.2	260
Maintenance	65	500	45%	10%	5%	4.6	40
Administration	130	-	0%	0%	30%	2.0	10
Total	620	5,500	100%	100%	100%	15.8	330

WENDY'S CHILI: A COSTING CONUNDRUM

What happens to a successful company when it loses its founder, senior chairman, advertising icon, and beloved leader? That was the question being asked about Wendy's International, Inc. in January 2002 after Dave Thomas, 69, passed away from cancer. In the words of Jack Schuessler, the company's chairman and CEO, "Dave was our patriarch. He was the heart and soul of our company." Without him, the company would never be the same. However, Dave Thomas left behind a legacy about values, ethics, product quality, customer satisfaction, employee satisfaction, community service and shareholder value that provided a solid foundation on which to continue the success the company had experienced for more than thirty years. Still, the patriarch was gone, and the future was uncertain.

HOW IT BEGAN

Wendy's International, Inc. was founded by Mr. R. David Thomas in Columbus, Ohio, in November 1969. Prior to that time, Mr. Thomas had purchased an unprofitable Kentucky Fried Chicken franchise in the Columbus area, turned it around, and subsequently sold it back to Kentucky Fried Chicken at a substantial profit. He then became a co-founder of Arthur Treacher's Fish & Chips. So, at the time he founded Wendy's, Mr. Thomas was no stranger to the quick-service restaurant industry.

Although he had been involved with businesses specializing in chicken and fish, Mr. Thomas's favorite food was hamburgers, and he frequently complained that there was no place in Columbus to get a really good hamburger without waiting thirty minutes or more. Someone finally suggested (whether in earnest or in jest was debatable) that he get into the hamburger business and do it his way. After thinking it over, that's just what he did, and he named his new company after his eight-y ear-old daughter, Wendy. His goal was to provide consumers with bigger and better hamburgers that were cooked to order, served quickly, and reasonably priced. By offering what he believed was a different product, Wendy's went after a different segment of the hamburger market—young adults and adults. In so doing, Mr. Thomas did not view his company as "just another hamburger chain."

Wendy's International, Inc. chose as its trademark what the company called the "old fashioned" hamburger. This was a hamburger made from fresh beef that was cooked to order and served directly from the grill to the customer. So that customers could see what they were eating, "old fashioned" hamburgers were square in shape so as to extend beyond the round buns on which they were served. The unique shape also differentiated a Wendy's hamburger from those of other restaurants. Mr. Thomas felt that one way for Wendy's to remain price competitive and still serve a better quality product was to limit the number of menu items. Thus, he decided on four main products: hamburgers, chili, french fries, and Wendy's Frosty Dairy Dessert. The standard soft drinks and other beverages were also included.

Wendy's old fashioned hamburgers were pattied fresh daily from 100 percent pure domestic beef and served "hot 'n juicy" in accordance with individual customer orders. Customers could choose either a single (one 1/4 lb. patty), a double (two 1/4 lb. patties), or a triple (three 1/4 lb. patties). With the many condiments available, Wendy's was able to offer variety (256 possible hamburger combinations) even though its menu was limited to four basic items. Wendy's chili was prepared daily using an original recipe. It was slow simmered from four to six hours and served the following day. Each eight ounce serving contained about a quarter pound of ground beef. The same beef patties were used in making chili as were served as hamburgers. Although it was sometimes necessary to cook beef patties solely for use in making chili, most of the meat for Wendy's chili came from "well-done" beef patties that could not be served as "hot 'n juicy" old fashioned hamburgers. These "well-done" hamburgers were refrigerated and used in making chili the following day.

Wendy's french fries were prepared from high quality potatoes and were cut slightly longer and thicker than those served by most other quick-service hamburger chains. The company used specialized fryers designed to cook the inside of these bigger potatoes without burning the outside. Wendy's Frosty Dairy Dessert was a blend of vanilla and chocolate flavors that was too thick to drink through a straw. It was served with a spoon to be eaten as a dessert, but some customers ordered a Frosty in place of a soft drink. Whether served as a dessert or as a dairy drink, the Frosty was a distinctive and popular menu item.

INITIAL GROWTH

The first Wendy's restaurant opened in Columbus, Ohio, in November 1969. The second Wendy's opened in 1970, restaurants three and four opened in 1971, and restaurants five, six, and seven opened in 1972. In addition to these seven company-operated stores, two franchised restaurants were opened in 1972. As shown in **Table 1**, a substantial increase occurred in the number of Wendy's restaurants opened between 1973 and 1978, the majority of which were franchised units.

Table 1
Number of Restaurants in Operation

	1973	1974	1975	1976	1977	1978
Company Restaurants	17	46	93	174	231	288
Franchised Restaurants	15	47	159	346	674	1119
Total Restaurants	32	93	252	520	905	1407

Both company and franchised restaurants were built to company specifications as to exterior style and interior decor. Most were free-standing, one story brick buildings, substantially uniform in design and appearance, and constructed on approximately 35,000 square foot sites with parking for 35-40 cars. Free-standing restaurants contained about 2,400 square feet and included a cooking and food preparation area, a dining room designed to seat 92 customers, and a pick-up window to serve drive-thru customers. Wendy's restaurants were usually located in urban or densely populated suburban areas, and their success depended upon serving a large volume of customers. As of December 31, 1978, the 288 company restaurants were located in 18 multi-county areas in and around the cities listed in **Table 2**.

Table 2
Company Restaurants
December 31, 1978

Columbus, Ohio	32	Indianapolis, Indiana	12
Cincinnati, Ohio	19	Fort Worth, Texas	9
Dayton, Ohio	24	Houston, Texas	18
Toledo, Ohio	10	Dallas, Texas	11
Atlanta, Georgia	28	Oklahoma City, Oklahoma	10
Tampa, Sarasota, St.		Tulsa, Oklahoma	10
Petersburg and		Memphis, Tennessee	11
Clearwater, Florida	20	Louisville, Kentucky	12
Jacksonville, Florida	11	Syracuse, New York	8
Detroit, Michigan	11	West Virginia	32

At this time, there were no franchised restaurants located in any of the market areas served by company restaurants.

COMPANY REVENUES

Wendy's initial revenues came from four principal sources. As shown in **Table 3**, these were: sales made by company restaurants, royalties paid by franchise owners (franchisees), technical assistance fees paid by franchise owners, and interest earned on investments. The increase in the percentage of total revenues that resulted from royalties during the five year period covered by **Table 3** was primarily caused by the substantial increase that occurred in the number of franchised restaurants relative to the number of company restaurants.

Table 3
Percentage Revenue Composition
1974-1978

	Year Ended December 31				
	1974	1975	1976	1977	1978
Revenues:					
Company restaurants	94.21%	93.37%	90.16%	87.10%	84.13%
Royalties	3.33	4.26	6.40	9.50	12.65
Technical assistance fees	1.53	1.70	2.16	2.04	1.87
Interest, other income	.93	.67	1.28	1.36	1.35
	100.00%	100.00%	100.00%	100.00%	100.00%

Revenue from sales made by company restaurants was recognized as soon after the sales occurred as was practicable. Because the amount of each company restaurant's daily net sales was to be reported to corporate headquarters in Dublin, Ohio, by 8:00 a.m. the next day, these sales were generally recorded by the corporate accounting staff the day after the sales were made.

Wendy's franchise agreements stipulated that every franchisee must pay to Wendy's International, Inc. a technical assistance fee for each restaurant the franchisee agreed to build within the franchised area.[1] The due date for payment of the technical assistance fee (sometimes referred to as a franchise fee) was negotiated with each franchisee. The earliest due date was at the time the franchise agreement was signed; the latest due date was 30 days prior to the opening of each restaurant.

According to Wendy's management, the technical assistance fees did not contribute substantially to company profits inasmuch as they were generally fully expended on providing a variety of services to franchise owners prior to the opening of each restaurant. These services included: site selection assistance, standard construction plans and specifications, initial training for franchise owners and restaurant managers, advertising materials and assistance, national purchasing agreements, and operations manuals. Technical assistance fees received anytime prior to the opening of the related franchised restaurants were recorded by the company as "deferred technical assistance fees." Technical assistance fees were recognized as revenue at the time the franchised restaurants commenced operations.

Once a franchised restaurant was opened, franchise owners had to pay Wendy's International, Inc. a royalty of 4 percent of gross sales. In connection therewith, franchisees were required to submit to the company weekly sales reports (due the following Monday) for each restaurant. Payment of the royalty was made on a monthly basis and was due, along with a monthly sales report, by the 15th of the following month. Royalties were recognized on an accrual basis at the end of each month based on the weekly sales reported by franchisees. If necessary, these monthly accruals were adjusted at the time the royalty payments were received from franchisees.

Wendy's did not select or employ any personnel for franchisees, nor did the company sell fixtures, food, or supplies of any kind to franchisees. Also, unlike many other restaurant chains, Wendy's did not derive revenue from owning the franchised units and leasing them to franchisees. All of Wendy's franchise owners either owned their franchised restaurants or leased them from independent third parties. Interest and other income represented the amounts earned on investments, principally certificates of deposit, bankers acceptances, and commercial paper. These amounts were recognized by the company on an accrual basis as earned.

---

[1] Unlike most other quick-service restaurant chains, Wendy's originally granted franchises for geographic areas (i.e., one or more counties) rather than for individual restaurants.

CHILI AND THE WENDY'S WAY

Wendy's was founded on the belief that the combination of product differentiation, market segmentation, quality food, quick service, and reasonable prices would produce a successful company. This combination was often referred to by Mr. Thomas as the "Wendy's Way." The decision to include chili as one of the original menu items was made after careful consideration of the most desirable product mix in keeping with the Wendy's Way.

The first and most important of Wendy's products was, of course, the "old fashioned" hamburger. French fries were the second item included on the menu, primarily because so many customers ate french fries with their hamburgers. It was at this point that a product decision needed to be made that would enhance the successful implementation of the Wendy's Way. Wendy's management knew that the only way their restaurants could serve old fashioned hamburgers directly from the grill in accordance with individual customer orders, and still be able to serve them quickly, was for the cooks to anticipate customer demand and have a sufficient supply of hamburgers already cooking when the customers arrived at the restaurants. The problem with such an approach, however, was what to do with the hamburgers that became too well done whenever the cooks overestimated customer demand and cooked too many hamburgers. Throwing them away would be too costly, but serving them as "hot 'n juicy" old fashioned hamburgers would result in considerable customer dissatisfaction. The solution to this dilemma was in finding a product that was unique to the restaurant industry and that required ground beef as one of the major ingredients. Thus, Wendy's "rich and meaty" chili became one of the four original menu items.

DIFFICULTIES IN THE 1980s

Wendy's continued its growth in total number of restaurants, revenues, and income throughout the first half of the 1980s. Responding to competitive pressures and changing customer demands, Wendy's added chicken to its menu through the acquisition of Sisters International, Inc. The company also expanded and improved its Garden Spot salad bar, added stuffed baked potatoes to the menu, and changed its restaurant decor to reflect a more upscale environment. As a means of providing more flexibility in dealing with franchisees and of facilitating expansion, Wendy's began the use of the single-unit franchise method whereby franchise rights were granted on a restaurant-by-restaurant basis, rather than on an area basis as had been the company's previous practice. In 1985, revenues exceeded $1 billion for the first time, and income set a new record at $76.2 million. Notwithstanding this impressive performance, management faced some formidable challenges. The U.S. economy was softening, and lower discretionary consumer spending served to increase competitive pressures in the quick-service restaurant industry. The company's major competitors had substantially improved the quality of their products, service, and facilities, and they had been aggressively introducing new menu items.

The year 1986 turned out to be the worst in the company's history. Total revenues increased less than two percent over the previous year's, and the company recorded a $75 million charge for business realignment expense. Consequently, Wendy's reported a loss for the year of approximately $5 million, its first loss ever. As an example of the competitive nature of the industry, Wendy's made a strategic decision to serve breakfast on a system-wide basis in June 1985. Shortly thereafter, the economy worsened, and Wendy's major competitors introduced new products targeted specifically at Wendy's customers. This created an environment where it was difficult to justify the investment necessary to accomplish a system-wide breakfast offering. Therefore, in March 1986, breakfast became an optional menu item for both company and franchised restaurants.

In 1987, Wendy's sold Sisters International, Inc. and began a systematic reduction in the number of company restaurants both inside and outside the U.S. The company also continued to expand the availability of its new three-section Super Salad Bar, and by year-end, it was installed at more than 90 percent of company restaurants and approximately 40 percent of franchised restaurants. Due to a $15 million income tax benefit and a $1 million extraordinary gain on early extinguishment of debt, Wendy's reported income of $4.5 million in 1987.

OPTIMISM IN THE 1990s

As Wendy's entered the 1990s, there were indications that the company was about to regain the momentum it had lost during the latter part of the previous decade. Company restaurant operating profit margins, return on average assets, and return on average equity had all begun to improve, and most of the unprofitable company restaurants had been closed. Wendy's was ready to begin a program of prudent, aggressive growth both domestically and internationally.

One of the interesting debates that occurred from time to time during the "realignment period" of the late 1980s and early 1990s had to do with the role of the company's original menu items in light of the introduction of what became known as Wendy's "balanced product and marketing approach." This approach had been introduced to enable the company to respond in a timely manner to ever-changing customer trends with respect to menu composition and pricing. Although Wendy's had abandoned its original "limited menu" concept during the late 1970s, the four original menu items continued to be sold as part of a group of product offerings that management referred to as the core menu.

As a guide for the 1990s, management identified six specific operating objectives, which then became known as "the keys to success." Key #1 was to grow the total number of Wendy's restaurants, with a goal of 5,000 by 1995. Key #2 was to generate consistent real sales growth (e.g., without prices increases) from quarter to quarter. Key #3 was to continue to improve restaurant operating margins. Key #4 was to manage corporate overhead expenses prudently. Key #5 was to enhance return on assets. And Key #6 was to continue to strengthen the entire restaurant system through the selective sale of company units to strong existing or new franchisees, while acquiring units in need of attention from existing franchises.

In addition to Wendy's new operating objectives, the company continued to experiment with new menu items throughout the 1990s. In March 1992, the company began offering five fresh salads to go. In addition, the company introduced a spicy chicken sandwich, and it then added a 5-piece chicken nugget item to its 99 cent Super Value menu. Management's hard work paid off, and the company added almost 2,000 restaurants during the decade.

A significant event occurred for the company in December 1995, when the company merged with Tim Horton, a coffee and baked goods company headquartered in Canada. This merger enabled both companies to expand their own operations across the United States/Canada border, and provided a strong foundation for further expansion of Wendy's and Tim Horton's franchise operations.

THE CHALLENGES OF THE 2000s

The new millennium brought many changes to Wendy's. John "Jack" T. Schuessler was named CEO and Chairman of the Board in March 2000, and the company opened its 6,000[th] restaurant in October 2001. However, these milestones were overshadowed by the death of Dave Thomas in January 2002. Maintaining the momentum of the past decade was going to depend on Wendy's ability to establish itself as the franchisor of choice for franchisees, the employer of choice for employees, and the restaurant of choice for customers. Thus, one of the most critical aspects of customer satisfaction had to do with the quality, price, and variety of the products sold. Menu decisions would likely become increasingly important as Wendy's continued to implement its portfolio approach of "super value" menu items, "specialty" menu items, and "core" menu items.

As the company began its post-Dave Thomas era, management thought that perhaps the time had come to give serious consideration to eliminating at least one of the original menu items. Of these, chili seemed to be the most likely candidate. In addition to being the menu "maverick," chili represented a relatively small percentage of total restaurant sales, and there was considerable controversy over its true profit margin. The issue, it seemed, had to do with determining the actual cost of a bowl of chili. This same issue had, in fact, been debated but never resolved back in 1979 when Wendy's salad bar was introduced. Thus, regardless of the ultimate menu decision, management was determined to figure out once and for all what a bowl of chili really cost.

COSTING THE CHILI

Wendy's chili was prepared daily by the assistant manager, in accordance with Wendy's secret recipe. It was slow simmered in a double boiler on a separate range top for a period of from four to six hours. While cooking, the chili had to be stirred at least once each hour, and at the end of the day it was refrigerated for sale the following day.

Normally, it took between ten and fifteen minutes to prepare a pot (referred to at Wendy's as a batch) of chili. First, the forty-eight 1/4 lb. cooked ground beef patties needed for a batch were obtained, if available, from the walk-in cooler. This took about one minute to do. These patties were ones that had been "well-done" sometime during the previous three days. Most of the time it was not necessary to cook any meat specifically for use in making chili, although the need to do so was more likely to occur during the months of October through March when approximately sixty percent of total annual chili sales occurred. If, as only happened approximately ten percent of the time, it became necessary to cook meat specifically for use in making chili, the number of beef patties needed were taken from the trays of uncooked hamburgers that had been prepared using a special patty machine, at the rate of 120 patties every five minutes, earlier that morning. On average, it took ten minutes to cook forty-eight hamburger patties.

Before placing the meat in the chili pot, it had to be chopped into small pieces. This generally took about five minutes to do. The remaining ingredients then had to be obtained from the shelves and mixed with the meat. This process also took about five minutes to complete, after which the chili was ready to be cooked. The quantities and costs of the ingredients needed to make a batch of chili, and the labor costs associated with the different classifications of restaurant personnel are shown in **Tables 4** and **5**. Other direct costs associated with the chili included: serving bowls, $.035 each; lids for chili served at the carry-out window, $.025 each; and spoons, $.01 each.

CHILI SALES

The selling prices for all of Wendy's products sold by company restaurants were set at corporate headquarters. Although some price differences existed among restaurants in different locations, representative prices for 2001 were $.99 for an 8 ounce serving of chili, $1.59 for a 12 ounce serving of chili, and $1.89 for a "single" hamburger. Chili sales were seasonal, and comprised about 5 percent of total Wendy's store sales compared to about 55 percent for hamburgers. As shown in **Exhibit l**, Wendy's consolidated cost of sales, as a percent of retail revenues, increased to 63.9 percent in 2001 from 63.1 percent in 2000. Food costs in 2001 reflected a 13.4 percent increase in beef costs, which was partially offset by a 1.6 percent selling price increase. Retail sales increased by 6.5 percent, and net income increased by about 14 percent during 2001.

Table 4
Chili Ingredients and Costs

Quantity	Description	Cost
1	No. 10 can of crushed tomatoes	$2.75/can
5	46 oz. cans of tomato juice	1.25/can
1	Wendy's seasoning packet	1.00/packet
2	No. 10 cans of red beans	2.25/can
48	Cooked 1/4 lb. ground beef patties (12 lbs. of ground beef)	3.50/lb.

Note: The batch of chili described above yielded approximately 57 eight-ounce servings.

Table 5
Restaurant Labor Costs

Description	Cost
Store Manager	$800.00/week (salary)
Co-Manager	12.50/hour
Assistant Manager	10.50/hour
Management Trainee	7.00/hour
Crew	5.75/hour

Note: Payroll taxes and other employee-related costs averaged about 10 percent of the above amounts.

REQUIRED

1. How was Wendy's able to achieve its initial success and to grow so rapidly at a time when the quick-service hamburger business appeared to be saturated?

2. What benefits might have resulted from Wendy's "limited menu" concept? What were the disadvantages of such a concept? Why was the concept eventually discontinued?

3. Why was Wendy's drive-thru window successful when other quick-service restaurant chains had been unsuccessful at implementing the same concept?

4. How much does a bowl of chili cost on a full cost basis? On an out-of-pocket basis?

5. For determining the true profitability of chili, how much does a bowl of chili really cost?

6. Would you recommend dropping chili from the menu? Why or why not?

Exhibit 1

WENDY'S CHILI: A COSTING CONUNDRUM

Statement of Income for the Years Ended
December 31, 2001 and 2000

(In thousands, except per share data)

	2001	2000
Revenue:		
Retail operations	$1,925,319	$1,807,841
Other, principally interest	465,878	429,105
	2,391,197	2,236,946
Costs and expenses:		
Cost of sales	1,229,277	1,140,840
Company restaurant operating costs	406,185	382,963
Operating costs	91,701	86,272
General and administrative expenses	216,124	208,173
Depreciation and amortization of property and equipment	118,280	108,297
International charges	-	18,370
Other expense	1,722	5,514
Interest, net	20,528	15,080
	2,083,817	1,965,509
Income before income taxes	307,380	271,437
Income taxes	113,731	101,789
Net income	$ 193,649	$ 169,648
Net income per common and common equivalent share	$1.65	$1.44
Weighted average of common and common equivalent shares outstanding	121,144	122,483
Dividends per common share	$.24	$.24

NARNIA, INC.

Once there was a company called Narnia, Inc. Its management developed three wonderful products and prepared to sell them. Prices would be set at 10 percent above cost so that a fair and reasonable profit would be made. Product A required six manual assembly operations, product B required three machining and three assembly steps, and product C required nine steps done on automatic numerically controlled machines. The projected costs and planned volumes were as follows:

Table 1
Narnia's Costs

	Product A	Product B	Product C
Material per unit	$6.00	$12.00	$18.00
Labor per unit	$10.00	$6.00	$4.00
Planned volume	1 million	1 million	1 million
Total material	$6M	$12M	$18M
Total labor	$10M	$6M	$4M

All other costs were expected to be $100M. Since Narnia's president wanted to know how much each product cost in order to set a price, she needed some way of dividing these other costs among the three products. Her accountant said that since usage of labor seemed to represent usage of capacity, it seemed fair to charge each product for its share of other costs according to the amount of labor that product used. Then, price would be based on each product's total cost plus 10 percent. On this basis, product A used 50 percent of direct labor and would be charged for 50 percent of the other costs, or $50 million. Product B would be charged $30 million, and product C $20 million. Projected costs and profit per unit would then be as follows:

Table 2
Narnia's Unit Costs, Profit and Selling Price

	Product A	Product B	Product C
Material	$ 6.00	$12.00	$18.00
Labor	10.00	6.00	4.00
Other Costs	50.00	30.00	20.00
Total	$66.00	$48.00	$42.00
Profit at 10%	6.60	4.80	4.20
Selling price	$72.60	$52.80	$46.20

Narnia began marketing its three unique products, and their sales built up nicely. Soon, demand for all these products was straining Narnia's capacity. Wishing to capitalize on its excellent products, Narnia's management began to make plans to increase capacity.

Now in the same land were three other companies preparing to start production and sale of products that were very similar to Narnia's. Each company was going to specialize in one of the products, and a peek at their cost projections revealed the following:

Table 3
Cost Projections of the Three Competitors

	Company X Product Ada	Company Y Product Beeta	Company Z Product Cema
Planned Volume	1 million	1 million	1 million
Total Material	$6M	$12M	$18M
Total Labor	10M	6M	4M
Total Other	20M	30M	50M
Per Unit:			
Material	$ 6.00	$12.00	$18.00
Labor	10.00	6.00	4.00
Other Cost	20.00	30.00	50.00
Total Cost	$36.00	$48.00	$72.00
Profit	3.60	4.80	7.20
Selling Price	$39.60	$52.80	$79.20

The Narnia company had been selling its three products about six months by the time the other three companies perfected their products. When companies X, Y, and Z entered the market, Narnia's management was surprised at their selling prices. Company X seemed to be trying to buy into the market by selling at a loss; soon they would either raise their price or go bankrupt. Company Y was going to be tough competition, but company Z was clearly much less efficient than Narnia.

Narnia's management decided to double the production of product C, but delay expanding production of products A and B.

What do you think happened next?

MONROE CLOCK COMPANY (B)

Jim Monroe, president of the Monroe Clock Company, had just finished saying he did not think they knew what the new household timer was going to cost. His controller, Tom Grant, had provided figures showing a full cost of $11.60, and Frank Tyler, his sales manager, had worked out a cost of $6.30. Frank said that was the timer's cost using only incremental costs. These computations are shown in the Monroe Clock Company (A) case.

"Alright," said Frank, "if you don't like our figures, what figures do you want to anoint?"

THE COMPANY

Monroe Clock Company was started by Jim Monroe, the company's president, in 1985. In 1998, Monroe had sold out to Piedmont Appliance Corporation, but he remained with the company as Monroe Clock's president. Originally, Monroe Clock made decorative electric clocks, but by 1992 Jim had decided he was much better at making the works than the decorations. So the company shifted to making accurate, durable, but inexpensive electric timing mechanisms. The company now made only three basic models, differing in size and strength. Slight modifications were made to fit each customer's needs. Sales had grown to over $50 million, and the timing mechanisms were made entirely for producers of timed electrical appliances. About half of Monroe's output went to Piedmont Appliance and about half to other companies.

THE NEW HOUSEHOLD TIMING DEVICE

After his house was burgled over the 2000 Labor Day weekend, Jim Monroe bought two timers that could be set to turn on house lights in the evening. Then, he had the idea to make a better timing mechanism for household use, one that had two features that he thought made his timer superior to those currently on the market. The Monroe timer had two options: a 48-hour cycle (so that lights would not turn on and off at the same time each day), or two different 24-hour cycles, so that one timer could operate two lights, each on a different 24-hour cycle. The design of these features was quite simple. There were two different 24-hour cycles, and for the 48-hour option, the timer switched back and forth.

Jim's sales manager, Frank Tyler, was not sure how important or valuable these options would be to the potential customer. Furthermore, this complete product would have to be sold through wholesalers and manufacturers' representatives, which were new to Monroe Clock. The company's sales force usually sold to a relatively small number of industrial customers. Frank thought price would be an important factor since other timers were on the market. But before Jim could set a price on the new timer, he needed to know how much it was going to cost.

THE ISSUE OF OVERHEAD COSTS

"Well," said Jim, after saying he did not think they knew what the new household timer was going to cost. "It seems to me this new household timer is different from the timers we usually make. There is a lot more wiring and assembly work involved. Our main products are timing mechanisms, and they all require about the same sequence of production steps. The heavy duty one is a bit different from the others in that it has more machined parts instead of stamped parts, and actually I've wondered for some time whether our plant-wide overhead rate was OK. If one type of work uses a lot more overhead than another, the products that require a lot of high overhead work may be getting a free ride. In the case of the new timer, since wiring and assembly work likely is a low overhead activity, the situation probably is reversed."

"That's true," said Tom, "but the only way to find out if there's much of a difference in overhead is to distribute overhead to the different functions. A lot of that overhead, like occupancy cost and plant administration, can only be distributed in a fairly arbitrary way."

Jim noted that parts of the overhead like machine depreciation and probably machine maintenance could be fairly accurately distributed. After some more discussion, Tom said he'd make some approximations, and they could then decide whether a detailed allocation would be worthwhile.

Tom set up three cost centers, each to have its own overhead rate. These were fabrication, machining, and assembly. If further subdivision into more cost centers was needed, he could do that later.

He then computed direct labor for last year by cost center. This was easy to do because workers were classified to show whether they were direct labor and did not shift among the three cost centers. Thus, payroll information quickly told him the direct labor by cost center.

Then he began allocating last year's functional overhead costs to the three cost centers. He did this mostly by guesswork, but when in doubt, he looked at detailed cost records and talked with the people involved. The result, which he was able to put together the next day, is shown in **Exhibit 1**.

As expected, the machining overhead rate was the highest. However, Tom was surprised that the fabrication rate was not higher in relation to assembly. He decided to check his figures, but did not expect to find any large changes.

Using the new overhead rates, Tom planned to recompute the timer's cost on a fully allocated basis to see what selling price that would suggest. Then he thought he would use $85,000 as a target contribution (from which advertising would be taken) and see how many timers would have to be sold at $8.00, $10.00 and $15.00 to achieve that contribution to fixed costs and profit.

Exhibit 1

MONROE CLOCK COMPANY (B)

Overhead Components as a Percent
of Direct Labor by Cost Center

Overhead Component	Fabrication	Machining	Assembly
Supplemental compensation for direct labor	35%	35%	35%
Supervision	10	20	20
Indirect labor	20	38	42
Machine maintenance	40	150	17
Machine depreciation	30	100	17
Manufacturing engineering	30	75	17
Plant administration	36	40	47
Electricity	10	18	5
Occupancy	35	50	42
Total	246%	526%	242%
Approximate ratio of direct labor dollars	50%	20%	30%

BREEDEN ELECTRONICS (A)

In October 1999, Herman Klein, President, and Marlene Baer, Controller, of Breeden Electronics USA were checking the budgeted figures for Breeden's 2000 operations. Breeden's parent company in Germany had established a target profit for Breeden of $210,000 for the upcoming year. Klein and Baer wanted to make sure they could meet that target.

THE COMPANY

In early 1999, Breeden Electronics, a large German manufacturer of radio equipment, had set up a subsidiary in the United States to manufacture two products Breeden had successfully marketed in Europe. One was a miniature signaling device used primarily for remote operation of garage doors. These "RC1" units consisted of a signal sender, about half the size of a pack of cards, and a receiver, which was a bit larger. A large manufacturer of motorized garage doors had agreed to take a minimum of 100,000 RC1 control units a year. Klein and Baer thought that 120,000 units was a reasonable target for 2000.

Breeden also had designed a similar device that could be used by a householder to turn on inside lights when arriving after dark. This unit, called "RC2," was slightly more expensive to make since the receiving part was a complete plug-in device, while the RC1 receiver was a component of the garage door unit. Initially, Breeden expected to sell the RC2 unit primarily through mail order catalogues. Klein and Baer projected sales of 60,000 units for 2000.

THE BUDGET

Looking at the budget, Baer indicated, "I'm relieved to see that our projection results in a budgeted profit that exceeds the target of $210,000 profit for next year expected by the parent company."

"Me, too," replied Klein. "But we're budgeting a monthly profit of $20,000, so we don't have a large margin for error. Let's see what level of sales would be required to provide the parent company with its target profit of $210,000 for the year."

To start, Baer pulled out the budgeted figures shown in **Exhibit 1**. She recognized that the budget was only approximate since she expected that changes would be made to improve efficiency and perhaps the product design. But she thought the numbers were solid enough for her to use in her analysis of what was necessary to reach the parent company's target profit. In preparing her analysis, she decided to assume that parts, direct labor, and supplies could be considered variable with units produced, and all the rest would be fixed within the time frame and volume range being considered.

Exhibit 1

BREEDEN ELECTRONICS (A)

2000 Monthly Budget

Sales Revenue	RC1	RC2	Total
Produce and sell per month	10,000 units	5,000 units	
Projected selling price	$ 20.00	$ 23.00	
Sales Revenue	$200,000	$115,000	$315,000
Manufacturing Cost			
Parts	$55,000	$32,000	$87,000
Direct labor	35,000	21,000	56,000
Overhead (a)	70,000	42,000	112,000
Total Manufacturing Cost	$160,000	$95,000	$255,000
Manufacturing cost per unit	$16.00	$19.00	
Selling and administrative			$40,000
Total expense			$295,000
Profit			$20,000

(a) Manufacturing overhead:

Supplies	$21,000
Occupancy (utilities, rent, maintenance)	15,000
Equipment maintenance	17,000
Equipment depreciation	8,000
Quality control and production engineering	15,000
Manufacturing administration	36,000
Total manufacturing overhead	$112,000

In this budget, overhead is allocated to the two products on the basis of direct labor estimated for the two products: $2.00 of overhead for each $1.00 of direct labor.

BREEDEN ELECTRONICS (B)

Marlene Baer, controller of Breeden Electronics USA, developed the figures requested by her boss and president of Breeden Electronics USA, Herman Klein. The numbers allowed her to see how the projected sales volume for 2000 related to breakeven, and examine the relative profitability of the two products, RC1 and RC2. (See Breeden Electronics (A) for background.) Baer thought the figures were OK as far as her analysis went, but she began to wonder about some of the assumptions built into her calculations. For example, she had used direct labor as a base for distributing indirect manufacturing overhead because that was the system traditionally used by the parent company. She recognized that the assumption on which that system was based was that the amount of direct labor used by a product was a good predictor of the amount of overhead that should be charged to it.

THE COMPANY

In early 1999, Breeden Electronics, a large German manufacturer of radio equipment, had set up a subsidiary in the United States to manufacture two products Breeden had successfully marketed in Europe. One was a miniature signaling device used primarily for remote operation of garage doors. These "RC1" units consisted of a signal sender, about half the size of a pack of cards, and a receiver, which was a bit larger.

Breeden also had designed a similar device that could be used by a householder to turn on inside lights when arriving after dark. This unit, called "RC2," was slightly more expensive to make since the receiving part was a complete plug-in device, while the RC1 receiver was a component of the garage door unit. Initially, Breeden expected to sell the RC2 unit primarily through mail order catalogues.

THE ALLOCATION OF OVERHEAD

On reflection, Baer didn't think that direct labor was a very good predictor of the amount of overhead that should be charged to a product. She considered whether units might be a good predictor, and decided that units worked well as a predictor of supplies usage. Supplies consisted of wire, connectors, solder, some general types of resistors, and other parts and pieces. To measure how each product actually consumed supplies would be tedious, but she thought a reasonable estimate could be made. She would deal with that later.

Though she thought units worked well for supplies, units did not seem to make any better sense than direct labor for use as a base for distribution of the other types of overhead. Equipment maintenance, for example, had more to do with the types of equipment used than with the units produced or direct labor, though she recognized that more units would probably cause more maintenance expense.

She had heard from the controller of another division in Germany that they were considering activity-based costing (ABC). Baer decided to consider whether ABC would have any value in her situation.

In reading about ABC, she learned that it was most useful where:

1. there was product diversity not recognized by the existing base(s) used for overhead distribution.

2. the amount of overhead was significant.

3. the competitive situation was such that accurate product costs would be helpful to company strategy.

Baer concluded that the amount of overhead was significant and that the competitive situation could well mean accurate product costs would be important. She was not sure, however, about the product diversity requirement. She wondered where, if at all, might use of direct labor as a base for overhead distribution introduce a distortion in product costs?

To get at that question, she decided she had to examine the processes used to manufacture each product. This was actually quite easy for her since she was very familiar with plant operations. Each product went through three kinds of processes:

1. Fabrication, where equipment operators made components such as insulated platforms for electronic parts and housings for the unit. The operation was quite highly automated with large punch presses and special molds together with belts and robots for moving and positioning parts.

2. Assembly, which was not so highly automated but did use some small machines and moving belts.

3. Packing and shipping, in which units were packed in preprinted boxes. The RC1 unit had one configuration of packaging for its single customer. The RC2 unit was currently being shipped to four mail order companies with a total of six configurations.

In addition, there was a significant quality control/production engineering activity and a number of activities related to production, such as purchasing, maintenance, payroll, and receivables/payables accounting. She decided to use the areas she thought might have some diversity between the products, and more important, she admitted to herself, those areas on which data would be the easiest to get. She considered her analytical approach to be a matrix, and began filling in the numbers as she obtained or estimated them. On the top, she listed the four activities she decided to work on first. Down the left side, she listed the budgeted expenses in the existing accounting categories. Her analysis then spread the budgeted expenses across the activities. (See **Exhibit 1**).

She had decided to treat the supplies expense differently from the other overhead expenses, since it was a variable expense and was likely to vary with unit volume. For her earlier calculations, she had used a flat $1.40 per unit ($21,000/15,000 units). Now she thought that number should be sharpened when it came to computing the cost of each product. Her knowledge of the process told her that the RC2 unit was a bit more complicated and would use slightly more supplies. After some more analysis, she decided that a more accurate per unit figure would be $1.37 per unit for the RC1 and $1.46 per unit for the RC2.

Along the way, she realized that some budgeted overhead expenses could not be distributed to the activities using any rational connection. Or put another way, there was not a clear causal relationship between the activities and the budgeted expense. So rather than force an artificial distribution, she designated a fifth "activity" that she called "general operations." She thought that later on, she might peel off some of the expenses in general operations and assign them to a newly designated activity. To make that work, however, she knew she would have to be able to relate the new activities to the products. Purchasing, for example, might be a new activity, but how to relate purchasing to products was a problem she was not ready to tackle. So the purchasing expenses were left in the general operations activity.

Baer distributed the overhead expense to the activities using the most logical method she could think of: square feet for occupancy expenses, estimates of time and parts costs for equipment maintenance expense, and equipment book values for depreciation. She filled in her spreadsheet with the resulting numbers.

Baer decided that the quality control/production engineering expense was driven more by the production activities than by any distinctive product characteristics. Therefore, she decided that the $19,000 total would be distributed to the three production activities. After talking with the people involved in quality control/production engineering about what caused their work, she made the distribution to the three main production activities as shown in **Exhibit 1**.

She now was ready to distribute the total activities cost to the two products. To do that, she wanted to consider what linkage reflected best the way product characteristics caused the activity. She thought of three possibilities: units of product, direct labor used by the product, or as a wild card, elapsed time in the activity. She discarded the units measure because she knew that, at least in fabrication, an RC2 unit used a lot more fabrication resources than an RC1 unit. Either direct labor or elapsed time would reflect that difference. Elapsed time, she thought, was interesting because it reflected not only the time items were worked on, but also the time they waited in a queue, which had some relationship to the way their complexity used the department's resources. But in the end, she chose direct labor, partly because she thought it did measure the product's use of the activity's resources, and partly because the data were easily available.

With a little work extracting existing data on direct labor use in the activities, Baer constructed the table shown in **Exhibit 2** and prepared to carry out the final step to compute the revised manufacturing cost of the two products. She would distribute each of the three overhead amounts for activities in proportion to direct labor in that activity. She would distribute the general operations overhead of $39,000 in proportion to total direct labor for all three activities.

Exhibit 1

BREEDEN ELECTRONICS (B)

Distribution of Direct Labor and Overhead to Activities

Expense	Total	Quality Control	Fabrication	Assembly	Packing & Shipping	General Operations
Direct Labor	$ 56,000		$ 18,500	$ 30,000	$ 7,500	
Overhead:						
Occupancy	15,000	$ 1,000	3,000	5,000	4,000	$ 2,000
Equip. Maint.	17,000	1,000	10,000	4,000	1,000	1,000
Equip. Dep'n.	8,000	2,000	4,000	1,000	1,000	
Qual. Contr.	15,000	15,000				
Mfg. Admin.	36,000					36,000
Total	91,000	19,000	17,000	10,000	6,000	39,000
Qual. Contr.		(19,000)	11,000	7,000	1,000	
Total	91,000	$ 0	$ 28,000	$ 17,000	$ 7,000	$ 39,000
Supplies	21,000					
Total Overhead	$ 112,000					

Exhibit 2

BREEDEN ELECTRONICS (B)

Estimated Direct Labor Per Month by Activity and by Product

	Total	RC1 10,000 Units	RC2 5,000 Units
Fabrication	$ 18,500	$ 10,000	$ 8,500
Assembly	30,000	21,000	9,000
Packing and Shipping	7,500	4,000	3,500
Total	$ 56,000	$ 35,000	$ 21,000

BREEDEN ELECTRONICS (C)

Early in 2001, Herman Klein, President, and Marlene Baer, Controller, of Breeden Electronics USA, were reviewing results for 2000. (See Breeden Electronics (A) and (B) for background.) Sales of the RC1 unit had just reached the minimum guarantee of 100,000 units, or 20,000 units below their target for the year. Offsetting their disappointment with those results was a high level of satisfaction with the mail order sales of the RC2 unit, which reached 80,000 units. During the year, the item had been picked up and featured by five new mail order customers. It was included, but not featured, in thirteen other catalogues.

Klein was proud of how his organization had responded to the mail order companies, particularly during the months leading up to Christmas. Their requirements were not easy to meet. Two of the largest companies ordered weekly from September through the second week in December, and twice in several weeks of November and December. Others ordered every two or three weeks. Most of the companies required shipment within five days and occasionally asked for shorter lead times.

Packaging also became a problem. With more customers, the variety of packaging increased. Packaging included printed display boxes, directions, and sometimes guarantee and repair information. While the garage timers were simple to package with just one customer, mail order timers seemed to involve endless problems.

Klein had been determined to provide satisfactory service and believed they had come through the holiday season with relatively few events that upset customers. He had added a full time expediter to see that the special needs of customers for delivery and packaging were met. Another person in packaging and shipping was also added. In addition to the temporary help used in purchasing and billing, he knew there were probably other expenses incurred to keep customers satisfied.

To get a quick picture of the unexpected expenses, he asked Baer to develop a rough listing of what she thought they had been. **Table 1** shows her list.

Table 1
List of Estimated Extra Expenses for 2000

Expediter (6 months)	$ 12,000
Added person in packaging and shipping (8 months)	12,000
Temporary help	12,000
Cost of expediting purchased components	8,000
Overtime	18,000
Depreciation on additional packaging equipment	8,000
Total extra expenses	$ 70,000

With this information, Baer decided to make a rough estimate of how they came out at the end of the year. (See **Exhibit 1**).

Though her figures were only approximate, they carried a message: Breeden had been much less profitable than they had hoped they would be, and much of the problem seemed to be in those extra expenses, which were mainly caused by the RC2 business. As she thought about how to get a better understanding of what went on, she began to think that they were actually running two factories: one made the two kinds of signaling devices, and the other serviced customers. The first factory produced two products with no variations on each up to the point where they were labeled, packaged and shipped. The second factory handled all the matters relating to packaging, shipping, and customer relations. There were many "products" of the second factory. The service of each customer was certainly a distinct product, and sometimes there were even several types of service (e.g., different packaging or shipment directions) for a given customer. Many activities were involved, and she realized there was wide diversity in the demands put on those activities. It was intuitively clear that not only was the RC2 less profitable than they expected, but some customers were also less profitable than others.

Though she did not want to make her analysis too complicated, she pressed on to get a clearer picture of what had happened. First, she listed the activities that went on in her second factory, which handled packing, shipping and customer communications:

- order processing, from receipt of an order to scheduling production
- setting up of the packaging line with matching boxes, directions, guarantees, etc.
- running the packing line
- assembling the shipment with delivery instructions
- billing
- collections
- cost of capital tied up in accounts receivable.

Except for running the packing line and the cost of tied up capital, she thought that the other activities were driven by orders, not by numbers of items. Beyond just orders as a driver, she recognized that some orders were harder than others to handle (those with short delivery, for example). She thought that at a later stage, she might use an index of difficulty (e.g., 1.2 for difficult, .8 for easy), but as a start, she decided to compute an average cost per order to use to get an estimate of customer profitability. To carry on her analysis, she needed three kinds of information:

1. Numbers of orders
2. Cost of order processing activities
3. Number of orders for each customer

The first was easy because each order had a number. She could simply subtract the year's starting number from the last number of the year. She came up with 420 orders, 20 for the RC1 unit and 400 for the RC2 unit.

The next two steps were harder. It took her several days to develop approximate figures. The activities driven by orders, including receipt of the order, producing and shipping it, together with billing and occasional follow-up, took place in a number of departments. Her plan was to segregate those costs and treat them as a single cost pool, and to treat the remaining costs as they had been treated before. She worked with actual units and budgeted dollar figures (except for the $70,000 extra expenses) because those figures were readily available. She thought the $70,000 in extra expenses should all be attributed to order handling since the total number of units sold was the same as had been budgeted. The following table is the result of her study.

Table 2
Separation of Order-Driven Cost Per Year

	Total	Driven by Orders	Remaining
Direct labor-pack & ship RC1	$40,000	$5,000	$35,000
Direct labor-pack & ship RC2	56,000	15,000	41,000
Overhead-pack & ship	84,000	16,000	68,000
General operations	468,000	38,000	430,000
Selling and Admin.	480,000	24,000	456,000
Total		$98,000	
Extra Expenses		70,000	
Total order handling cost		$168,000	
Number of orders		420	
Cost per order		$400	

Next, she examined the sales records to find out how many orders and how many units each customer ordered. There was one customer for the RC1 unit and 18 customers for the RC2 unit.

Table 3
Customer Orders

	Orders	Total Units Ordered
RC1 Customer	20 orders	100,000 Units
RC2 Customers:		
1	50	15,000
2	40	5,000
3	36	7,200
4	30	2,400
5-14 (Total)	200	40,000
15	12	4,800
16	12	2,400
17	12	1,200
18	8	2,000
Total RC2	400 orders	80,000

Finally, she began to reconstruct the cost sheets for the two products, first as originally budgeted and then recognizing actual volumes and order handling costs. (See **Exhibit 2**).

When she took a break, she had four things left to do:

1. Complete her cost sheets for the "two factory" approach.

2. Using those figures, compute the profitability of the RC1 and the RC2 sales to the eight single customers shown in **Table 3**.

3. Compute RC2 profitability for orders of 100 units, 200 units and 400 units.

4. Figure out how 2001 could be more profitable than 2000.

Exhibit 1

BREEDEN ELECTRONICS (C)

Revised Profit Estimates for 2000

	RC1	RC2	Total
Selling price	$ 20.00	$ 23.00	
Variable cost-original	10.40	12.00	
Adjustment in supplies	(.03)	.06	
Variable contribution	$ 9.63	$ 10.94	
Sales in units	100,000	80,000	
Total contribution	$963,000	$875,200	$1,838,200
Normal fixed manufacturing cost	$91,000 x 12		1,092,000
Normal selling admin. cost	$40,000 x 12		480,000
Total cost			$1,572,000
Profit before extra expenses			$266,200
Less extra expenses			70,000
Projected profit			$196,200

Exhibit 2

BREEDEN ELECTRONICS (C)

Per Unit Product Costs

	ABC #1 Budgeted Volume		"Two Factory" Cost Actual Volume	
Driven by units	RC1	RC2	RC1	RC2
Parts	$ 5.50	$ 6.40	$ 5.50	$ 6.40
Supplies	1.37	1.46	1.37	1.46
Fabric. labor	1.00	1.70	1.00	1.70
Fabric. overhead	1.514	2.573	1.514	2.573
Assembly labor	2.10	1.80	2.10	1.80
Assembly overhead	1.191	1.020	1.191	1.020
Subtotal (unchanged)	12.675	14.953	12.675	14.953
Pack & Ship labor	.40	.70	.35	.512
Pack & Ship overhead	.373	.653	.313	.458
General Operations	2.436	2.923	2.227	2.592
Total Manufacturing Cost	$15.884	$19.229	$15.565	$18.514
Driven by orders Total: $168,000	-0-	-0-		
Selling & Admin.				
$480,000/180,000 units	2.667	2.667		
$456,000/180,000 units			2.533	2.533
Total cost	$18.551	$21.896		
Unit price	20.00	23.00	$20.00	$23.00
Profit	$ 1.45	$ 1.104		

ZAUNER ORNAMENTS

As she put the finishing touches on the annual financial statements for Zauner Ornaments, Chia-yi Yu contemplated her schedule for the next few weeks. As the new controller for Zauner Ornaments in Taiwan, Yu thought the slow-sales period in January would be the perfect time for her to focus on Zauner's management-accounting procedures. Yu had recently returned to Taiwan from graduate business school in Europe, and she was anxious to apply the knowledge she had gained at school to her new job. As a first step, Yu decided to research Zauner's current costing methods.

BACKGROUND

Zauner Ornaments was a wholly owned subsidiary of Zauner Crystal, Inc., a large manufacturer of crystal and glass products headquartered in Vienna, Austria. Although originally established as an industrial-glass producer, Zauner Crystal reinvented itself after the Second World War as a producer of fine crystal, glass tableware, and other similar products. The company enjoyed an international reputation as a producer of high-quality glass and crystal at affordable prices owing to the skills of its master artisans, as well as the application of innovative technology in the manufacturing process. Zauner crystal was used in fine restaurants, hotels, and residences throughout the world.

ZAUNER ORNAMENTS

Several years previously, management at Zauner Crystal recognized that growth in the fine-crystal and glass-tableware markets was beginning to slow, forcing the company to search for other growth opportunities. After extensive research, management concluded that expanding into glass Christmas-tree ornaments would allow the company not only to continue to grow, but also to take advantage of Zauner Crystal's unique capabilities. The company leased a small manufacturing facility in Taiwan, and began producing the following three products there:

	Ornaments per Box	Sales Price per Box*
Small glass ball ornaments	12	$9.00
Large glass ball ornaments	6	$11.00
Specialty glass ball ornaments	1	$17.00

*Note: All monetary amounts are expressed in U.S. dollars

COST ACCOUNTING AT ZAUNER ORNAMENTS

In the third week of January, Yu called the sales department to inquire about price-setting procedures for the different product lines. She quickly discovered that the sales department investigated the prices of similar products available in the marketplace and set Zauner's prices accordingly. Yu knew that the company was profitable overall, but wondered if the prices set by the sales department were sufficient to ensure that the individual product lines were profitable. She decided to have one of her senior analysts, Yung Chen, prepare an analysis of unit-product costs for each of Zauner's three products. She thought this might be helpful in determining whether any adjustments in the product prices were warranted. To assist Chen in his task, Yu provided him with a schedule of the factory's annual overhead costs, as follows:

Overhead Item	Annual Cost
Production scheduling	$ 85,000
Machine setups	160,000
Equipment depreciation	220,000
Plant depreciation	150,000
Quality inspection	70,000
Packing	185,000
Plant administration	300,000
Total overhead	$1,170,000

Later that day, Chen returned to Yu's office with a schedule showing his calculation of product costs for each of Zauner's three products (**Exhibit 1**). Chen calculated the cost per box for each product, using a traditional volume-based costing system. Budgeted overhead was allocated to each product line, based on the planned production of ornaments. Chen and Yu were dismayed by the results of Chen's analysis; according to his calculations, Zauner was selling small glass ornaments for $9.00 a box, but it was costing the company $21.12 a box to produce those ornaments!

Yu took these results to the director of Operations, David Metz. "I'm really worried about our pricing and the efficiency of our manufacturing processes," Yu told Metz. "According to this product-cost analysis, we are losing money on both the small and large glass ornaments we produce, while making money on the specialty ornaments. Surely, that can't be the case, can it? Are our costs really that much higher than other firms in the industry?" Metz looked at Chen's schedule and shook his head. "I think I see the problem here," he told Yu. "You've allocated overhead to each product based on production units. Why don't you try this analysis again, this time allocating overhead to each product based upon direct materials and direct labor? I think that method better approximates the actual use of the overhead resource by each product line, and it should fix your problem."

Yu returned to her office and instructed Chen to redo his analysis using direct materials plus direct labor as the allocation base for overhead expenses. Chen soon returned with the product-cost schedule shown in **Exhibit 2**. "Look!" he told Yu. "I think Metz was correct. Allocating overhead based on direct materials and direct labor gives us product costs that are below our current sales price for each product line. I think we're fine now."

Yu felt better after seeing Chen's second analysis, but she was not fully convinced that the revised schedule captured Zauner's product costs in the most accurate manner. While Chen was working on his analysis, Yu met with the manufacturing department to gain a better understanding of Zauner's operations. The results of these meetings are summarized in **Exhibit 3**. She learned that, while all three ornaments were made on the same production lines, specialty ornaments underwent an additional painting process. In the specialty-painting department, 24 fully utilized workers hand-painted intricate designs on the inside of each specialty ornament. Yu also discussed with Manufacturing the types of overhead at Zauner and the specific activities that could be generating the company's overhead costs. She discovered that both production-scheduling and machine-setup costs appeared to be driven primarily by the number of batches required for the annual production volume. Because the number of batches varied by product type, Yu concluded that total yearly batches might be an appropriate means of allocating production-scheduling and machine-setup costs to the different product lines.

In addition, she had a little more difficulty ascertaining the root cause of equipment depreciation. It was unclear whether equipment depreciation occurred because of the number of machine operations performed or because of the machine run time. Based on feedback from the manufacturing department, she decided that the number of machine operations was the better indicator of equipment depreciation. She also thought that plant depreciation could reasonably be based on the factory square footage used to manufacture, paint, and store each box. Her discussions also led her to conclude that the number of inspections performed drove inspection costs, while the number of boxes used drove packaging costs. Plant administration (which included supervision, labor relations, and clerical costs) appeared to be the most problematic in deciding how best to allocate these costs. Yu would have to make that decision soon, and in the meantime, had gathered the data in **Exhibits 4** and **5**, which she thought might be useful in her deliberations.

After seeing Zauner's manufacturing process, Yu recalled reading about activity-based costing (ABC) in graduate school. She remembered that companies used ABC systems to assign indirect manufacturing costs to products based on the activities performed on those products. Yu thought she might be able to use ABC to reflect Zauner's product costs more accurately, thereby improving product-pricing decisions.

REQUIRED

1. Determine the best base for allocating plant-administration costs.

2. Calculate the ABC costs for each product on a per-box basis.

3. What do these results tell you about activity-based costing versus costing based on standard volume or direct materials plus direct labor?

4. What changes, if any, should management make to Zauner's pricing strategy?

Exhibit 1

ZAUNER ORNAMENTS

Calculation of Product Costs: Volume-Based Costing System

Product	Number of Ornaments	Ornaments per Box	Number of Boxes	DM & DL per Box	Total DM & DL	Allocated Overhead	Total Cost	Total Cost per Box
Small colored glass	420,000	12	35,000	$4.00	$ 140,000	$ 599,268	$ 739,268	$ 21.12
Large colored glass	300,000	6	50,000	$5.00	250,000	428,049	678,049	$ 13.56
Specialty ornaments	100,000	1	100,000	$7.00	700,000	142,683	842,683	$ 8.43
	820,000		185,000		$ 1,090,000	$ 1,170,000	$ 2,260,000	

Exhibit 2

ZAUNER ORNAMENTS

Calculation of Product Costs: DM- and DL-Based Costing System

Product	Number of Ornaments	Ornaments per Box	Number of Boxes	DM & DL per Box	Total DM & DL	Allocated Overhead	Total Cost	Total Cost per Box
Small colored glass	420,000	12	35,000	$4.00	$ 140,000	$ 150,275	$ 290,275	$ 8.29
Large colored glass	300,000	6	50,000	$5.00	250,000	268,349	518,349	$ 10.37
Specialty ornaments	100,000	1	100,000	$7.00	700,000	751,376	1,451,376	$ 14.51
	820,000		185,000		$ 1,090,000	$ 1,170,000	$ 2,260,000	

Exhibit 3

ZAUNER ORNAMENTS

Activity Data by Product

Product	Number of Ornaments	Number of Batches	Machine Operations per Ornament	Ornaments per Box	Inspections per Box	Sq. Footage Per Box
Small colored glass	420,000	800	4	12	1	1
Large colored glass	300,000	750	4	6	2	0.5
Specialty ornaments	100,000	500	5	1	4	0.2

Exhibit 4

ZAUNER ORNAMENTS

Historical Five-Year Plant-Administration Costs and Other Data

	Total Plant Administration Costs	Ending Inventory Cost	Plant Personnel	Number of Customers	Total Direct Labor Costs	% of Plant Capacity Used
2003	$300,000	$90,000	122	1200	$520,000	70%
2002	295,000	83,000	122	1250	515,000	75%
2001	285,000	58,000	119	1100	555,000	85%
2000	280,000	50,000	112	800	540,000	90%
1999	290,000	76,000	116	600	500,000	95%

Exhibit 5

ZAUNER ORNAMENTS

Plant Data by Product Line

	Small Colored Glass Ornaments	Large Colored Glass Ornaments	Specialty Ornaments	Total
Ending inventory costs	$26,100	$51,300	$12,600	$90,000
Plant personnel:				
Non-specialty	N/A	N/A	N/A	98
Specialty (painting)			24	24
Number of customers	600	420	180	1,200
Total direct labor costs	$83,200	$93,600	$343,200	$520,000
% Plant capacity used	N/A	N/A	N/A	70%

DATA SERVICES AT ARMISTEAD

It was Thursday afternoon, November 18, 2002, and JoAnne Deacon had just returned to her office at Armistead Insurance Company after a two-week assignment working with one of Armistead's subsidiaries, Data Services, Inc. Deacon had landed a position as financial analyst with Armistead in the summer of 2002, but the work with Data Services was the first real assignment she had been given. James Watkins, Armistead's chief financial officer, had called her into his office, had welcomed her to the company, and had asked her to make a business analysis of Data Services and help him decide about the future of the subsidiary.

In their initial meeting, Watkins had talked about Data Services, and described its current situation as follows:

> Data Services, Inc. began operations in 1997, and its sales have grown rapidly since then. This growth has been the result of an aggressive selling effort by the management of the subsidiary. Unfortunately, Data Services has been operating at a loss since its formation. This subsidiary has become a very controversial subject in the company, and I find that I am caught in the middle. The corporate officers are complaining about the increasing cash investment in a subsidiary that continues to lose money. On the other hand, the management of Data Services is enthusiastic and optimistic about the company's future and wants additional funds for continued growth.

> There are two questions that I would like to have answered concerning the company. Is it a good business for Armistead to invest in? If it is, is it being well managed?

BACKGROUND

Armistead Insurance Company was a large company by industry standards. It had experienced substantial growth over the past 20 years, and had been one of the first insurance companies to automate its operations. By 2002, the company was operating a state-of-the-art Sun data-base server, running Oracle data-base management applications, and two Pentium-based Internet servers, running the Microsoft Windows NT and Linux operating systems, to support the company's actuarial and underwriting functions, claims, sales and marketing, finance, and other operations. These computers usually operated close to capacity for two shifts, but the company had never been successful at getting its managers to schedule work for the third shift, and that large block of time was largely idle. Watkins believed that most managers who used the computer facilities were reluctant to schedule processing in advance and were averse to overnight delays. Data

Services had been established as an application service provider in the hope that the subsidiary would find profitable uses for this third-shift computer time without interfering with the processing of normal operations.

Data Services provided flexible, scalable data-processing and information-storage services designed especially for the fast-food industry. The company received weekly sales, operations, and human-resources data from its restaurant customers via on-line data-entry systems, electronic data uploads, or by scanning custom-designed forms or other documents prepared by the restaurants. Data Services then processed the data and compiled information data bases that were then queried to provide customer managers with information about their labor and materials costs and averages or trends in those costs. Restaurant management could access Web-based real-time or customized reports prepared and maintained by Data Services. In addition, Data Services compiled hard copies of standard operating reports that were mailed to the managements of the customer companies once a month. This information could then be used by restaurant management to analyze the historical performance of any shift at any location, compare shifts within the company, and compare company performance relative to the overall fast-food industry. The objective of Armistead in establishing Data Services as an application service provider was to provide comprehensive analytical services and data storage to fast-food companies to increase their efficiency and productivity while reducing labor costs and other operating expenses.

A shift-month was chosen as a single reporting unit because customer surveys indicated that analysis of similarities and differences among shifts could provide useful comparisons. The number of shifts for a fast-food company depended on the number of outlets that chose to report and the number of shifts at each outlet. An "outlet" was a single location (franchised or owned) of the fast-food chain, and could have as many as four shifts.

The fees charged to fast-food companies by Data Services were based on a monthly rate per reporting shift. Rates were negotiated by the Data Services sales team, and were intended to represent less than 2 to 3 percent of the direct labor costs of the shift-reporting unit for a franchise outlet. In many instances, the information prepared by Data Services resulted in customer cost savings of 10 to 20 percent.

CURRENT DATA SERVICES PERFORMANCE

Exhibit 1 presents the results of operations for Data Services for 2002 as reported to Armistead management. The subsidiary's sales came from four sources:

1. Initial installation of services

2. Standard and custom data summaries

3. Continuing operations

4. Electronic data storage and retrieval

It was generally agreed that Data Services faced only one direct competitor. That company was a subsidiary of the nation's largest fast-food chain, and had been established several years previously to provide computer services to its own outlets. It had standardized its operations, and had begun marketing its services to other fast-food chains in 1990. In 2002, its sales were about three times larger than Data Services' sales.

The rates charged by its competitor were about the same as the rates charged by Data Services, but Mike Nunnally, the president of Data Services, believed that Data Services' product was better:

> Our competitor adapted its internal procedures and services for use by other companies. Data Services started from scratch, and studied the fast-food industry to determine the most useful information that could be accumulated with the least paperwork. We were not biased by established procedures, and for that reason, our services are generally considered to be superior to those of our competitor.

SALES AND MARKETING

JoAnne Deacon became familiar with the operations of Data Services during her meetings with the management. Data Services' top managers and their staffs performed sales duties in addition to handling their general-management responsibilities. They had recruited the 14 new customers who had been acquired over the past fiscal year. They had no established procedures for soliciting customers, but the managers spent a majority of their time visiting prospective buyers. An average of three visits to a customer was needed before a decision was made concerning the service. Approximately one sale was made for every six companies that decided against using the service. Nunnally estimated that the top management and staff spent 75 percent of their time on the selling function.

After a sale was made, a service agent had to make a series of visits to the customer to analyze the required system and assist in its implementation. During these visits, the service agent would usually train the customer's management in recording the necessary data and in understanding the usefulness of the reports from Data Services. On average, an agent spent approximately one day each month with a new customer during the three months of system implementation.

A great volume of scanning, systems integration, and data upload was also necessary to add a customer to the Data Services system. The subsidiary had its own scanning and data-entry staff, but made extensive use of the corporate information-technology (IT) staff "pool" to set up the files for a new customer. Occasionally, the system would have to be modified to meet the needs of a new customer, and, again, Data Services would call upon the corporate IT unit to help with that start-up activity. Data Services was charged for its use of the time of the corporate IT staff.

A one-time charge per shift-reporting unit was made to each new customer in addition to the regular monthly rate. This fee partially offset the costs of installation incurred by Data Services.

Data Services' policy was to grant volume discounts to new customers based on the number of shift-reporting units in the customer's systems. These discounts took the form of reduced monthly rates per shift-reporting unit. In practice, however, the discounts were not applied uniformly, and they were not updated to conform to changes in the number of shift-reporting units per customer. Data Services gave Deacon a customer list as of September 30, 2002, showing the customer number, the number of shifts, the monthly rate for that customer, and the total fees for the month of September (see **Exhibit 2**).

CONTINUING OPERATIONS

As current data were received from customers each week, they were reviewed, organized, and entered into the computer. The files were updated, and reports were run. Data Services staff used a continuous process of manual inspection of documents to detect any recording errors or computer malfunctions. Programmers continually performed program maintenance to fine-tune the system and to ensure a smooth flow of information to all customers.

The service agents, in addition to their implementation duties, periodically visited all customers and performed a supervisory and trouble-shooting function. Each regular customer was visited about once a month.

Occasionally, a customer would ask Data Services to provide the former's management with special data-storage facilities and retrieval services. Data Services was happy to oblige, and billed the customer based on the amount of storage space and computer time required. The costs incurred in connection with those special services were accumulated separately, in designated expense accounts.

SUBSIDIARY OUTLOOK

In the two weeks that Deacon had spent at Data Services, she had become aware of the emotionally charged attitudes that existed among management on the future of the subsidiary. She also knew that many members of corporate management were in favor of limiting investment in the subsidiary. Some Armistead people had even suggested selling the entire system if a suitable buyer could be found. The management of Data Services was opposed to these suggestions. Tom Griffin, the vice president of Data Services, stated the following:

> We have to continue to solicit new customers aggressively. Although the rising costs of labor and materials have increased the number of customers interested in our service, these customers will be lost to competition if we do not get them now. Once a customer implements a system such as ours, the initial costs of manpower and installation generally prohibit that buyer from changing the source of these services, regardless of the advantages to be derived from any new system.

Deacon knew that many factors should be considered in determining the value of Data Services to Armistead. She also knew that James Watkins had to make a decision in the next two weeks regarding the future of Data Services. Deacon was concerned about the recommendations she should make to Watkins regarding the decision about Data Services that Armistead was facing. She was pondering the two questions posed earlier:

1. Does this subsidiary operation constitute a viable business?

2. Is it being managed well?

In order to get started, Deacon decided to allocate the revenues and costs shown in **Exhibit 1** to provide separate profit-and-loss statements for forms, special reports, sales and installation, and continuing operations. The Data Services people had explained that some of the expenses in their income statement were from their own accounting unit, and that some were a result of charges from the Armistead corporate IT department. Armistead corporate IT personnel billed Data Services based on "units of service," where each unit of service represented four hours of corporate IT staff time. Corporate charges to Data Services were as follows:

Charges per Unit of Service:

Data entry	$400
Data control	200
Programming	120
General and administrative	80
Total	$800

Allocated Expenses:

Computer, base charge	$1,600
Computer, processing time	400
Rent and depreciation	360
Total	$2,360

Based on her understanding of the operations at Data Services, Deacon decided that it would be reasonable to allocate all the units-of-service charges to sales and installation because those costs were incurred to cover overflow conditions—as when a new account was being set up. She decided to allocate the computer-processing-time charge to continuing operations, but she was not sure what to do with the computer-base charge or the allocation of rent and depreciation. For the moment, she decided to leave them out of her product-line-profitability calculation.

She studied the other costs and expenses, and, based on the data she had gathered at Data Services, allocated them between sales and installation and continuing operations (her calculations are shown in **Exhibit 3**).

Based on this work, Deacon developed her analysis of revenue and expenses, as outlined in **Exhibit 4**. It occurred to her that it might be useful to know what size customer was break-even for Data Services. In fact, as she thought about that, it also occurred to her that she ought to know what the break-even number of customers would be for the subsidiary. She set about to make those calculations, but she knew that it would soon be time to stop analyzing and begin strategizing.

She knew that Watkins would expect a recommendation from her, and she understood that she would be expected to outline a game plan for both Armistead and Data Services. Watkins had told her that she had the advantage of bringing an unbiased perspective to the problem, but the fact that others in management had some strong biases made her more than a little nervous.

Exhibit 1

DATA SERVICES AT ARMISTEAD

Results of Operations
for the Year Ending September 30, 2002
(in thousands of dollars)

Sales:

Sales and installation	$ 800	
Data summaries	320	
Continuing operations	6,400	
Electronic data storage and retrieval	480	$ 8,000

Expenses:

Data entry	2,000	
Service agents	1,000	
Selling and general management	1,800	
Computer*	2,000	
Travel	1,200	
Data control	600	
Programming	520	
Storage	400	
Data	400	
General and administrative, including postage and communications	480	
Rent, depreciation of office equipment	$ 360	10,760

Profit (loss) $(2,760)

*Computer expense consisted of a fixed charge of $1.6 million, assessed by the corporate group, plus a variable charge for processing time.

Exhibit 2

DATA SERVICES AT ARMISTEAD

Revenue from Customers
for the Month Ending September 30, 2002

Customer	Shifts	Monthly Rate	Monthly Amount
1	266	$18.82	$ 5,006
2	80	45.84	3,667
3	1,143	13.51	15,442
4	192	17.91	3,439
5	38	20.94	796
6	398	13.77	5,480
7	99	22.17	2,195
8	197	20.39	4,017
9	434	20.14	8,741
10	7,364	14.85	109,355
11	1,445	16.75	24,204
12	677	16.17	10,947
13	1,032	14.85	15,325
14	3,080	14.14	43,551
15	272	13.37	3,637
16	448	14.87	6,662
17	562	27.68	15,556
18	629	16.34	10,278
19	492	26.24	12,910
20	641	21.61	13,852
21	316	25.46	8,045
22	501	15.71	7,871
23	919	18.45	16,956
24	313	14.87	4,654
25	1,241	17.47	21,680
26	4,460	11.92	53,163
27	574	12.58	7,221
28	114	19.80	2,257
29	613	25.19	15,441
30	582	20.45	11,902
31	518	16.26	8,423
32	1,789	9.81	17,550
33	1,792	10.64	19,067
34	1,998	11.04	22,058

Exhibit 2 (continued)

DATA SERVICES AT ARMISTEAD

Customer	Shifts	Monthly Rate	Monthly Amount
35	294	$20.79	$6,112
36	419	12.50	5,238
37	375	24.19	9,071
38	77	19.99	1,539
39	3,450	12.86	44,367
40	114	20.06	2,287
41	122	22.90	2,794
42	117	9.65	1,129
43	363	20.80	7,550
44	185	20.35	3,765
45	823	18.36	15,110
46	243	18.96	4,607

Total Customers	Total Shifts		Total Revenue
46	41,801		$634,917

Weighted average monthly rate = $15.19

Note: Variations in monthly fees charged by Data Services to its customers resulted, in part, from the volume discounts that were granted. In addition, the type of service provided by Data Services would often affect the monthly charge per shift-reporting unit. Different customers might require different details and reports about their operations because of differences in their sizes, shift-reporting units, or management-information needs.

Exhibit 3

DATA SERVICES AT ARMISTEAD

Distribution of Expenses for Service Agents ($1,000,000), Selling
and General Management ($1,800,000), and Travel ($1,200,000)
to Two Activities: Sales & Installation and Continuing Operations

Service Agents

Continuing operations:
Average number of customers over year = $32 + (1/2 \times 14) = 39$
39 customers $\times$ 12 visits = 468 visits for continuing operations

Installation:
14 customers $\times$ 3 visits = 42 visits for installation
Total = 510 visits
$1,000,000/510 visits = $1,961 per visit
468 visits $\times$ $1,961 per visit = $920,000 for continuing operations

- $920,000 to continuing operations
- $ 80,000 to sales and installation

Selling and General Management

75% of management and staff time $\times$ $1,800,000 = $1,350,000

- $1,350,000 to sales and installation
- $ 450,000 not allocated

Travel

Management (selling)
14 sales $\times$ 7 companies per sale $\times$ 3 visits per company = 294 visits per installation

Service agents (installation)
14 customers $\times$ 3 visits = 42 visits per installation

Service agents (continuing operations)
39 customers $\times$ 12 visits = 468 visits for continuing operations

294 + 42 + 468 = 804 visits total

$1,200,000/804 visits = $1,493 per visit
468 visits $\times$ $1,493 per visit = $700,000 for continuing operations

- $700,000 to continuing operations
- $500,000 to sales and installation

Exhibit 4

DATA SERVICES AT ARMISTEAD
Analysis of Revenue and Expenses
for the Year Ending September 30, 2002
(in thousands of dollars)

	Expenses not Allocated	Data Summaries	Electronic Storage	Sales & Installation	Continuing Operations Varies with # of Customers	Continuing Operations Varies with # of Shifts	Total
Sales		$320	$480	$800			$6,400
Expenses:							
Data entry				$400		$1,600	$1,600
Service agents				80	$920		920
Selling and general management[1]	$450[1]			1,350			
Computer[2]	1,600[2]						
Travel				500		400	400
Data control				200	700	400	700
Programming				120		400	400
Data Storage costs		$400	$400				
General and administrative					400		400
Rent and depreciation[3]	360[3]			80			400
	$2,410	$400	$400	$2,730	$2,020	$2,800	$4,820
Profit (loss)		$(80)	$80	$(1,930)			$1,580

[1] This is 25% of Data Services' expense for management and staff, which is the portion not used on sales activity. It is not allocated because it is assumed not to vary with sales or operations level. It would vary, however, with the keep or drop decision on Data Services as a whole.

[2] This computer cost is likely fixed over a range of activity levels, and would probably not go away if Data Services is dropped. Its relevance to the keep or drop decision would depend on whether there were other valuable uses of the third shift of computer time.

[3] The relevance of this expense is similar to the computer item.

PART IV

MANAGEMENT CONTROL SYSTEMS: BASIC VARIANCE ANALYSIS

WILMONT CHEMICAL CORPORATION

The Wilmont Chemical Corporation produced a variety of industrial products, including a specialty chemical called SC. SC was packaged and sold by the company in 25 liter plastic containers. At the beginning of each year, the company's controller estimated the unit cost of SC for the coming year as one factor in the development of the product's pricing and promotion strategies. In addition, the estimated cost for SC was used as a benchmark against which to compare the actual cost of production. The estimated direct cost per unit (omitting any manufacturing overhead allocation) of SC for the current year was as follows:

Raw material (10 pounds at $3.00/pound)	$30.00
Direct labor (0.5 hours at $12.00/hour)	6.00
Total direct cost per unit	$36.00

Wilmont Chemical also prepared monthly budgets for production volume, sales volume, and non-manufacturing expenses. In general, management strove to achieve actual results similar to the budgeted amounts and tried to minimize the company's working capital investment by maintaining just-in-time inventory levels. Unfortunately, the market demand and sales price for SC were difficult to predict. In addition, the company's actual direct labor costs were somewhat erratic, primarily due to equipment problems and high employee turnover. Also, the cost of the raw material used to produce SC was significantly affected by unstable crude oil prices and variability in the quality of the available material. Due to the general instability of the environment in which the company produced and sold SC, it was not unusual for actual results to deviate from budgeted amounts. For example, the actual operating results for the most recent month differed from the budgeted amounts as follows:

	Actual	Budget
Production volume, units	11,000	11,000
Sales volume, units	10,000	11,000
Sales price per unit	$45.00	$46.00
Direct labor hours	5,610	5,500
Direct labor cost	$66,759	$66,000
Raw materials purchased, lbs.	120,000	110,000
Raw materials purchased, cost	$384,000	$330,000
Raw materials used in production, lbs.	115,500	110,000
Non-manufacturing expenses	$84,000	$80,000

Wilmont Chemical's accounting policy was to use the actual raw material cost and the actual direct labor cost in applying the LIFO inventory method as the basis for ending inventory valuation and cost of goods sold determination. Work in process inventory was not a factor because it was negligible. Each month, the actual unit cost of SC was compared to the estimated unit cost to see if there was a difference. Significant differences were investigated by management as part of Wilmont Chemical's continuous improvement program.

Based on what he had learned at a recent professional development conference, the company's controller thought the financial statements might be more managerially relevant if raw material inventory were kept at estimated costs and finished goods inventory were kept at estimated production costs. Cost of goods sold would be determined using estimated costs, and differences between actual and estimated costs would be treated as adjustments to the current month's income. The controller thought this new approach would facilitate the identification of any variances from plan, which could be broken down into the price and quantity impacts for both materials and labor. In his opinion, this new approach would enhance management's ability to take appropriate corrective actions.

REQUIRED

1. Prepare an income statement for the most recent month using the company's actual costing system. Assume raw material and finished goods inventory were both zero at the beginning of the month. Calculate the ending inventory costs for raw materials and finished goods.

2. Prepare an income statement for the most recent month using the controller's "managerially relevant" approach. Calculate the ending inventory costs. Explain the differences in the two income statements and in the ending inventory balances.

3. A variation of the controller's "managerially relevant" approach would be to keep raw material inventory at actual cost, recognizing any differences between the actual and estimated cost only for the material used in production. Using this modified approach, prepare an income statement for the most recent month and calculate the ending inventory costs. Explain how this income statement and ending inventory balances differ from the other two approaches.

4. As a manager, which of these three financial statement approaches would you prefer? Why?

HYDROCHEM, INC.

Hydrochem, Inc. processed polychloric oxide to make blank condutronic plates. The company maintained an actual process costing system as the basis for cost of goods sold determination and inventory valuation. However, the company's new controller, Mohini Dang, was considering adopting a standard costing system for management reporting purposes. She believed a standard costing system would provide Hydrochem management with better information and would facilitate the identification of any deviations from plan. To test her hypothesis, Dang decided to compare Hydrochem's financial statements for the month based on actual costs with those same financial statements based on standard costs.

As a first step, Dang calculated the company's current standard cost per plate to be $21.65 as follows:

Raw material (4 pounds at $2.50/pound)	$10.00
Direct labor (0.6 hours at $12.00/hour)	7.20
Manufacturing overhead (allocated)	4.45
Total standard manufacturing cost per plate	$21.65

Typically, the company produced and sold 70,000 plates each month at an average sales price of $27.00 per plate. Budgeted manufacturing overhead for factory rent, equipment depreciation, supervision, utilities, and other manufacturing-related costs was $311,500 per month, or $4.45 per plate at normal production volume. Of this amount, $175,000 was considered to be fixed, and the remainder varied primarily on the basis of machine hours. Each plate manufactured by Hydrochem required 1.5 machine hours to produce.

The company's account balances at the beginning of the month were as follows:

Assets

Raw materials (36,000 pounds at $2.50/pound)	$ 90,000
Finished goods (6,100 plates at $21.70/plate)	132,370
Other assets	668,000
Total Assets	$890,370

Liabilities and Equity

Accounts payable and accrued expenses	$170,370
Other liabilities	140,000
Capital stock	120,000
Retained earnings	460,000
Total Liabilities and Equity	$890,370

The following things occurred during the month:

1. 360,000 pounds of raw material were purchased on account at a price of $2.60 per pound.

2. 328,000 pounds of raw material were used in production.

3. 49,600 hours of direct labor were incurred on account at an average cost of $11.80 per hour.

4. 116,000 machine hours were incurred.

5. Actual manufacturing overhead costs incurred were as follows. Ignore depreciation and assume these overhead costs were all paid.

Fixed	$174,000
Variable	162,000
Total	$336,000

6. 80,000 plates were produced, and 60,000 plates were sold on account at a price of $26.95 per plate.

7. $1,400,000 of accounts receivable were collected.

8. $800,000 was paid on accounts payable and accrued expenses.

Hydrochem used the LIFO inventory method to determine cost of goods sold and ending inventory balances. The company had no work in progress inventory at the beginning or at the end of the month.

REQUIRED

1. Prepare two income statements for the month and two balance sheets as of the end of the month. One set of financial statements should be based on the company's actual process costing system using actual production and inventory costs. The second set should be prepared using the proposed standard costing system, where both raw materials and finished goods inventories reflect standard costs.

2. Explain the differences between the two sets of financial statements. Which costing method should Dang use? Why?

GOMEZ ELECTRONICS, INC.

Gomez Electronics produced three models of portable compact disc (CD) players which it sold under its own brand name. It sold Model A for $47.00, Model B for $52.00, and Model C for $37.00. The company had three production departments: Department 1 performed the component assembly, Department 2 performed the chassis assembly, and Department 3 performed the final assembly where the headphones, controls, and purchased plastic case were added to the CD player. Models A and B went through all three departments, but Model C was handled only by Department 3. For this model, a Japanese chassis was purchased in 1,000 unit lots and assembled with a unique purchased case that Gomez Electronics had designed. Model C had been added to the company's product line in 1999 to take advantage of excess production capacity in Department 3 and to extend the company's product line to a less expensive CD player. Departments 1 and 2 worked two shifts, and management did not believe a third shift would be needed any time soon. Department 3 worked a single shift and, even after the addition of Model C, operated slightly above 50 percent of physical capacity.

The company used a full cost, standard costing system. Standard costs were reviewed and, if necessary, revised annually. **Exhibits 1** and **2** contain information regarding standard costs, budgets, production, sales, and actual costs and expenses. Ending inventories were costed at standard cost. Although the company's president had been reasonably satisfied with the existing costing system, she was evaluating the benefits of changing to a standard direct costing system for internal company use.[1]

In January 2003, the company received an offer to supply a large discount company with 5,000 CD players similar to the present Model C. Deliveries were to be made at a rate of 1,000 a month beginning in March. The only difference between this CD player and the company's Model C player was a different plastic case costing $2.00 per unit less than the case used in the Model C player. The president knew the cheaper case was available in sufficient quantity. The discount company offered to pay Gomez Electronics $28.75 for each CD player, and the president did not expect this cheaper model to affect sales of the company's Model C player.

The president asked her controller to put together information that would help her evaluate the discount company's proposal. In addition, she suggested to the controller that this would be a good opportunity to evaluate the desirability of changing from a full costing system to a direct costing system.

In response, the controller prepared comparative standard cost sheets for Gomez Electronics (see **Exhibit 3**). In addition, the controller was about to prepare income statements for the last six months of 2002 using both the present full costing system and the proposed direct costing system.

---

[1] In this case, "direct costing" is the same as "variable costing."

REQUIRED

1. Using **Exhibit 4**, prepare the comparative income statements for the period July 1 through December 31, 2002.

2. Explain why net income is different under the full costing and direct costing systems. Which approach is more useful in evaluating the discount company's proposal?

3. What conclusions can you draw about the company's performance during the last six months of 2002?

4. What advice would you give the president regarding the discount company's request?

5. Which costing system would you recommend?

Exhibit 1

GOMEZ ELECTRONICS, INC.

Standard and Budgeted Costs
July 1 – December 31, 2002

Standard Labor and Material Cost		Model A	Model B	Model C
Department 1:	Direct Labor	$ 3.80	$ 4.00	
	Material	4.20	5.00	
Department 2:	Direct Labor	5.00	5.30	
	Material	3.80	3.50	
Department 3:	Direct Labor	5.25	6.50	$ 9.00
	Material	5.50	7.00	16.00
Normal volume of CD players (units)		10,000	8,000	6,000

Manufacturing Overhead Budget	Dept. 1	Dept. 2	Dept. 3
Normal unit volume for six months	18,000	18,000	24,000
Variable Mfg. Overhead	$31,500	$36,000	$33,600
Fixed Mfg. Overhead	22,500	21,600	14,400
Variable Mfg. Overhead per CD player	1.75	2.00	1.40
Fixed Mfg. Overhead per CD player	1.25	1.20	0.60

Notes:
1. Within a department, manufacturing overhead was applied on the basis of a single departmental rate per radio for all models.
2. The budget for selling, general and administrative expenses amounted to 20 percent of all other expenses at normal volume.

Exhibit 2

GOMEZ ELECTRONICS, INC.

Actual Costs and Volume
July 1 - December 31, 2002

		Production	*Sales*	
Model A		8,000	7,000	
Model B		10,000	10,000	
Model C		5,000	4,000	

	Direct Labor	*Material*	*Variable Mfg. Overhead*	*Fixed Mfg. Overhead*
Department 1	$ 68,000	$ 86,000	$ 33,000	$ 18,200
Department 2	95,000	61,400	31,400	19,800
Department 3	155,800	198,200	35,500	16,400
Total	$318,800	$345,600	$ 99,900	$ 54,400

Note: Actual selling, general and administrative expenses were $165,300.

Exhibit 3

GOMEZ ELECTRONICS, INC.

Standard Cost Sheets

		Model A		Model B		Model C	
		Full Costing	Direct Costing	Full Costing	Direct Costing	Full Costing	Direct Costing
Dept. 1	Direct Labor	$ 3.80	$ 3.80	$ 4.00	$ 4.00		
	Material	4.20	4.20	5.00	5.00		
	Variable Mfg. Overhead	1.75	1.75	1.75	1.75		
	Fixed Mfg. Overhead	1.25		1.25			
	Total	$11.00	$ 9.75	$12.00	$10.75		
Dept. 2	From Dept. 1	11.00	9.75	12.00	10.75		
	Direct Labor	5.00	5.00	5.30	5.30		
	Material	3.80	3.80	3.50	3.50		
	Variable Mfg. Overhead	2.00	2.00	2.00	2.00		
	Fixed Mfg. Overhead	1.20		1.20			
	Total	$23.00	$20.55	$24.00	$21.55		
Dept. 3	From Dept. 2	23.00	20.55	24.00	21.55		
	Direct Labor	5.25	5.25	6.50	6.50		
	Material	5.50	5.50	7.00	7.00	$ 9.00	$ 9.00
	Variable Mfg. Overhead	1.40	1.40	1.40	1.40	16.00	16.00
	Fixed Mfg. Overhead	0.60		0.60		1.40	1.40
						0.60	
	Total Mfg. Cost	$35.75	$32.70	$39.50	$36.45	$27.00	$26.40
Selling, General and Administrative Expenses (20%)		7.15		7.90		5.40	
	Total Cost	$42.90	$32.70	$47.40	$36.45	$32.40	$26.40
	Selling Price	$47.00		$52.00		$37.00	

Exhibit 4

GOMEZ ELECTRONICS, INC.

Comparative Income Statements
July 1 - December 31, 2002

	Full Costing		Direct Costing	
	Budgeted Sales & Budgeted Production Volume	Actual Sales & Actual Production Volume	Budgeted Sales & Budgeted Production Volume	Actual Sales & Actual Production Volume
Sales	$1,108,000	$997,000	$1,108,000	$997,000
Standard COGS				
Standard Gross Margin				
Variances				
Direct Labor				
Material				
Variable Mfg. Overhead				
Fixed Mfg. Overhead				
Total Variances				
Total Fixed Overhead				
Actual Gross Margin				
Selling, General and				
Administrative Expenses	167,100	165,300	167,100	165,300
Net Income				

Note: Variances for material *prices* and wage *rates* were insignificant. Assume these variances were zero.

PART V

MANAGEMENT CONTROL SYSTEMS: PLANNING, BUDGETING, AND STRATEGIC PROFITABILITY ANALYSIS

BLACKHEATH MANUFACTURING COMPANY—REVISITED

PART I

Mr. Blackheath had promoted Lee High to vice president of finance. Lee had practically been running the firm for several years during which time sales and profit had been declining. On November 15, 2000, Mr. Blackheath announced that his son, Trafalgar Blackheath, would take over as owner and president on January 1, 2001. Trafalgar was a graduate of an MBA program and for several years had been working for a large consulting firm as a marketing specialist. In their private discussions, Mr. Blackheath told his son that the problems in the family firm were marketing rather than financial, so the situation was ready made for Trafalgar. Mr. Blackheath, it seems, had been completely taken by Lee High.

When Trafalgar arrived on December 1, 2000, and began to read various internal reports, he realized Blackheath Manufacturing did not have a cash budget, and there didn't seem to be much in the way of financial planning. Trafalgar asked Lee High about this. Lee's response was that Blackheath Manufacturing ran on the basis of several well-developed decision rules, and budgets weren't necessary because if the firm ever ran out of funds, Mr. Blackheath simply deposited $10,000 or $20,000 in the bank. Trafalgar's response was clear: "My father is a millionaire, but I am not!' Lee indicated he didn't know much about budgeting, but he would get an assistant to work up some "stuff."

Trafalgar decided to call his old friend Crofton Brockley. Brockley was in charge of several large budgeting projects for a consulting firm, and Trafalgar knew Crofton to be a recognized expert on budgeting for small companies. Fortunately for Trafalgar, Brockley wasn't busy that week and was able to fly down the next day.

Crofton spent two days going over the accounting records, interoffice memos, and everything else he could find. On Friday morning, Trafalgar found the following note on his desk:

Dear Trafalgar:

Had to leave last night for Pittsburgh. During the two days I spent in the office, I discovered:

1. You have no budget or control system at all.
2. Lee High's decision rules are all wrong.
3. High doesn't know the first thing about finance, budgeting or manufacturing.

Will be back on Monday morning to talk to you. By the way, if you can find Adelaide Ladywell, I would like to speak to her.

Your friend,
Crofton

Trafalgar was perplexed by the note but decided he had better find out who this Ladywell was. Lee told Trafalgar that Adelaide was a file clerk who had been fired a couple of years ago because she refused to follow company policy. Trafalgar asked Lee if he could find Adelaide. Lee said that he heard she was working for some firm in town and would find out where.

Eventually, Trafalgar found Adelaide working as a bookkeeper for Maze Woolwich. During a phone conversation Adelaide explained about her being fired by Mr. Blackheath. She went on to explain that after she got fired she went to see Mr. Woolwich. Apparently, Woolwich realized that Adelaide was right and that Lee High and Blackheath were wrong. Adelaide went on to say that Mr. Woolwich felt bad about her getting fired. Woolwich had intended to retire but decided to hire Ms. Ladywell as a bookkeeper because he needed additional help and thought that this would give her a chance to find another job. Adelaide had been working for Woolwich ever since.

Shortly after Trafalgar finished talking to Adelaide, Crofton entered the office. With his usual efficiency, Crofton made the following points:

- We had better get a budgeting system immediately and try to see where we are. (Any complex cost accounting would have to wait.)
- Lee has got to go.
- We must decide on how to get a budgeting system put together quickly because Blackheath's might be broken.

Crofton concluded by asking, "Did you find Adelaide Ladywell? She is the only person around here in the last three years who did anything right, and she got fired."

Trafalgar indicated that Ms. Ladywell was going to stop by after work and talk to them. Crofton then suggested Trafalgar fire Lee High and try to rehire Adelaide as the bookkeeper-analyst. That afternoon Lee was fired, given two months pay, and asked to leave the office by 3 o'clock; that evening Adelaide agreed to work for Trafalgar on the condition she would not have to deal with either the older Mr. Blackheath or Lee High. Trafalgar explained that Lee was already gone, and his father left for Florida several days previously.

Adelaide agreed to be at work the following Monday morning. She indicated that Mr. Woolwich was all but out of business and had no need for her services anymore. With that, she left after assuring Trafalgar she would be back on Monday.

PART II

After Lee High had left the office, Crofton Brockley went through all the available records and files and, as a result, was able to establish the following information as a basis to begin the budgeting process.

Items about which Lee High seemed to be correct

Variable Direct Costs	
Direct materials cost per unit	$ .75
Direct labor cost per unit	1.25
Total	$2.00

Variable Overhead

Indirect labor cost per unit	$ .20
Electricity cost per unit	.10
Other overhead per unit produced	.50
Total	$.80

Fixed Costs

Indirect labor per week	$100
Indirect materials per week	300
Electricity per week	75
Factory insurance per week	125
Other overhead per week	110
Total	$710

The office expenses are very close to $781 per week. Of this amount, the breakdown seems to be:

Salaries (including fringe benefits and payroll tax)	$400
Rent on office	200
Depreciation on office equipment	81
Utilities	100
Total	$781

Direct labor is paid on a piece rate basis. Workers are paid $1.25 per unit produced.

Average rate of collection is as follows:

During the month in which sale is made	30%
1st month after sale	40%
2nd month after sale	20%
3rd month after sale	10%
	100%

Several other notations made by Crofton Brockley

(a) Trafalgar expected to draw $1,400 per month for personal use.

(b) Consulting fees will be billed at about $225 per week or $900 per month.

(c) A reasonable estimation of the value of factory and equipment is $70,000. Depreciation should be monthly on the basis of an average useful life of five years. This equipment will have a salvage value of $2,500.

(d) The production process to produce the Great Heath is fairly simple. Raw materials consist of a single item, which is usually entered into the process in the morning. Various machining operations take place during the day. At the end of each day, all the finished units are moved into the storeroom. Because started units are always finished before the workers go home, there is never a work-in-process inventory overnight.

(e) Assume that 2001 net income will be relatively low and, therefore, compute income tax on the basis of 25 percent of net income. Taxes will be paid quarterly at the end of the last day of the quarter.

(f) The inventory of raw materials at the end of December will be 800 units, and there will be 750 units of finished product.

General guidelines set by Crofton Brockley

These guidelines should be followed through the end of 2001, at which time they are to be reviewed and revised.

(a) The estimates of variable costs of production are almost certainly correct.

(b) Fixed costs of production are almost certainly correct at $710 per week, except that there is no estimation or allowance for depreciation. Take fixed cost of production to equal $710 plus depreciation.

(c) Charge fixed factory overhead on a monthly basis. Since the $710 per week amount seems reasonable, charge a monthly amount of $710 times 4½. The over or under applied overhead existing at the end of a month will be charged as part of that month's cost of goods sold.

(d) Establish cost accounting records on the basis of full cost, assuming that normal output is 500 units per week, or 2,250 units per month.

(e) Selling commission should be 10 percent on all sales, and the price on regular sales should be set at $7.00 per unit for at least the first quarter of 2001.

(f) All depreciation should be on a straight-line basis.

Following is an estimation of the balance sheet as it will appear on January 1, 2001, when Trafalgar Blackheath takes over complete control of the business:

Cash	$10,000	Accounts payable	$ 1,275
Receivables	14,000	Notes payable	30,000
Raw material inventory	600	Capital: Trafalgar Blackheath	85,687
Finished goods inventory			
($4.72/unit)	3,540		$116,962
Office equipment	13,122		
Factory equipment	70,000		
Land	5,000		
	$116,962		

REQUIRED

1. Production Budget

Adelaide's first important step in budgeting was to develop a production budget and a raw materials schedule for the first quarter of 2001. Actual sales for October and November of 2000 were available, and reasonable estimates of sales for December and the first four months of 2001 were made.

Actual sales (units)		Expected sales (units)	
October 2000	1,500	December 2000	1,800
November 2000	2,300	January 2001	2,000
		February 2001	2,200
		March 2001	1,900
		April 2001	2,100

Since there was no established policy on production scheduling, inventory planning, or raw materials inventory, it was necessary to establish one. Crofton, Trafalgar, and Adelaide agreed that a policy based on experience would have to wait until some data were collected over the next 6 to 8 months. In an effort to "get things going," they settled on a two-part operational statement of policy:

(a) Production in any month should be scheduled so that an ending inventory of Great Heaths will equal one-half of the next month's expected sales.

(b) Purchase of raw material should be made so that on average there is enough raw material on hand to produce 700 Great Heaths. Thus, no end of month inventory should have fewer than 700 units of raw material.

Prepare a production schedule, schedule of raw material use, and a schedule of raw material purchases for January, February, and March.

2. Cost of Production and Flexible Budget

Adelaide's next task was to prepare a flexible budget that could later be used to prepare a budgeted income statement and would also help Trafalgar tell whether actual expenditures were as they should be. She decided to use the format shown in the variable budget table. On the left she would write in the cost formula which would show how much should be spent on each item for any given production volume. Then she would fill in the amounts for the volume of production she had projected for the first three months of 2001.

Projected number of units produced		*January*	*February*	*March*
Cost Formula	*Cost Item*			
	Materials used			
	Direct labor			
	Indirect labor			
	Electricity			
	Indirect materials			
	Factory insurance			
	Other overhead			
	Depreciation			
	Total cost			
	Cost per unit			

3. Income Statements

Having developed the data in assignments 1 and 2, Adelaide decided to project income statements for January, February, and March 2001.

4. Cash Budgets

After developing the income statements, Adelaide decided to see what would happen to the cash position of Blackheath during the quarter. When Mr. Blackheath actually turns the business over to Trafalgar, Mr. Blackheath will withdraw all cash. All receivables will be due to Trafalgar, and all payables will be his responsibility. Trafalgar expects to pay $30,000 for the business, which will be a liability of the business, and he intends to deposit $10,000 in the firm's checking account to establish a working balance.

- Purchases of raw materials are always made on a 30-day-due basis. Consequently, payments are always made in the month following the purchase of materials.

- It is expected that 1,700 units of materials will be purchased during December 2000.

- Direct labor, all overhead, commissions, salaries, rent, and utilities are paid in the month incurred.

5. Balance Sheet

As a final step in the general budget process Adelaide decided to project a balance sheet as of April 1, 2001.

6. Evaluation of the Budget

Armed with the material developed in items 1 through 5, Adelaide, Crofton, and Trafalgar had a meeting to discuss problems which were likely to arise. What points would be likely to dominate such a meeting? Why?

7. January Activity

In early February, the following information was available on January's activity. Prepare an analysis of the results:

Sales: 2,250 units @ $7.00 per unit
Actual production: 2,250 units
Expenses actually paid:

Direct materials bought	$1,166.00
Direct labor	2,812.50
Indirect labor	895.00
Electricity	325.00
Indirect materials	1,570.00
Factory insurance	562.50
Other overhead	1,600.00
Office expense	2,260.00
Commissions	1,400.00

Ending raw materials were 600 units
Neither Crofton nor Trafalgar had been paid anything yet.

8. Variable Costing

At a meeting in early February, Crofton suggested that Adelaide rework the data under an assumption of variable costing. He argued that seeing the data assuming variable costing would be useful. Furthermore, he suggested that after the variable costing data were developed for actual and projected sales at $7.00 per unit, it would be interesting to see what would happen to profit, cash, and retained earnings if 500 additional units could be sold at an average of $6.00 per unit each month. These additional units, he stressed, would be special offers and should not in any way affect regular sales or selling price. Furthermore, no credit would be given on such sales.

THE SQUEAKY HORN

Eugene Decker hung up his office phone and frowned. As part owner of the Squeaky Horn, a musical-instrument repair shop, Decker was responsible for setting the charges for various types of repairs. A potential customer had just called to inquire about the cost to repair the bridge on her cello. After Decker quoted an estimated price for the job, the woman had remarked, "Thank you for the quote, but I'll be going to Best Instrument Repair. I've heard they give good service, and their prices are lower than yours." Unfortunately, Decker had heard similar statements many times during the past few months. Ever since Best Instrument Repair had opened across town, Decker and his partners had found themselves having to compete for business more than ever before. To attract repair jobs and avoid layoffs, Decker and his partners had lowered prices for minor repairs for the first time in 10 years. Decker looked at the budgeted versus actual operating-profit statement on his desk (**Exhibit 1**). How could he tell what portion of the company's lost profits was due to the price decreases and how much was related to other factors?

BACKGROUND

The Squeaky Horn was a musical-instrument repair shop that specialized in the repair and restoration of band and orchestral instruments. The shop was owned and managed by Decker and two partners, who were all well regarded for their exacting repair work and attention to detail. Professional musicians from all over the country sent their instruments to the Squeaky Horn for minor adjustments or major overhauls. Demanding concert and travel schedules placed great stress on the delicate parts of musical instruments, and professional musicians were careful to keep their instruments in peak condition.

SERVICE LINES

Currently, the Squeaky Horn offered four main services: major and minor repairs and restorations of band instruments such as saxophones and French horns, and major and minor repairs and restorations of orchestral instruments such as violins and cellos. Historically, minor repairs were billed at a rate of $35.00 an hour for band instruments and $32.50 an hour for orchestral instruments. Major repairs and restorations were performed under individual flat-fee arrangements that were quoted to customers based on the type of work needed for each instrument. The Squeaky Horn's three owners performed all major repairs and restorations in the shop. Minor repairs of band instruments were performed by hourly employees, and minor repairs of orchestral instruments were performed by three full-time salaried employees.

In addition, rush jobs for minor repairs were occasionally performed for local customers only. These jobs were subcontracted to a retired employee of the Squeaky

Horn, who performed the repairs for $25 an hour. Rush jobs were billed under flat-fee arrangements that averaged $150 per job. The average rush job took three hours to complete.

THE ANNUAL OPERATING PLAN

At the beginning of the current year, Decker's CPA had prepared the annual operating plan for the Squeaky Horn (**Exhibit 1**). The Squeaky Horn's business was small and relatively straightforward, which enabled the CPA to develop the company's operating budget using specific volume and revenue data for each product line. The following information was used in preparing the annual plan:

1. Based on prior years' work orders, the shop was expected to perform the following number of jobs in the coming year: 390 major band repairs, 1,830 minor band repairs, 540 major orchestral repairs, 1,560 minor orchestral repairs, and 50 rush jobs. Average major repairs were quoted at $400 and $300 for band and orchestral jobs, respectively. The average minor band repair took two hours to complete, whereas the average minor orchestral repair took four hours to complete.

2. All three partners drew annual base salaries of $60,000 plus bonuses of 5 percent of sales revenue.

3. The hourly employees were paid $20 an hour for work performed.

4. The salaried employees were paid annual base salaries of $38,000. To the extent that the number of minor orchestral repairs exceeded 1,560 the orchestral repairers were paid a flat rate of $80 per job to complete those repairs.

5. Replacement parts and other supplies were budgeted at $50 for each major job and $10 for each minor job (including rush jobs), based on experience.

6. Approximately 35 percent of the instruments that the Squeaky Horn worked on were shipped to the shop from out of town. The company expected to incur average shipping charges of $30 per package to ship the instruments back to their owners.

7. Advertising, depreciation, office rent, and miscellaneous expenses were budgeted as fixed expenses.

ACTUAL RESULTS FOR THE YEAR

At the end of the year, Decker's CPA prepared the actual operating-profit statement shown in the last column of **Exhibit 1**. Although Decker knew the Squeaky Horn had experienced significant changes during the past year, he was still shocked to discover that the company's profit was $50,745 less than planned even though revenues had increased by $7,770. In order to understand fully the decrease in profits, Decker sat down and compiled the following information:

1. Owing to increased competition, minor band repairs were billed at $30 an hour, and minor orchestral repairs were billed at $28 an hour.

2. Planned versus actual jobs and average hours per job were as follows:

Job Type	Plan Volume No. of Jobs	Plan Hrs./Job	Actual Volume No. of Jobs	Actual Hrs./Job
Band major repairs	390	7.0	450	7.0
Band minor repairs	1,830	2.0	1,740	3.0
Orchestral major repairs	540	6.0	510	7.0
Orchestral minor repairs	1,560	4.0	1,650	3.6
Rush jobs	50	3.0	55	2.8
Total	4,370		4,405	

3. On average, major repairs and restorations required more replacement parts than in past years. Therefore, replacement-parts expenses for major repairs increased an average of $10 per job for the year. In addition, shipping expenses increased by approximately $5 per package.

4. Advertising expenses were $500 more than budgeted owing to an unplanned printing of flyers for band camp. Miscellaneous expenses, however, were $100 less than budgeted.

REQUIRED

1. Conceptually, what specific factors are likely to explain the difference between planned and actual results for the Squeaky Horn?

2. Prepare a revised budget with all prior planning assumptions retained, but use the total actual number of jobs the Squeaky Horn worked on (i.e., 4,405).

3. Prepare a profit reconciliation of planned versus actual profit by quantifying, in dollar terms, all significant contributing factors. (Hint: What did you identify in question 1?)

4. How do the different compensation arrangements at the Squeaky Horn impact profits?

5. What changes should Decker and his partners make based on the results of your analysis?

Exhibit 1

THE SQUEAKY HORN

Schedule of Planned versus Actual Operating Results

	Plan	Actual
Revenue	$ 656,400	$ 664,170
Owner Salaries - Base	180,000	180,000
Owner Salaries - Bonus	32,820	33,209
Band Repairers Wages	73,200	104,400
Orchestral Repairers Salaries	114,000	121,200
Rush Job Wages	3,750	3,850
Replacement Parts	80,900	92,050
Delivery	45,885	53,961
Contribution	125,845	75,500
Advertising	12,000	12,500
Depreciation	3,600	3,600
Office Rent	48,000	48,000
Miscellaneous	4,500	4,400
Profit	$ 57,745	$ 7,000

CHARLEY'S FAMILY STEAK HOUSE (A)

Charley Turner was in an unusually good mood as he pulled into the parking lot of Charley's Family Steak House No. 2. It was a beautiful day in mid-December 2002, and he was about to have a meeting he had been looking forward to for several weeks. Mr. Turner was scheduled to meet with Alex Pearson, the new manager of Charley's Family Steak House No. 2, to finalize the 2003 operating plan for the restaurant. He hoped this meeting would be a good first step toward increasing sales and improving profitability at all of his restaurants.

BACKGROUND

Unit No. 2 was one of four Charley's Family Steak Houses owned by Mr. Turner through a privately-held corporation. He opened his first family steak house in 1992 on the west side of a rapidly growing cosmopolitan city in eastern Texas. He managed this restaurant for three years, experimenting with various menus, pricing strategies, and customer service concepts. Mr. Turner's goal was to create the best steak house in the city – one that was known for having a pleasant atmosphere, fast and courteous service, high-quality, freshly prepared food, and reasonable prices. As with many other family steak houses, the menu was posted on the wall, and customers went through a cafeteria-style line to place their orders, pick up their beverage, and pay the cashier. The food was then prepared and brought to the tables by a staff of servers. The servers also provided chocolate mints and comment cards to customers once they had finished their meals, and Mr. Turner utilized the customer comments and suggestions to make continuous improvements at his restaurants.

By 1995, Mr. Turner knew he had developed a solid recipe for success. Customers raved about his restaurant's food, service, cleanliness and overall value. During the next few years, he took his finely-tuned formula and replicated it on the east, north, and south sides of the city. As each new restaurant was opened, Mr. Turner would manage the unit himself until operations had achieved the "Charley's Style" of friendly customer service and consistent, high-quality food. By the end of 2001, Mr. Turner owned four restaurants, all of which were similar in size and appearance. None of Charley's Family Steak Houses served breakfast, although Mr. Turner was thinking seriously about test marketing the idea at Unit No. 2 as a means of obtaining greater utilization of his facilities and covering some of his fixed costs.

All Charley's Family Steak House restaurants had identical menus, and prices were similar, although not necessarily the same. Each restaurant manager had the authority to raise or lower specific prices by an amount not to exceed five percent of the suggested prices provided by Mr. Turner. His restaurant pricing strategy was intentionally simple: he determined the expected food cost for each menu item and then applied a predetermined uniform markup to that cost. Food purchases were done centrally by Mr. Turner or his assistant in response to orders placed by the restaurant

---

managers. The chain's menu, shown in **Exhibit 1**, had from four to seven items in each of four categories, ranging in price from $1.99 for a side salad to $16.99 for a lobster dinner. Menu prices were reviewed semi-annually by Mr. Turner.

MANAGEMENT CONCERNS

Charley Turner truly enjoyed restaurant management, but he was becoming increasingly frustrated by the challenge of managing Unit No. 4 while continuing to support and monitor the activities of the other three restaurants. As an entrepreneur, Mr. Turner was extremely attached to his restaurants, and he often wished he could be in all four locations at once. Although he controlled the advertising and purchasing for all four locations, he felt removed from the day to day operations of Units 1, 2, and 3. Consequently, he felt like he didn't really know everything that was going on at these restaurants.

In addition, Mr. Turner was troubled by the fact that every year the restaurant with the highest sales and the largest profit was the one he managed. He wondered if this was because he just happened to be a particularly gifted manager, or if other factors caused his restaurant to outperform the others. Furthermore, he was concerned about the quality of the information he was receiving from each restaurant. A few months earlier, Mr. Turner had discovered that Unit No. 2's previous manager had been falsifying the weekly financial reports sent to headquarters, and he couldn't help but wonder if he needed to improve his overall planning and control system.

Mr. Turner knew he should probably promote one of his assistant managers to be the manager of Unit No. 4, which would enable him to spend all of his time overseeing the operations of all four restaurants. In addition, Mr. Turner was interested in implementing some type of bonus system in 2003 that would make each restaurant manager eligible to earn up to an additional 25 percent of his or her salary. He hoped this system would encourage improved performance, which would increase sales and profits at all of his of restaurants.

Although he had not finalized all the details of the management bonus program, Mr. Turner knew that one of the most important performance measures of the program would be the achievement of predetermined annual sales and profit goals. In the past, each restaurant manager had prepared a forecasted operating statement for the year. However, Mr. Turner had been busy getting new locations up and running, and thus had not had much time to oversee each manager's planning and budgeting process or to analyze fully any differences between budgeted and actual results. He believed the implementation of a bonus system would significantly increase the level of attention his managers paid to their own annual forecasts. In addition, he felt that a more rigorous budgeting and planning process might lead to improved sales and profitability at all four restaurants. He scheduled budget planning meetings for 2003 with each manager, and he viewed these meetings as opportunities to influence their thinking.

FORECASTING REVENUES

Mr. Turner and Alex Pearson began their December planning meeting by discussing Unit No. 2's 2002 sales volume. Toward the end of 2001, Mr. Turner had installed a new touch screen restaurant POS system at each of the four restaurants. Cashiers entered customer orders into the computer system, and orders were immediately transmitted to a computer screen located in the kitchen. Each week, Alex obtained a printed report from the POS system, which showed gross sales by menu item, discount coupon usage, and net sales for Unit No. 2.

Based on the POS reports for the first 50 weeks of 2002, Mr. Turner estimated that a total of 182,000 meals would be sold during the entire year. He suspected this figure was low due to mismanagement of the restaurant throughout much of the year, and could be improved. In addition, he knew that a 100-room economy motel with no restaurant was scheduled to open very close to Unit No. 2 in June 2003. He estimated the hotel would generate an additional 100 to 120 meals per week for the steak house during the latter six months of 2003. Therefore, he targeted a ten percent increase in meals sold in 2003 over the 182,000 meals sold in 2002. Alex thought these projections were rather optimistic, but Mr. Turner insisted the sales target was achievable.

The POS reports also showed that about 38% of the unit's meals were sold during the hours of 11:00 am – 3:00 pm. Alex knew the restaurant was underutilized at lunch-time, and he expected that some of the planned increase in meals sold would occur then through greater promotion of lunch services and healthy, affordable menu items. At the same time, Alex wanted to grow the restaurant's profitable dinner business. With Mr. Turner's consent, Alex decided to set a target of 40% of meals sold at lunch-time in 2003. Average gross revenues per meal were forecasted to be $7.50 for lunches and $10.50 for dinners.

Mr. Turner and Alex turned once again to the POS data, this time to determine the effect of the use of discount coupons on the steak house's net sales. At least once a month, Mr. Turner placed coupons in local newspapers to attract customers. The coupons expired after two weeks, and they could be used any time at any Charley's Family Steak House location. Based on the POS data, coupon usage was expected to average fifty cents per meal for both lunch and dinner.

FORECASTING EXPENSES

Alex was aware of Charley Turner's menu pricing methodology, and he actually thought it worked rather well. Thus, Alex readily accepted Mr. Turner's suggested prices for each menu item. Therefore, food costs for Unit No. 2 were based on the expected total sales of each menu item and the predetermined markup. For 2003, food costs were expected to be 55% of gross sales.

Labor costs at the steak house varied by type of employee. Unit No. 2 employed four full-time cooks, each of whom worked 2,000 hours per year, and sixteen cashiers and servers who worked an average of 1,800 hours during 2002. Labor cost for the cooks was expected to be fixed, while labor cost for the servers and cashiers was expected to vary with the number of customers. In 2002, cooks were paid an average of $12.00 per hour, while cashiers and servers were paid an average of $3.00 per hour.[1] Alex planned to give his cooks a wage increase of $1.00/hour beginning January 1, 2003, but wages for the cashiers and servers were expected to remain unchanged.

---

[1] Consistent with industry practice, cashiers and servers at Charley's Family Steak Houses were paid low hourly wages but garnered additional income from shared tips. Employers of tipped employees were required to pay only $2.13 per hour in direct wages if that amount plus the tips received at least equaled federal and state minimum wage requirements.

Other operating expenses for the steak house included supplies, maintenance and utilities. Alex thought these costs were primarily driven by customer count, but Mr. Turner disagreed. He felt these expenses were primarily fixed in nature and that they varied with customer volume only above a certain base amount. Alex eventually agreed, but he noted that it would be very time consuming to identify the fixed and variable portions of each of these operating expenses. Although Mr. Turner wanted the 2003 forecasted operating plan to be as accurate as possible, he admitted that Alex had a point. Actual other operating expenses were 8% of gross sales in 2002, and Mr. Turner and Alex compromised and agreed to budget these same operating expenses for 2003 at the same percentage of gross sales.

Mr. Turner managed the advertising for all four steak houses at corporate headquarters. Advertising campaigns promoted Charley's Family Steak Houses across the city, promoting the chain's friendly service and great food. In addition, the restaurant managers were allotted a small budget for unit-specific promotion. For 2003, Mr. Turner planned to incur advertising expenses of approximately 3.5% of gross sales for the entire chain. Of the 3.5% of gross sales included in the plan, 0.5% was for use by the restaurant manager, 1% was for broadcast media, 1% was for print media, and 1% was for ad preparation.

Throughout the course of a year, each restaurant incurred certain miscellaneous expenses that were hard to predict. Some of these expenses were fixed, and others varied with customer count. Based on past experience, Mr. Turner and Alex decided to budget the 2003 miscellaneous expenses at a fixed amount of $3,000. Depreciation on furniture, the POS cashier system, and other equipment historically approximated $2,000 per month. Alex informed Mr. Turner that no new equipment would be needed for Unit No. 2 during 2003.

Mr. Turner's corporation held a property and liability insurance policy which covered all four Charley's restaurants. Premiums expense was allocated to each restaurant based on square footage. In 2002, Unit No. 2's portion of the insurance premiums was $9,400. Mr. Turner thought his insurance company might increase the premiums in 2003, but he had no way of estimating the potential increase. In addition, he was considering adding another restaurant in 2003, and he realized that any expansion would raise the total insurance premiums paid and affect the premiums allocated to Unit No. 2. After some discussion, Alex and Mr. Turner decided to assume the 2003 insurance premiums for Unit No. 2 would remain unchanged from 2002 for budgeting purposes.

Mr. Turner paid all of the licenses and fees for all four steak houses at corporate headquarters. In 2002, the licenses and fees applicable to Unit No. 2 were $11,250. He expected the total amounts for all four restaurants to increase by 4% in 2003. Mr. Turner had signed a ten-year lease on the restaurant property in 1996 which required minimum rent payments of $6,000 per month. In addition, the lease terms stipulated that additional year-end rent payments be made equal to 5.0% of the excess of actual gross sales above $1,800,000.

The only other expense listed in the 2003 operating plan was titled "Management." This expense consisted of salaries for Alex and his assistant manager, an allocated charge to cover Mr. Turner's salary, and Unit No. 2's portion of the purchasing, accounting, and other service activities that occurred at corporate headquarters. This expense was estimated to be $95,000 for 2003. The comprehensive operating plan for 2003 for Unit No. 2 is shown in **Exhibit 2**.

REQUIRED

1. Verify and be prepared to explain the amounts presented in the 2003 operating plan for Charley's Family Steak House No. 2 shown in **Exhibit 2**.

2. Assume that the forecasted sales volume for Unit No. 2 in 2003 is reduced to 3,700 meals per week from 3,850 meals per week. What is Unit No. 2's revised projected profit for the year?

Exhibit 1

CHARLEY'S FAMILY STEAK HOUSE (A)

MENU

<u>Top of the Line</u>
Lobster Dinner	$ 16.99
New York Strip	11.99
Jumbo Shrimp	10.99
Prime Rib	9.99

<u>Popular</u>
Sirloin	8.99
BBQ Ribs	8.99
Seafood Platter	8.99
Sirloin Tips	8.79
Chicken Breast	8.29
Rib Eye	8.19

<u>Value</u>
Chopped Sirloin	6.99
Country Fried Steak	6.79
Baked Fish	6.79
Fried Shrimp	5.99
Ham Steak	5.79

<u>Sandwiches and Salad Bar</u>
Chopped Steak	3.99
Fish Fillet	3.79
Beef BBQ	3.79
Barbeque Chicken	3.59
Jumbo Hot Dog	2.99
Salad Bar Buffet	5.99
Side Salad	1.99

Exhibit 2

CHARLEY'S FAMILY STEAK HOUSE (A)

2003 Operating Plan

Gross Sales	$ 1,861,860
Net Sales	1,761,760
Food	1,024,023
Labor	200,096
Other Operating Expenses	148,949
Contribution	388,692
Advertising	65,165
Miscellaneous	3,000
Depreciation	24,000
Insurance	9,400
Licenses and Fees	11,700
Rent (Base)	72,000
Rent (Overage)	3,093
Management	95,000
Profit	$ 105,334

Supporting Data:

Average weekly customer count	3,850
% customers - lunch	40%
% customers - dinner	60%
Average gross check - lunch	$7.50
Average net check - lunch	$7.00
Average gross check - dinner	$10.50
Average net check - dinner	$10.00

CHARLEY'S FAMILY STEAK HOUSE (B)

"I guess I'll just have to find out if I can still cook like I used to," thought Alex Pearson, manager of Charley's Family Steak House No. 2, as he hung up the telephone. One of his cooks had just called in sick, one was in the hospital, and the other two were on vacation. He wasn't too concerned, however, because the first two weeks in January were typically not very busy. Many of his steady customers made annual New Year's resolutions about losing weight, and it usually took at least a week for them to resume their former eating habits. Alex's only real concern that morning was how Charley Turner, the owner of the steak house, would assess Alex's performance now that he had completed his first full year as manager.

Unit No. 2 was one of four Charley's Family Steak Houses owned by Mr. Turner. Alex had been promoted from assistant manager to manager of the restaurant in September 2002 after the previous manager was caught falsifying the weekly financial reports that were submitted to Mr. Turner. Alex had previously worked as a cook at Unit No. 1 and as assistant manager of Unit No. 4. He was moved to Unit No. 2 in June 2002 because Charley Turner had serious concerns about the manner in which that restaurant was being managed.

Unlike the other three restaurants, Unit No. 2 was located next to a small shopping center and close to a large office complex. In July 2003, a 100-room economy motel with a pool but no restaurant opened within easy walking distance of the steak house. Except for a sandwich shop and pizza place located in the shopping center, there were no other eating establishments within about one mile of Unit No. 2. Charley Turner considered it to be an excellent location.

In September 2003, Alex developed an express service innovation at Unit No. 2 for frequent lunch-time customers who didn't have much time to eat. It consisted of a "quick-serve" menu (see **Exhibit 1**), prepaid meal cards, and a separate ordering and payment line. This innovative service became very popular with people who worked in nearby office buildings, and it enabled the restaurant to establish a brisk lunch-time business throughout the work week.

Soon after his promotion to manager, Alex had met with Mr. Turner to develop the 2003 operating plan for Unit No. 2. Although the plan was not unreasonable, Alex viewed the sales projections as being very aggressive. Nevertheless, he was delighted with his new position and the opportunities it would provide. He felt confident he would find a way to meet the high expectations Mr. Turner had for Unit No. 2 and for Alex as its manager. Besides, Mr. Turner had informed him that he was considering implementing a bonus system that would make Alex eligible to earn up to an additional 25 percent of his salary. Alex believed the most important performance measure of the bonus program was likely to be the achievement of predetermined annual sales and profit goals. However, he wasn't sure what other performance factors might be used, and he was never asked for his thoughts regarding the implementation of the new bonus plan.

He hoped to have an opportunity to make his views known when he met with Mr. Turner later that week to review the operating performance of Unit No. 2 for 2003.

In planning for his upcoming meeting, Alex had prepared an operating statement comparing the actual results with the original plan for 2003 (see **Exhibit 2**). His task over the next few days was to prepare himself to explain to Charley Turner why Alex thought both he and Unit No. 2 had performed extremely well in 2003 despite the fact that the restaurant's profit was more than 40% less than originally planned. Alex knew that Mr. Turner would not be pleased with Unit No. 2's lower profit, as the actual gross sales volume was greater than expected for the year.

Alex tried to think of all the factors that had affected Unit No. 2's results for 2003, and he jotted them down on a notepad (see **Exhibit 3**). In addition, he prepared a schedule of actual vs. budgeted staff labor hours and wages for the year (see **Exhibit 4**). He knew he had done a good job, and all he had to do now was to convince Charley Turner. Doing so would entail responding to Mr. Turner's two favorite questions: How did actual sales compare with planned sales? and; How well were costs and expenses controlled? Alex suspected that his only hope for receiving a bonus was to prepare an explanation of the 2003 operating results for Unit No. 2 that was comprehensive, logical, and very convincing.

REQUIRED

1. Now that you know 2003's actual gross sales and overall customer count, use that information to prepare a revised budget for all of the restaurant's <u>expenses</u>. In essence, prepare a new budget for each of the restaurant's expenses as if, at the time of making the original budget, you had predicted gross sales and total customer count to be what they actually ended up being. This revised expense budget is often referred to as a <u>flexible</u> expense <u>budget</u>. How do the actual expense amounts compare to the flexible budget amounts? Do you think it is more meaningful to compare the actual expenses incurred to the flexible budget amounts or to the original budget amounts? Why?

2. What were the major factors that contributed to the difference between actual net sales and planned net sales in 2003?

3. Prepare a detailed reconciliation of actual profit with planned profit for 2003.

Exhibit 1

CHARLEY'S FAMILY STEAK HOUSE (B)

Menu for Unit No. 2

Top of the Line

	Lobster Dinner	$ 16.99
✦	New York Strip	11.99
✦	Jumbo Shrimp	10.99
	Prime Rib	9.99

Popular

✦	Sirloin	8.99
✦	BBQ Ribs	8.99
	Seafood Platter	8.99
	Sirloin Tips	8.79
✦	Chicken Breast	8.29
	Rib Eye	8.19

Value

✦	Chopped Sirloin	6.99
	Country Fried Steak	6.79
✦	Baked Fish	6.79
✦	Fried Shrimp	5.99
	Ham Steak	5.79

Sandwiches and Salad Bar

✦	Chopped Steak	3.99
✦	Fish Fillet	3.79
✦	Beef BBQ	3.79
✦	Barbeque Chicken	3.59
✦	Jumbo Hot Dog	2.99
✦	Salad Bar Buffet	5.99
✦	Side Salad	1.99

✦　Quick-serve menu item

Exhibit 2

CHARLEY'S FAMILY STEAK HOUSE (B)

Operating Statement

	2003 Actual	2003 Plan
Gross Sales	$ 1,936,025	$ 1,861,860
Net Sales	1,726,725	1,761,760
Food	1,025,870	1,024,023
Labor	185,800	200,096
Other Operating Expenses	152,450	148,949
Contribution	362,605	388,692
Advertising	78,625	65,165
Miscellaneous	3,320	3,000
Depreciation	24,000	24,000
Insurance	9,780	9,400
Licenses and Fees	10,940	11,700
Rent (Base)	72,000	72,000
Rent (Overage)	6,801	3,093
Management	98,000	95,000
Profit	$ 59,139	$ 105,334

Supporting Data:

Average weekly customer count	4,025	3,850
% customers - lunch	50%	40%
% customers - dinner	50%	60%
Average gross check - lunch	$7.50	$7.50
Average net check - lunch	$6.50	$7.00
Average gross check - dinner	$11.00	$10.50
Average net check - dinner	$10.00	$10.00

Exhibit 2 (continued)

CHARLEY'S FAMILY STEAK HOUSE (B)

Explanation of Operating Statement

Gross Sales: Total sales using menu prices. All menu prices remained the same during the year.

Net Sales: Gross sales minus discounts that were mainly from use of coupons. The coupons were good at any of the four Charley's Family Steak Houses.

Food: The annual food cost in the plan was based on the expected total sales of each menu item and the predetermined markup for that item. For 2003, food costs were expected to be 55% of gross sales. Alex learned that the actual prices of food purchased by Mr. Turner had been about 2% below the level used in the plan.

Labor: The annual labor cost varied by type of employee. Labor cost for cooks was expected to be fixed, while labor cost for servers and cashiers was expected to vary with the number of customers. Actual vs. budgeted staff hours and wages for 2003 are shown in **Exhibit 4**.

Other Operating Expenses: These included supplies, maintenance and utilities. Alex thought they were driven primarily by customer count, and the plan set them at 8% of gross sales.

Advertising: Mr. Turner managed the advertising for the four units. Of the 3.5% of gross sales included in the plan, 0.5% was for use by the restaurant manager, 1% was for broadcast media, 1% was for print media, and 1% was for ad preparation.

Miscellaneous: A catchall for small items, some fixed and some responding to customer-count variations.

Depreciation: This represented straight-line depreciation on furniture, the POS system, and other equipment.

Insurance: This represented both property and liability insurance.

Licenses and Fees: This represented a combination of federal, state, and local business licenses and fees. Some of the amount represented a corporate allocation.

Base Rent: A fixed annual rent paid on the restaurant property.

Rent Overage: A variable amount equal to 5.0% of the excess of actual gross sales above $1,800,000.

Management: This consisted of the restaurant manager's and assistant manager's combined salary of $55,000, a charge assessed to cover Mr. Turner's salary, and Unit No. 2's portion of the purchasing, accounting, and other service activities that occurred at corporate headquarters.

Exhibit 3

CHARLEY'S FAMILY STEAK HOUSE (B)

Alex's Notes for Unit No. 2

<u>Sales Factors:</u>
      Number of customers
      Customer lunch/dinner mix
      Average gross check at lunch and dinner
      Discount coupon usage

<u>Expense Factors:</u>
      Food prices
      Food usage
      Labor rates
      Labor usage
      Spending variances

Exhibit 4

CHARLEY'S FAMILY STEAK HOUSE (B)

Schedule of Staff Hours and Wages

	2003 Actual	2003 Plan
Cooks		
Hours worked	8,000	8,000
Average wages per hour	$12.50	$13.00
Cashiers and Servers		
Hours worked	26,400	32,032
Average wages per hour	$3.25	$3.00

CHARLEY'S FAMILY STEAK HOUSE (C)

As Alex Pearson reviewed the financial results of Charley's Family Steak House No. 2 for 2004, he could hardly believe that a whole year had gone by since he had met with Charley Turner to explain to him why the restaurant had not reached its planned profit for 2003 and to agree on an operating plan for 2004. His recollections of that meeting were actually quite pleasant, as Mr. Turner had been surprisingly receptive to Alex's analysis and explanation of all of the factors that had contributed to the 2003 profit shortfall. Alex was convinced that his decision to prepare a detailed reconciliation of the 2003 planned profit with the 2003 actual profit, including the identification of those factors for which Alex had control and those for which Mr. Turner had control, had been the major cause for the successful outcome of last year's meeting. However, Mr. Turner's subsequent decision to award Alex a $5,000 bonus for 2003 had come as a most pleasant surprise.

This year, Alex was looking forward to discussing Unit No. 2's 2004 performance with Mr. Turner. To prepare for that meeting, Alex reviewed the 2004 operating plan that he and Mr. Turner had agreed upon a year ago for Unit No. 2. The expenses shown in the 2004 plan were determined just as they had been in the 2003 operating plan. Labor costs were expected to average $13.00 per hour for four full-time cooks and $3.25 per hour for cashiers and servers. The lease agreement on the restaurant was not up for renewal until 2006, and so the terms of the monthly rent remained the same as in 2003. A $6,000 increase in management expense over the planned amount for 2003 was expected due to a $4,000 salary increase given to Alex and a $2,000 salary increase given to the assistant restaurant manager.

As further preparation for his upcoming meeting with Mr. Turner, Alex prepared an operating statement comparing the actual results with the original plan for 2004 (see **Exhibit 1**). In addition, he reflected on some of the trends he had noticed at the restaurant over the course of the past year. Customer count continued to rise, which pleased both Alex and Mr. Turner immensely. Furthermore, the restaurant's 2004 POS reports showed a reduction in coupon use as compared to 2003, and Alex thought this trend should result in a more favorable relationship between gross sales and net sales. However, Alex also noticed a continued unfavorable shift in customer mix toward lunch and away from dinner. Actual prices of food purchased by Mr. Turner were one percent higher than expected in 2004, and actual labor hours for cooks and actual hourly wages for cooks, cashiers and servers were as planned. There were no menu price changes during 2004.

Alex knew Mr. Turner would want to understand the profit impact of any deviations from plan. Therefore, he decided to prepare a detailed reconciliation of the 2004 planned profit with the 2004 actual profit. Alex hoped this year's meeting with Mr. Turner would go as well as last year's meeting and that he would receive another bonus for his management of Unit No. 2 in 2004.

REQUIRED

1. Using the actual data for 2004, prepare a flexible expense budget that reflects what each expense should have been for 2004. How do the actual expenses compare to the flexible budget expenses?

2. What were the major factors that contributed to the difference between actual net sales and planned net sales in 2004?

3. Prepare a detailed reconciliation of actual profit with planned profit for 2004. What conclusions might you draw from this reconciliation?

4. Assess Alex Pearson's performance during 2004. Does he deserve a bonus? If so, how much?

5. What type of management bonus system would be appropriate for Charley Turner's restaurants.

Exhibit 1

CHARLEY'S FAMILY STEAK HOUSE (C)

Operating Statement

	2004 Actual	2004 Plan
Gross Sales	$ 1,900,600	$ 1,972,100
Net Sales	1,790,100	1,812,200
Food	1,050,533	1,084,655
Labor	192,400	191,360
Other Operating Expenses	150,168	157,768
Contribution	396,999	378,417
Advertising	70,921	69,024
Miscellaneous	3,260	3,000
Depreciation	24,000	24,000
Insurance	9,650	9,500
Taxes and Licenses	11,170	11,000
Rent (Base)	72,000	72,000
Rent (Overage)	5,030	8,605
Management	100,500	101,000
Profit	$ 100,468	$ 80,289

Supporting Data:

	2004 Actual	2004 Plan
Average Weekly Customer Count	4,250	4,100
% Customers-Lunch	60%	50%
% Customers-Dinner	40%	50%
Average Gross Check - Lunch	$7.00	$7.50
Average Net Check - Lunch	$6.50	$7.00
Average Gross Check - Dinner	$11.00	$11.00
Average Net Check - Dinner	$10.50	$10.00

BELLAIRE CLINICAL LABS, INC. (A)

Joe Mack, chief financial officer of Bellaire Clinical Labs, Inc., looked at the clock on his desk and frowned. He had a busy day ahead of him, and he was fairly sure he would have to work late into the evening for the third night in a row. By the end of the day, Mack had to finalize Bellaire Lab's 2003 operating plan in preparation for his meeting tomorrow with Wilma Lands, the company's chief executive officer. Mack had spent numerous hours developing the current draft of the operating plan, and he was getting pretty comfortable with the process. However, Lands was known to be both detail-oriented and demanding, and Mack knew he had better be fully prepared to answer any questions she may ask.

THE CLINICAL LABORATORY TESTING INDUSTRY

Revenues for the clinical laboratory testing industry in the United States totaled more than $32 billion in 2002. Clinical laboratory tests were used by physicians and other health-care providers to help diagnose and treat patients' medical conditions. The tests were usually performed on blood, urine, tissue, or other specimens. Testing services were provided by hospital labs (approximately 49 percent of industry revenues), labs in physicians' offices (approximately 13 percent of revenues), and approximately 5,000 independent clinical labs (approximately 38 percent of revenues). Although there were some national independent clinical labs, most of the independent labs were relatively small and served regional and local markets.

The primary customers for testing services were hospitals, physicians, and other organizations (e.g., large corporations). Labs billed and obtained payment for the tests, however, from one of several parties: the ordering party (e.g., hospital or physician), the patient, or an other party making payment on behalf of the patient (e.g., the patient's employer, private insurance company or governmental payors such as Medicare [which primarily covered patients over the age of 65] and Medicaid [which primarily covered indigent patients]). Payment for lab testing provided to Medicare beneficiaries was made according to a fee schedule established by the U.S. Congress, which imposed a cap on such payments. In addition, payment for lab testing provided to Medicaid beneficiaries was subject to similar ceilings. In effect, labs had limited ability to influence the price paid for testing services provided to Medicare and Medicaid beneficiaries. In many instances, these amounts were lower than the prices paid by other parties.

BELLAIRE CLINICAL LABS, INC.

A small, high-quality, privately-owned independent clinical laboratory located just outside Boston, Massachusetts, Bellaire Clinical Labs, Inc., provided laboratory-testing services to local physicians' offices, hospitals, and other companies. Founded in 1982, the company specialized in providing swift, accurate medical testing services and electronic communication of results. Bellaire Labs provided both routine blood-testing services (primarily simple blood tests that patients received as part of routine physical examinations) and specialty testing services for more complicated medical problems. Routine tests were highly automated and required lower-skilled personnel than did specialty tests, which were more labor intensive and required highly skilled technologists to administer, conduct analyses, and prepare reports explaining the results.

Although physicians ordered the laboratory tests to be performed on their patients by Bellaire Labs, the costs of billing and collection varied greatly among the parties being billed. These costs were lowest when the physician was billed, highest when the patient was billed, and in-between when other parties—Medicare, Medicaid, private insurance companies, or employers —were billed. To reflect these significant cost differences, Bellaire charged different prices for the tests depending on the party being billed. In addition, the price differential between tests billed to third parties and tests billed to the physician or patient reflected limitations imposed by the fee schedules under which Medicare and Medicaid made payments.

At the end of 2002, Bellaire Labs faced intense competition from national and local independent laboratories. The greater Boston metropolitan area was well known for its high concentration of exemplary physicians and hospitals, and many clinical laboratory companies were attracted to the area. In addition, managed care organizations, Medicare and Medicaid had all increased their efforts to control the cost and utilization of health care services, and these efforts had negatively impacted Bellaire Labs' operating margins for the past several years.

In response to the intense competition and price pressure, Wilma Lands planned to launch a media campaign in 2003 to promote Bellaire Labs' accuracy, responsiveness, and flexibility. In addition, she hoped to position the company as a state-of-the-art clinical laboratory to attract additional contracts for clinical research trials of new drugs, oncology testing, occupational drug testing, and other specialized services. As support for the marketing initiative, the company also planned significant investments in the latest laboratory equipment. Joe Mack knew the future success of Bellaire Labs depended largely upon the success of the media campaign and on the company's performance in 2003. Therefore, he expected Lands to scrutinize the company's operating plan for next year very carefully.

ESTIMATION OF REVENUES

Early in November 2002, Mack had begun the budgeting process by estimating the lab's planned revenues for 2003. Mack knew the revenues for the company were a function of the following four factors: the volume of tests performed, the specific types of tests performed, the mix of billing parties, and negotiated prices. Each year, Mack and his staff employed a five step process to determine planned revenues as follows:

- Estimate future test volume based upon prior year actual test volumes, customer needs, competition, demographic shifts and contract negotiations;

- Estimate how many tests are expected to be routine tests and how many tests are expected to be specialty tests;

- Estimate what proportion of tests will be billed to physicians, patients, or other payors such as Medicare, Medicaid, or private insurance companies;

- Determine the expected average price per test for routine and specialty tests based upon planned tests and negotiated fee schedules; and

- Calculate overall revenue and review total volumes and revenues for reasonableness.

As a first step in his planning process, Mack compiled the 2002 year-to-date annualized volume and revenue data for Bellaire Labs shown in **Exhibit 1**. He knew that the 980,000 tests performed in 2002 represented a 1.5% increase over the number of tests performed by the company in 2001. Furthermore, Mack believed that demographic shifts in the area's population and customer response to Bellaire Lab's planned advertising campaign would generate an additional 1.5% to 2.5% of test volume in 2003 for the company despite increased local competition. Therefore, he projected the lab's overall test volume in 2003 to increase by slightly more than 2.0% over 2002, to 1,000,000 tests.

As the company's CFO, Mack was also well aware of certain uncertainties in the company's contract negotiations with physicians for 2003. A large national laboratory chain had recently opened up several locations in the Boston area, and several physicians had told Bellaire that the larger company was able to provide routine lab work very efficiently and at a low cost. Mack knew that several contracts with local physicians had not been renewed, and that his company was in danger of losing some of the routine lab work ordered by these providers. Therefore, he projected that the total number of routine tests performed by the lab would fall by 23,200 tests in 2003 as compared to 2002.

At the same time, Mack knew that Wilma Lands was working hard to establish Bellaire Labs as a leader in specialized or niche testing services such as clinical research, occupational, diagnostic genetics, oncology, and other complex procedures. Mack expected Land's efforts and the media campaign planned for 2003 to result in increased specialty tests billed to all payors. Therefore, he estimated specialty tests performed by Bellaire Labs to increase by 3,600 tests per month in 2003 as compared to 2002.

As the next step in his planning process, Mack forecasted what proportion of 2003 tests would be billed to physicians, patients, or other payors. Due to the expected loss of several physician contracts, he estimated that only 50 percent of the total routine and specialty tests performed by Bellaire Labs in 2003 would be billed to physicians. In addition, Mack expected a shift towards tests billed to hospitals and pharmaceutical companies due to new contracts to provide certain clinical trials testing procedures and specialized oncology testing services. Thus, the percentage of tests billed to other parties was projected to increase from 28% of total tests in 2002 to 30% of total tests in 2003.

In order to determine the estimated revenues for 2003, Mack obtained the forecasted average price for routine and specialty tests for each billing party from Jennifer Russell, the company's director of billing and reimbursement. To calculate these amounts, Russell utilized an Access database of historical test data and forecasted assumptions of customer needs to break down the 2003 overall volume projections by billing party provided by Mack into estimated test volumes for each of the 2,600 different clinical laboratory tests offered by the company. Then, negotiated fee schedules with Medicare, Medicaid, physicians, hospitals, and other companies were loaded into the Access database, and Russell queried the database to determine the expected weighted average price per routine and specialty test for each billing party. As they reviewed the results generated by the queries, Russell and Mack noted that the expected average revenue per test for both routine and specialty tests by billing party for 2003 remained unchanged from 2002 except for routine tests billed to physicians, which decreased an average of $0.50 per test, and specialty tests billed to other parties, which increased an average of $0.25 per test. Prices for routine tests billed to physicians were expected to decrease due to price pressure from the increased local competition, and prices for specialty tests billed to other parties were projected to increase due to the shift towards high-end tests for clinical trials and oncology testing services in 2003. Overall, the forecasted average prices per test generated by the Access database were consistent with the expectations of Russell and Mack.

As the final step in his revenue budgeting process, Mack reviewed the estimated volumes by test type and billing party and calculated Bellaire Lab's total projected revenue for 2003 (see **Exhibit 1**). In his opinion, the projected volumes and revenues were reasonable given the competitive clinical laboratory industry and the current state of contract negotiations with local physicians, hospitals and other companies.

ESTIMATION OF EXPENSES

To prepare the lab's initial operating expense budget for 2003, Mack sat down with Marty Walters, the company's manager of Operations. Walters had been with Bellaire Labs for only a few months, but he had been hired because of his reputation for astute management and cost control while previously employed at a competing clinical lab. In fact, Walters's employment contract stipulated that he could receive as much as a 20 percent annual bonus based on how effectively and efficiently he managed the overall operations of the lab.

Mack and Walters' first task was to estimate the materials cost for the lab. Materials cost was expected to vary with the number of tests, and the materials cost related to both routine tests and specialty tests was expected to be approximately the same. In 2002, the materials cost per test was $2.80. Walters told Mack that this figure appeared to be high, and that the materials cost per test at his previous employer was only $2.65 per test. He estimated that he could reduce Bellaire Lab's materials cost per test to $2.70 in 2003, and Mack readily agreed to incorporate these savings in the company's 2003 operating plan.

The labor cost for routine tests was expected to vary with the number of routine tests performed during the year. Likewise, the labor cost for specialty tests was expected to vary with the number of specialty tests performed. Based upon the projected test volumes for 2003, Mack and Walters planned a staffing complement of 140 employees for routine tests and 50 employees for specialty tests. Then, Mack and Walters utilized current wage rates, company turnover and expected wage increases of 2.0% to determine average wage rates of $8.25 an hour for routine test staff and $19.50 an hour for specialty test staff.

The company recorded annual depreciation expense using the straight-line method. In 2002, depreciation expense totaled $3.2 million. To support the forecasted shift towards more complicated specialty tests, Walters had purchased new laboratory equipment for $3.0 million which was expected to arrive in January 2003. Mack planned to depreciate the new equipment over ten years using the straight-line method of depreciation and no salvage value.

Bellaire Labs incurred other costs of testing including additional labor, utilities, maintenance, and sanitation expenses. In 2002, these expenses approximated $1.106 per test, and Mack initially used this amount to calculate the expected other costs of testing for 2003. However, Walters disagreed with this approach. In his opinion, the company incurred certain support costs to keep the lab functioning regardless of test volume, while other expenses varied directly with the number of tests performed. After much discussion, Mack agreed with Walters and revised the operating plan as follows: of the total amount budgeted, approximately $300,000 was expected to be fixed, and the remainder was expected to vary with the number of tests performed.

Bellaire Labs employed about 25 full time personnel dedicated to perform billing and collection activities for the company. As noted previously, the costs of billing and collection varied greatly among the parties being billed. Physicians, hospitals, and employers were billed once a month for all tests performed by the lab during that month. Likewise, tests performed for Medicare and Medicaid patients were billed monthly via electronic filing arrangements with these payors. However, self-pay patients were billed individually, and these bills were often hard for the company to collect. To accurately calculate the average billing and collection cost for each payor, Mack had ordered a bi-annual time study for the billing and collections department. For a period of two weeks, department personnel tracked the actual time spent on all billing and collections activities by payor, and this data was used to calculate the total labor cost per test by payor for billing and collection activities. In addition, a resource analysis was conducted to determine the cost per test of materials, postage, computer time, bad debts, and other expenses for billing and collection activities by billing party.

In 2002, the time study and resource analysis showed total billing and collection expenses of $0.50 per test for tests billed to physicians, $3.50 per test for tests billed to individual patients, and $3.00 per test for tests billed to other parties. Both Mack and Walters agreed that a continued focus on process improvement in the billings and collection department should offset the 2.0% wage increase planned for that department in 2003. Therefore, billing and collection costs per test were held constant at 2002 actual cost levels for the company's 2003 operating plan.

Historically, Bellaire Lab's annual advertising and promotion expenses averaged approximately $550,000. However, the latest estimates from the company's director of marketing showed a cost of $820,000 for the proposed media campaign and ongoing marketing efforts in 2003. Furthermore, Mack knew that Wilma Lands had authorized the total expenditures for promotion and marketing efforts in 2003 to vary directly with changes in revenue.

In addition to advertising and promotion expense, the company incurred management and other administrative costs to support the lab. For 2003, executive management salaries and bonuses were expected to total $700,000. Other administrative costs were expected to be fixed at $500,000.

As he put the final touches on the 2003 operating plan for Bellaire Labs, Joe Mack tried to predict Wilma Land's reaction to his work. He predicted that she would not be happy with an increase in test volume of only 20,000 tests over 2002, and he needed to be prepared to defend his assumptions. Personally, Mack wondered if this projected increase in test volumes was too aggressive given the heightened level of clinical lab competition in the Boston area. He knew that Lands was expecting great results from the company's new marketing campaign, and he suspected that she would ask him to run several sensitivities of the operating plan based upon various test volumes.

Exhibit 1

BELLAIRE CLINICAL LABS, INC. (A)

2002 Actual Annualized Volumes, Revenues per Test

Number of tests per year	980,000
% tests, routine	84%
% tests, specialty	16%
% tests paid for by physician	52%
% tests paid for by patient	20%
% tests paid for by other parties	28%
Price, routine test	
when physician pays	$ 14.50
when patient pays	$ 17.00
when other party pays	$ 16.00
Price, specialty test	
when physician pays	$ 20.00
when patient pays	$ 23.00
when other party pays	$ 21.75

BELLAIRE CLINICAL LABS, INC. (B)

Joe Mack, chief financial officer of Bellaire Clinical Labs, Inc., had not anticipated the surprise and concern expressed by Wilma Lands, the company's chief executive officer, during their initial meeting to begin the review of the 2003 financial results for the company. With actual net profit for 2003 slightly above planned profit, and actual net revenue almost $1 million above planned revenue, Mack had expected a more favorable reaction from the CEO. Instead, she responded by asking, "What's been going on? How did we manage to do a million dollars more business without generating significantly more profit? Don't we know how to manage our expenses?" Mack readily acknowledged the relevance of Lands's questions but stated that he had just finished compiling the 2003 results and had not yet had time to "get behind the numbers." He assured her that he would have some answers when they met the following week. Between now and then, Mack knew he had a lot of work to do.

Just prior to his meeting with Lands, Mack had prepared an operating statement comparing the 2003 actual results with the 2003 operating plan (see **Exhibit 1**). He had noticed the disparity between the incremental revenue and the incremental profit, but he had not had time to undertake any detailed investigation. After meeting with Lands, his investigation broadened in scope and took on an added sense of urgency.

THE CLINICAL LABORATORY TESTING INDUSTRY

Revenues for the clinical laboratory testing industry in the United States totaled more than $34 billion in 2003. Clinical laboratory tests were used by physicians and other health-care providers to help diagnose and treat patients' medical conditions. The tests were usually performed on blood, urine, tissue, or other specimens. Testing services were provided by hospital labs (approximately 49 percent of industry revenues), labs in physicians' offices (approximately 13 percent of revenues), and approximately 5,000 independent clinical labs (approximately 38 percent of revenues). Although there were some national independent clinical labs, most of the independent labs were relatively small and served regional and local markets.

The primary customers for testing services were hospitals, physicians, and other organizations (e.g., large corporations). Labs billed and obtained payment for the tests, however, from one of several parties: the ordering party (e.g., hospital or physician), the patient, or an other party making payment on behalf of the patient (e.g., the patient's employer, private insurance company or governmental payors such as Medicare [which primarily covered patients over the age of 65] and Medicaid [which primarily covered indigent patients]). Payment for lab testing provided to Medicare beneficiaries was made according to a fee schedule established by the U.S. Congress, which imposed a cap on such payments. In addition, payment for lab testing provided to Medicaid beneficiaries was subject to similar ceilings. In effect, labs had limited ability to influence the price paid for testing services provided to Medicare and Medicaid beneficiaries. In many instances, these amounts were lower than the prices paid by other parties.

BELLAIRE CLINICAL LABS, INC.

A small, high-quality, privately-owned independent clinical laboratory located just outside Boston, Massachusetts, Bellaire Clinical Labs, Inc., provided laboratory-testing services to local physicians' offices, hospitals, and other companies. Founded in 1982, the company specialized in providing swift, accurate medical testing services and electronic communication of results. Bellaire Labs provided both routine blood-testing services (primarily simple blood tests that patients received as part of routine physical examinations) and specialty testing services for more complicated medical problems. Routine tests were highly automated and required lower-skilled personnel than did specialty tests, which were more labor intensive and required highly skilled technologists to administer, conduct analyses, and prepare reports explaining the results.

Although physicians ordered the laboratory tests to be performed on their patients by Bellaire Labs, the costs of billing and collection varied greatly among the parties being billed. These costs were lowest when the physician was billed, highest when the patient was billed, and in-between when other parties—Medicare, Medicaid, private insurance companies, or employers —were billed. To reflect these significant cost differences, Bellaire charged different prices for the tests depending on the party being billed. In addition, the price differential between tests billed to third parties and tests billed to the physician or patient reflected limitations imposed by the fee schedules under which Medicare and Medicaid made payments.

In 2003, Bellaire Labs faced intense competition from national and local independent laboratories. The greater Boston metropolitan area was well known for its high concentration of exemplary physicians and hospitals, and many clinical laboratory companies were attracted to the area. In addition, managed care organizations, Medicare and Medicaid had all increased their efforts to control the cost and utilization of health care services, and these efforts had negatively impacted Bellaire Labs' operating margins for the past several years.

In response to the intense competition and price pressure, Wilma Lands had launched a media campaign in 2003 to promote Bellaire Labs' accuracy, responsiveness, and flexibility. In addition, she positioned the company as a state-of-the-art clinical laboratory to attract additional contracts for clinical research trials of new drugs, oncology testing, occupational drug testing, and other specialized services. As support for the marketing initiative, the company also made significant investments in the latest laboratory equipment.

PREPARATION OF THE 2003 OPERATING PLAN

In November 2002, Wilma Lands had approved the 2003 profit plan prepared by Joe Mack (shown in the second column of **Exhibit 1**). To estimate planned revenues, Mack had first considered the existing customer base and industry trends to project the total number of tests the laboratory would perform in 2003. Then, he projected how many of those tests would be routine tests and how many would be specialty tests. Next,

Mack estimated what proportion of tests would be billed to physicians, patients, or other payors such as Medicare, Medicaid, or private insurance companies. Then, Mack had obtained the forecasted average price per test by type and billing party from Bellaire Lab's director of billing and reimbursement (see **Exhibit 1**). Finally, Mack performed a final review of the estimated volumes by test type and billing party and calculated Bellaire Lab's total projected revenue for 2003.

In preparing the 2003 budgeted expenses, Mack had worked with Marty Walters, the company's manager of Operations. Walters had joined Bellaire Labs in September 2002, and he had been hired because of his reputation for astute management and cost control while previously employed at a competing clinical lab. In fact, Walters's employment contract stipulated that he could receive as much as a 20 percent annual bonus based on how effectively and efficiently he managed the overall operations of the lab. The following information was used by Mack and Walters in preparing the budgeted expenses.

1. Materials cost was expected to vary with the number of tests, and the materials cost related to both routine tests and specialty tests was expected to be approximately the same.

2. Labor cost for routine tests was expected to vary with the number of routine tests. The projected annual labor cost for routine tests was based on 140 employees at an average wage of $8.25 an hour. Labor cost for specialty tests was expected to vary with the number of specialty tests. The projected annual labor cost for specialty tests was based on 50 employees at $19.50 an hour.

3. Depreciation represented straight-line depreciation on furniture and equipment.

4. Other costs of testing consisted primarily of additional labor, utilities, maintenance, and sanitation. Of the total amount budgeted, approximately $300,000 was expected to be fixed, and the remainder was expected to vary with the number of tests performed.

5. Billing and collection costs were budgeted at $0.50 per test for tests billed to the physician, $3.50 per test for tests billed to the patient, and $3.00 per test for tests billed to the patient's insurance company.

6. Advertising and promotion costs were budgeted at 5 percent of revenues.

7. The executive management team expected to receive salaries and bonuses totaling $700,000.

8. Other administrative costs were expected to be fixed at $500,000.

ACTUAL RESULTS COMPARED WITH THE ORIGINAL PLAN

As part of his analysis of actual profit compared with planned profit, Mack summarized several statistics relative to 2003 actual performance regarding the number of tests, the mix of routine and specialty tests, the mix of payors, and the price of the tests (see **Exhibit 1**). He noted that the actual lab prices per test during 2003 were as predicted. In addition, the company's actual labor cost reflected the use of 133 employees for routine tests at an average wage of $8.22 an hour, and 67 employees for specialty tests at an average wage of $19.60 an hour. Actual routine-labor hours were 276,640; actual specialty-labor hours totaled 139,360. Actual prices for lab materials used were the same as those included in the plan. The actual fixed costs included in "other costs of testing" were $8,000 higher than expected.

During the year, Mack had heard that Walters was doing a good job as the lab's operations manager; Walters had initiated some significant process improvements to reduce the amount of materials use and waste and routinely recognized employee initiatives for improving efficiencies. Mack knew that Walters hoped to receive a bonus for his performance in 2003, and this added another dimension to the importance of learning more about the actual operating expenses for the year. Therefore, Mack arranged a meeting with Walters to go over the 2003 actual operating results. He hoped his investigation would not only enable him to answer Lands's questions, but would also give him useful insights into why actual expenses differed from the original plan. He was still puzzled by the fact that Walters's process improvements had not seemed to enhance profits much at all.

Exhibit 1

BELLAIRE CLINICAL LABS, INC. (B)

2003 Operating Statement

		Actual		Planned
Net revenue				
Routine testing	$	11,676,904	$	12,160,000
Specialty testing		5,709,496		4,240,000
Total net revenue		17,386,400		16,400,000
Materials		2,760,000		2,700,000
Labor, routine		2,273,981		2,402,400
Labor, specialty		2,731,456		2,028,000
Depreciation		3,503,000		3,500,000
Other costs of testing		1,120,000		1,100,000
Billing and collection costs		2,080,000		1,850,000
Advertising and promotion		892,000		820,000
Management salaries		710,000		700,000
Other administrative costs		510,000		500,000
Total expenses		16,580,437		15,600,400
Net profit	$	805,963	$	799,600
Number of tests per year		1,030,000		1,000,000
% tests, routine		74%		80%
% tests, specialty		26%		20%
% tests paid for by physician		44%		50%
% tests paid for by patient		20%		20%
% tests paid for by other parties		36%		30%
Price, routine test				
when physician pays	$	14.00	$	14.00
when patient pays	$	17.00	$	17.00
when other party pays	$	16.00	$	16.00
Price, specialty test				
when physician pays	$	20.00	$	20.00
when patient pays	$	23.00	$	23.00
when other party pays	$	22.00	$	22.00

DISTILLERS DELIGHT IN THE U.K

"I sure am looking forward to a new and better year," thought Tony Hamilton, brand manager for Distillers Delight in the United Kingdom. Tony had been with Global Distillers, Inc. for over twenty years, and he had never experienced a more challenging and unpredictable year than the company's 2003 fiscal year that had ended just two weeks earlier. He reflected back to the numerous planning meetings he had held over fourteen months ago, when he and his key associates had prepared the 2002-2003 operating budget (see **Exhibit 1**). He recalled the enthusiasm and the optimism that had characterized those meetings, as well as the frequent conversations about Delight's glorious past and fantastic future.

The emergence of the European low-proof alcoholic beverage category and the recent success of Distillers Delight in the U.K. were well known throughout the company. From "Project Hurricane" of the mid-1980s had come the introduction of Distillers Delight in the United States in 1990. Before long, annual sales of Delight exceeded four million nine-litre cases. After a series of product reformulations, Delight was introduced in the U.K. in 1996, and it quickly became the market leader in the low-proof category. Sales doubled by 1998 as successful product introductions occurred throughout Europe. By the end of 2001, Distillers Delight was making a significant contribution to corporate profitability, and the U.K. market was leading the way. Thus, Tony was both shocked and humbled by the realization of how wrong so many of their planning and budgeting assumptions had been.

Neither Tony nor any of his associates had anticipated any excise tax increase, let alone the 60% increase that took effect shortly after the 2003 fiscal year began. From that point on, almost nothing went according to plan. The entire low proof industry was caught by surprise, and it seemed as if no one really knew how to respond. At first, Global Distillers and its major competitors tried to price low proof products just as they previously had done in an attempt to preserve their margins. Not surprisingly, customers resisted the increase in the total purchase price, and sales declined rather sharply. This resulted in considerable discussion within the company regarding the possible need for a new pricing strategy. Tony and his boss, Charlotte Hardy, Managing Director for the U.K., originally decided to continue with the existing pricing policy. Before long, however, competitors began cutting prices, and Global Distillers was forced to do the same. To make matters worse, key competitors also began aggressive new advertising campaigns. Consequently, the anticipated continued growth of Delight sales and profitability was seriously threatened. As the year progressed, sales improved slightly, but the Delight market did not experience anything close to the aggressive performance that had been included in the 2003 fiscal year operating plan.

As Tony reflected on the key value driver meetings that he had participated in each month, he was reminded of just how difficult the entire year has been. Still, as he prepared for his upcoming meeting with Charlotte, during which he and the other U.K. brand managers would be providing a detailed analysis of the 2003 fiscal year results, he knew that simply stating that actual results were considerably below planned results because it had been a very challenging and unpredictable year would not be a sufficient explanation. What he needed to do was to create a method of explaining and reconciling the actual results and the planned results in a way that was accurate, informative and understandable.

Exhibit 1

DISTILLERS DELIGHT IN THE U.K.

Operating Statement
(In Thousands of U.K. Pounds)

	Fiscal Year Ended March 2003	
	Actual	Plan
	£	£
Gross Sales	327,360	399,750
Excise Taxes	79,360	66,625
Discounts	86,800	83,282
Net Sales	161,200	249,843
Cost of Sales	52,800	66,625
Production Costs	26,600	33,312
Gross Profit	81,800	149,906
Advertising Expense	12,850	16,656
Promotion Expense	20,600	26,650
Direct Contribution	48,350	106,600
Selling Expenses	5,100	6,662
Distribution Costs	7,220	9,994
Net Sales Contribution	36,030	89,944
General & Administrative Expenses	19,150	20,000
Operating Profit	16,880	69,944

Supporting Data:

Sales volume (Thousands of 9 litre cases)	6,200	8,200
% Sales on-premise	40%	50%
% Sales off-premise	60%	50%
Gross average price on-premise	£ 57.75	£ 52.50
Net average price on-premise	£ 28.44	£ 32.80
Gross average price off-premise	£ 49.50	£ 45.00
Net average price off-premise	£ 24.38	£ 28.12
Excise taxes	32%	20%

Exhibit 1 (continued)

DISTILLERS DELIGHT IN THE U.K.

Explanation of Operating Statement

Gross Sales:	Total sales, including excise taxes.
Excise Taxes:	Taxes on sales of alcoholic beverages.
Discounts:	Price discounts and rebates granted to customers. Budgeted at 25% of gross sales minus excise taxes.
Net Sales:	Gross Sales minus excise taxes, price discounts and rebates.
Cost of Sales:	Standard material costs of products sold. Budgeted at 20% of gross sales minus excise taxes.
Production Costs:	Standard conversion manufacturing costs (i.e., direct labor and manufacturing overhead) of products sold. Budgeted at 10% of gross sales minus excise taxes.
Gross Profit:	Net sales minus standard cost of sales and production costs.
Advertising Expense:	Total advertising costs (e.g., print, television, radio and billboards). Budgeted at 5% of gross sales minus excise taxes.
Promotion Expense:	Total promotion costs (e.g., displays and price incentives) associated with selected products. Budgeted at 8% of gross sales minus excise taxes.
Direct Contribution:	Gross profit minus advertising and promotion expenses directly attributable to products sold.
Selling expenses:	Sales-related expenses, some of which were indirect to the products sold and were therefore allocated. Budgeted at 2% of gross sales minus excise taxes.
Distribution Costs:	Costs, some of which were allocated, related to the distribution of products sold (e.g., transportation and shipping). Budgeted at 3% of gross sales minus excise taxes.
Net Sales Contribution:	Direct contribution minus selling expenses and distribution costs.
General and Administrative Expenses:	Other expenses (e.g., accounting, legal, personnel, information systems and supervision) related to products sold, many of which were allocated. Budgeted at a fixed amount.
Operating Profit:	Net sales contribution minus general and administrative expenses.

ENTERTAINMENTNOW. COM

It was a chilly December evening, and Mark Dibbs was working late again. As the vice president of Financial Analysis for EntertainmentNow.com, Dibbs had been charged with analyzing the company's financial results for the past year. EntertainmentNow.com's operating budget for the past year showed an expected net loss per item sold of $2.95. The company's actual financial results, however, showed a net loss per item sold of $3.10. Dibbs was expected to explain this variance fully and to make recommendations to senior management based on his analysis.

BACKGROUND

EntertainmentNow.com offered a comprehensive array of books, music, videos and DVDs, toys, and small electronics on the company's international Web site, EntertainmentNow.com. Considered one of the world's leading Internet retailers of entertainment products, the company focused on providing superior customer service. Similar to Amazon.com, EntertainmentNow.com purchased products from vendors, held the products in inventory, and fulfilled customers' orders directly. EntertainmentNow.com marketed and sold primarily to individual customers. Recently, however, the company had begun serving corporate and institutional customers as well.

During the past few years, EntertainmentNow.com's management had spent a significant amount of capital on the company's technology and infrastructure. Now, the company needed to gain scale in order to generate positive returns on those capital investments. Therefore, EntertainmentNow.com's operating results for the past year were extremely disappointing to management and to the company's stockholders. Furthermore, the increase in net loss per item sold was surprising given that the company's actual sales volume was greater than expected for the year. Dibbs knew he had to be able to explain fully what caused EntertainmentNow.com's increased shortfall.

ANNUAL OPERATING BUDGET

Dibbs looked at EntertainmentNow.com's annual operating budget (**Exhibit 1**). The following information was used in preparing the annual budget:

1. Basing its projections on prior years' data, management expected to have approximately 4 million customer accounts[1] and sell 29.76 million items at an

---

[1]Just for comparison purposes, as of December 31, 2001, Amazon.com had approximately 26 million customer accounts.

average sales price of $15.90 each. Cost of goods sold was expected to be 76 percent of sales revenue.

2. Fulfillment expenses represented costs incurred for warehouses, customer-service centers, and packaging orders for shipment. These costs were budgeted at $2.50 per item sold. This amount included the estimated cost of opening a new warehouse and distribution center in Phoenix, Arizona, to handle projected growth in the Southwest.

3. Marketing expenses were expected to be $0.78 per item sold.

4. Technology and content expenses had been high over the last few years, as the company expended significant effort to develop the EntertainmentNow.com Web site. These expenses, however, were expected to remain fairly level over the next few years, as the major work on the site had already been completed. Thus, technology and content expenses were budgeted as a fixed expense of $23.6 million.

5. Both general and administrative expenses and depreciation and amortization expenses were budgeted as fixed costs.

ACTUAL RESULTS

As a first step in his analysis, Dibbs decided to compile a schedule of budgeted versus actual sales volume and unit prices (**Exhibit 2**). As he knew, total sales volume for the year had increased as compared with budgeted levels. In September, the company had launched a brand-new advertising campaign to boost lagging sales, and sales had rebounded significantly during the last quarter of the year. The advertising campaign was expensive, however, and marketing expenses were raised by $0.05 per unit for the year. Cost of goods sold averaged 76.5 percent of actual sales revenue, and fulfillment costs increased to $2.53 per item owing to cost overruns on the Phoenix distribution center. General and administrative expenses, however, fell by $250,000 because of lower-than-planned salary increases. In addition, technology and content expenses were $350,000 higher than expected owing to a significant increase in the number of product offerings, as well as an increase in partnerships with other Web sites, both of which required additional Web-site maintenance. Dibbs knew he had to consider all this information in his variance analysis.

REQUIRED

1. Conceptually, what factors explain the difference between planned and actual results?

2. Prepare a flexible budget for EntertainmentNow.com for the past year, flexing solely on total actual units sold.

3. Quantify the impact on the net loss per item sold of each factor you noted in question 1.

4. Assume that technology and content, general and administrative, and depreciation and amortization costs are fixed costs that total $73.7 million

---

annually. Based on EntertainmentNow.com's current sales revenue, cost of goods sold, fulfillment expenses, and marketing, what is the company's breakeven sales in units? Is this level of sales realistic? Why or why not?

Exhibit 1

ENTERTAINMENTNOW.COM

Schedule of Planned versus Actual Operating Results

	Plan	Actual
Revenue	$ 473,280,000	$ 475,980,000
Cost of goods sold	359,692,800	364,124,700
Gross profit	113,587,200	111,855,300
Fulfillment	74,400,000	76,557,800
Marketing	23,212,800	25,115,800
Technology and content	23,600,000	23,950,000
General and administrative	19,000,000	18,750,000
Depreciation/amortization	31,000,000	31,000,000
Loss from operations	$ (57,625,600)	$ (63,518,300)
Net loss per item sold	$ (1.94)	$ (2.10)

Exhibit 2

ENTERTAINMENTNOW.COM

Schedule of Planned versus Actual Volumes and Prices

	Plan Volume	Plan Revenue per Unit	Actual Volume	Actual Revenue per Unit
Books	9,000,000	$18.00	10,000,000	$17.50
Music	12,000,000	$13.00	11,000,000	$14.00
DVD/Video	7,980,000	$16.00	8,300,000	$14.00
Toys	600,000	$34.00	750,000	$29.00
Electronics	180,000	$40.00	210,000	$43.00
Total	29,760,000		30,260,000	

ORIOLE FURNITURE, INC. (A)

Bernard Mente, Vice President of the Rattan Furniture division of Oriole Furniture, Inc., was faced with a difficult decision in mid-June. He was wondering what he should do in light of his division's failure to meet sales and profit goals during the first five months of the year. Despite the recession, the division had managed to meet the sales and profit budget for the first three months, but the deepening recession had severely affected the results of the following two months.

THE COMPANY

Oriole Furniture, Inc. is a 30-year old distributor of high quality, imported furniture. Currently, the company was organized into four divisions: Teakwood, Antiques, Rosewood, and Rattan. Four centralized staff departments were organized to support the product groups: finance and control, marketing, purchasing, and engineering. Each of the four product divisions was a profit center.

THE RATTAN FURNITURE DIVISION

The division was established four years ago after the company decided to import completely-knocked down (CKD) rattan furniture for assembly and sales to the mid-Atlantic states. The division had been an immediate success. Indeed, the division had had an annual sales growth of 35 percent for the past three years and sales were $60 million last year. The division offered three main product lines: a living and dining room line, a bedroom line, and an outdoor patio line. Half of last year's sales came from the living and dining room line with the remainder from the other two product lines. Mr. Mente was in charge of the sales and production activities of all three lines. His performance was measured by the profits earned by the division and he had always been pleased to receive a healthy year-end bonus based on his division's performance.

THE PROFIT PLAN

Each division Vice President prepared an annual profit plan, starting about six months before the beginning of the plan year. The first step in the process involved estimating sales for the next year. Two sales estimates were prepared for each division: one by the field sales force and another by the product specialists.

For the coming year, the individual product specialists estimated rattan furniture sales at $75,130,000 and the field sales force estimated sales at $77,010,000. After a discussion with the sales manager, Mente decided to use $77,010,000 as his division's sales estimate even though there was a high degree of uncertainty about the direction of the economy. He was confident, however, that sales would continue to grow, although not at the same rate as in past years.

The next step in the budget cycle had been estimating manufacturing costs. The production manager, Kay Gray, was given the rattan furniture sales estimate and she then forecasted direct material, direct labor, variable manufacturing overhead, and fixed manufacturing overhead costs for each assembly area, or cost center. Gray organized production processes and work flow around three cost centers, one for each product line.

Most of the direct materials (e.g., CKD rattan parts) were imported from Singapore. The Singapore suppliers had informed Oriole to expect a 6 percent increase in price for the coming year. Gray used this information to increase the budgeted cost of production's direct materials. She had then estimated the hourly labor cost for each of her cost centers. Using the most recent productivity data she had for the factory, Gray had estimated the budget year's salaries and wages and then had reduced that figure by 5 percent to account for projected increased efficiencies (based on a learning curve tabulated for the division). For variable manufacturing overhead, she had assumed an historical percentage of direct production costs and reduced this by 5 percent to again account for planned, increased efficiencies. For fixed manufacturing overhead costs, she had used actual costs reported on the most recent monthly income statement and applied a 4 percent increase.

As part of the budgeting process, the sales, administration, logistics support, and quality control departments in the Rattan Furniture division had had to also estimate their expenses for the coming year. In addition to the expenses incurred directly by the Rattan Furniture division, the division was also allocated a share of the corporation's administrative costs. These costs were allocated to the divisions based on a division's sales as a percentage of total corporate sales. A division's own departmental fixed costs, plus the corporate allocated costs, comprised the fixed costs for the Rattan Furniture division.

Using the data described above, the accountant, George Jeffrey, had prepared the Rattan Furniture division profit plan. The result was an estimated division operating profit of $22,720,000 on a sales volume of $77,010,000. This plan was submitted to Mr. Mensan, the company president, right on schedule for his review. (Generally, this review occurred three months before the start of the year being budgeted.) When Mr. Mensan reviewed the division's plan in relation to the specific sales and profit goals which he had established for the company at large, the combined plans of the four divisions had not met his profit expectations. In a heated discussion with Mr. Mensan, Mente had agreed to revise his division's sales up to $81,060,000 and operating profit to $23,900,000 (**Exhibit 1**). He had no real plan for reaching the new sales budget, but he realized that Mr. Mensan was not going to budge from his adamant push for continued sales growth at least equal to past levels. Thus, he had agreed to the upward revision, trusting that he had time to figure out how to get the division to that level.

ACTUAL PERFORMANCE

The past eight months had flown by. As Mente was looking at his January through May results, the actual performance of the division was disappointing. A comparison of actual performance with the budget showed that sales were 11 percent below plan, the backlog was down 20 percent, and profit was 18 percent below plan (**Exhibit 2**). Mente knew his sales people were working harder than ever and he believed they were doing a good job in view of the poor economic picture. Improving sales would not be easy—if it could be done at all.

Mr. Mensan had told all the division managers, as recently as two weeks ago, that he still expected to reach the profit objective set for the year. He said, "We have been successful for 20 years and I expect us to continue our growth in sales and profits. Over the years, our profit plans have helped in achieving our success. They tell us where we want to go and how we will get there. It's tough sometimes, and that is when we have to buckle down and plow ahead."

Mente's relatively new division had always been fast growing and very profitable. Thus, he had no experience in managing during a slowdown in sales. He realized, however, that he must come up with a plan, one that he had not yet been able to work out, for reaching the division's profit objective. One idea he was contemplating was to delay the purchase of some new machinery which was scheduled for delivery in September. This machinery, which cost $500,000 would replace some existing machinery which broke down frequently and led to overtime labor and, sometimes, late delivery schedules.   Another possibility he thought of was to forego hiring two new furniture designers he had been looking for all year, without any success. If he didn't hire the designers, this would save about $100,000 in salary for the rest of the year.

"What will I tell Mr. Mensan if he stops by today?" mumbled Mente, as he continued to ponder a new plan and wonder if his days were numbered with Oriole Furniture.

Exhibit 1

ORIOLE FURNITURE, INC. (A)

Rattan Furniture Division
This Year's Original and Revised Annual Profit Plans

	Original	**Revised**
Sales (Net)	$77,010,000	$81,060,000
Variable Costs		
Direct Material	23,100,000	24,320,000
Direct Labor	11,550,000	12,020,000
Variable Manufacturing Overheads	2,310,000	2,430,000
Total Variable Costs	36,960,000	38,770,000
Contribution	40,050,000	42,290,000
Fixed Costs		
Manufacturing Overheads	2,690,000	2,810,000
Sales and Marketing	9,050,000	9,550,000
Administration	2,350,000	2,400,000
Engineering and Purchasing	3,240,000	3,630,000
Total Fixed Costs	17,330,000	18,390,000
Operating Profits	$22,720,000	$23,900,000
Average Assets	$23,000,000	$24,000,000

Exhibit 2

ORIOLE FURNITURE, INC. (A)

Rattan Furniture Division
Comparison of Actual Performance with Budget
January – May

	Actual	**Budget**	
Sales	$30,060,000	$33,780,000	-11%
Variable Costs			
Direct Material	8,990,000	10,130,000	
Direct Labor	4,470,000	5,010,000	
Variable Manufacturing Overheads	900,000	1,010,000	
Total Variable Costs	14,360,000	16,150,000	
Contribution	15,700,000	17,630,000	
Fixed Costs			
Manufacturing Overheads	1,040,000	1,170,000	
Sales and Marketing	3,920,000	3,980,000	
Administration	1,020,000	1,000,000	
Engineering and Purchasing	1,520,000	1,510,000	
Total Fixed Costs	7,500,000	7,660,000	
Operating Profits	$ 8,200,000	$ 9,970,000	-18%
Average Assets	$23,000,000	$24,000,000	
Backlog	$28,520,000	$35,650,000	-20%

CONSUMER SERVICE COMPANY (A)

Consumer Service Company was established to take advantage of the young, professional and affluent baby-boomer population. It was apparent to Mr. John Hurdle, the founder of the company, that a major part of the economy was composed of upscale consumers, where both adults in the household were employed as professionals or where both had significant other interests which occupied their time. These two consumer segments seemed to offer great opportunity for a company which provided a variety of quality services, saving the consumers' time and enhancing the quality of their life.

The company began with a home cleaning service. Initially, its regional offices were headquartered in the larger East coast suburbs and each had staffs of well-trained janitorial people who were available to perform inside home cleaning on a weekly, bi-weekly, or monthly contract basis. Recent additions to the service portfolio included exterior home maintenance, vehicle maintenance, and landscape maintenance. The concept was powerful and the business grew explosively.

ORGANIZATIONAL STRUCTURE

The basic concept was demonstrably sound, and was the root of the company's success. Part of the company's success could also be traced to its organization structure (see **Exhibit 1**). All four services were performed from regional offices located in a number of cities across the United States. Regional offices were staffed with a manager for each one of the four service lines and it was that manager's responsibility to hire and train the staff, supervise the day-to-day work, and conduct the local marketing. The local office administrators managed the offices, but were not involved in the functional operations. Each of the four service lines was managed as a division, by a national director. The national directors were responsible for the supervision of their respective field service managers and for the national marketing of their service lines. Mr. Hurdle had rightly understood that the four services the company offered involved different consumer decisions, and his decision to orient the company's marketing and service directly to the interests of the buyer had fueled a large part of the company's growth.

The four product service directors had small marketing and administrative staffs, working out of the company's headquarters in Morristown, N. J. The corporate office provided accounting, computing, legal, and administrative assistance to the divisions and the regions. Each of the four service line directors (and an administrative vice-president) reported to Mr. Hurdle, the chief executive officer. He was the model of an entrepreneur. In addition to being the founder of the company and the developer of the consumer services idea, Mr. Hurdle had put all of his personal capital at risk in the venture. Consumer Service's stock was owned by several institutions and by about 300 individuals. Mr. Hurdle remained a 30 percent stockholder and his stock holdings made him a wealthy man. Of late, he had begun thinking about opening a European operation modeled on the successful U. S. operations. After all, he could finance the start up himself, the challenge was intriguing, and his two sons could head it up.

THE PLAN PROCESS

Each year in the Fall, the division directors developed a profit plan for their divisions, committing their group to a deliverable level of sales and profits before taxes. Sales were billed to customers based on time spent on the job by the Consumer Service employee, multiplied by a standard hourly rate. Because employees were paid only for time they actually worked on jobs, and because fixed costs were relatively small, profit levels for the company were fundamentally a factor of sales levels. Indeed, division directors primarily focused their efforts on hours sold and average rates charged.

To help develop the sales plan, each division director asked their field service managers to provide an estimate of the sales level they expected during the next year. In addition, each division's marketing staff was asked for their projections as to what the division's sales would be. In previous years, the division directors had met with Mr. Hurdle during the first week in October in a seaside resort to establish the profit plan for the divisions and for the company as a whole. Together, they reviewed the prior years' results for each division, and in a collegial discussion established their coming year's sales and profit plans. Mr. Hurdle always made an inspirational speech at the start of the proceedings and he challenged any division director who seemed to be proposing a lazy plan. But he also believed the directors were to be treated as managers of their own businesses and so he did not pry too deeply into the details of the division plans.

The profit plans were used to keep things on track during the year—if a division was falling behind plan, the director would investigate, and if necessary, change marketing programs, increase field training, or take some other action deemed necessary. The division plans were also used to forecast demand for accounting and computer services from the headquarters group. In fact, once the division plans were established, the headquarters budget was crafted and each division profit plan was allocated a share of the corporate costs. This allocation was not changed during the year regardless of the division's actual sales results.

The division plans were important to the company and to the division directors. The division directors' annual compensation was based on the following formula:

Base Pay $25,000	+	2.5% of Planned Sales for the year	+	.5% of Sales over plan	-	7.5% of Sales under plan

The time for establishing the profit plan for the coming year was fast approaching and Mr. Hurdle suggested a modification to the previous years' procedure. He suggested that the company would save time and money if each of the division directors met with him in his office to finalize plans for their individual divisions. He asked Ms. Forthright to meet with him at 2 o'clock next Thursday, October 17. She was relieved because that appointment would give her a week to study the data from her field managers and division marketing staff. However, as the week passed she became anxious. She learned from the grapevine that she was the last of the four directors to meet with Mr. Hurdle. The other three had found the meetings to be quite unpleasant and each had left their meeting committed to a plan they thought would be difficult to meet.

(Additional facts available only to Ms. Forthright and to Mr. Hurdle are available separately from your professor.)

Exhibit 1

CONSUMER SERVICE COMPANY (A)

Organization Chart

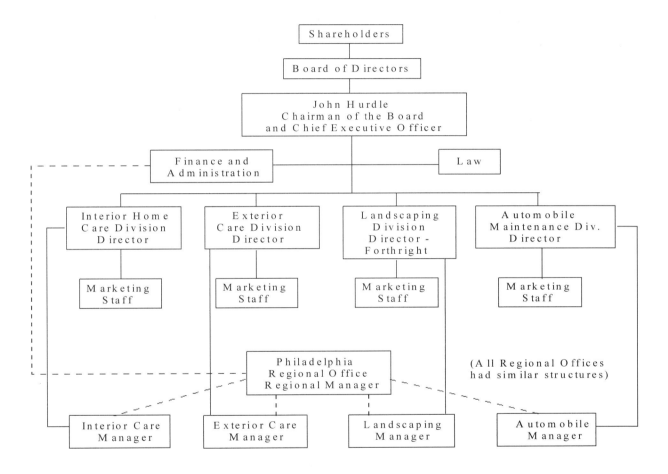

PART VI

MANAGEMENT CONTROL SYSTEMS: PERFORMANCE MEASUREMENT AND INCENTIVE SYSTEMS

PERFORMANCE MEASUREMENT AT THOMAS J. LIPTON

As associate director of Financial Analysis for Thomas J. Lipton, Incorporated, Don Logan was contemplating the poor reception given to the latest changes in product line profit statements and the measures by which product line financial performance was evaluated.

After working with his staff through the summer implementing the new system, Logan realized that many of the product managers, whose performance would be measured by the new system, did not understand it. Some of the product managers questioned the principles involved. Others wondered how the new system would affect their particular products.

THOMAS J. LIPTON, INCORPORATED

Thomas J. Lipton, Inc. was established in 1915 in New York City as a tea-importing firm by Sir Thomas Lipton, a flamboyant multimillionaire tea merchant. After his death in 1931, a holding company owned by the Anglo-Dutch corporation Unilever NV purchased the company from his estate. The company grew and became one of the largest diversified food companies in the United States.

Lipton's stable of products consisted both of products developed internally and products that had been obtained through acquisition. The 30 product lines were divided into three operating divisions: Beverage, Food, and General Management. Lipton brands were among the leaders in tea, soup, and salad-dressing markets. Lipton was the dominant supplier of tea to the retail trade in the United States, and tea continued to account for over 40 percent of Lipton's revenues.

Within the industry Lipton had positioned itself in the growing market for convenience and instant foods. Looking toward the future, Lipton's marketing strategy was to strengthen the position of its tea business and other segments in which the company held a dominant position. For product lines that were profitable, but whose growth prospects were limited, Lipton's objective was to maintain sales at their present level. Lipton also sought to develop new products in high-growth segments of the food industry. Its long-term marketing objective was to continue to broaden its base through internal growth and acquisition. The table below shows the diversity of sales volumes and growth patterns of Lipton's product lines.

Brand Sales Volume

25 brands or product groups:
- 11 with sales under $10 million
- 10 with sales between $10-50 million
- 4 with sales over $50 million

Some were growing fast, some were declining, and some were quite stable.

Lipton had a very good relationship with Unilever, its parent company. Indeed, it had one of the best financial performance records of any Unilever subsidiary; consequently, Unilever did not maintain tight control over Lipton's day-to-day operations. Biannually Lipton and Unilever would agree to a basic strategic plan and determine projected profits and growth rates.

For the future Lipton had several financial and operating objectives. Sales were projected to continue to grow by 10.5 percent per year and the after-tax profit margin to improve to 6 percent. Another objective was to achieve a 15 percent after-tax return on average invested capital, defined as assets minus current liabilities. Other important financial objectives revolved around Lipton's current and potential cash needs. Lipton wished to maintain its AA bond rating to minimize borrowing costs and maximize future borrowing flexibility because all growth had to be financed from retained earnings or by borrowing.

FINANCIAL PERFORMANCE MEASUREMENT AT LIPTON

The primary measure that Lipton's management used to evaluate its corporate performance was after-tax return on average invested capital (ATRIC).[1] A problem with the use of ATRIC was that it was only calculated for the whole company, since assets and current liabilities had never been accurately broken down by product line. Thus ATRIC did not provide information as to how the individual product lines contributed to overall corporate return on invested capital.

The basic measure of product-line financial performance used by Lipton's management was trading profit as shown in **Exhibit 1**. Product lines and product-line managers were evaluated on the basis of trading profit and delivered profit, profit as a percentage of sales, and growth in unit volume. Thus the format for product line P&Ls seemed to match the information needs of a marketing-oriented manager.

Unilever evaluated Lipton's overall financial performance on the basis of three measures:

- Ratio of net sales to average gross capital employed (capital turnover)
- Trading profit before tax as a percent of net sales (return on sales)
- After-tax return on average gross capital employed (return on capital)

Though internally Lipton, like other U.S. companies, did not adjust its financial measures for the effects of inflation, Lipton was required to adjust for inflation on it reports to Unilever. In these three measures both profits and assets were adjusted to account for the effect of inflation on fixed assets. On the corporate P&L, depreciation expense was calculated on the basis of the current replacement value (CRV) for fixed assets. On the balance sheet the net book value of fixed assets was stated as Gross CRV less accumulated CRV depreciation. Gross Capital Employed equaled Net CRV of fixed assets plus working capital. **Exhibit 2** shows an example of these calculations.

---

[1]Invested capital equals assets less current liabilities.

Logan concluded there were three weaknesses in the present method of calculating product line profits. First, he recognized that inflation had distorted product line P&Ls. Increased product line revenue and profits did not necessarily indicate improved performance. Furthermore inflation increased the costs of replacing fixed assets. Historic cost depreciation did not accurately reflect the cost of replacing those assets in the future. Thus in an inflationary environment, nominal profits gave misleading information as to the ability of a product line to operate in the future. Second, the cost of using working capital and fixed assets did not appear on product line P&Ls. Therefore, trading profit did not reflect the cost of all cash invested in a particular brand. Logan thought that failure to allocate that expense encouraged product managers to increase working capital balances more than necessary.

The third problem Logan observed was that many product expenses were not allocated, or if so, were improperly allocated among product lines. The unallocated corporate Other Income and Deductions (OI&D) account contained many items that applied to individual product lines. **Exhibit 3** lists corporate OI&D items that applied to product lines. Other allocation problems centered on the New Product Development Charge and on manufacturing and corporate overhead. The New Product Development Charge was allocated to established products on the basis of profits; Logan thought it should not be charged to established products. Manufacturing and corporate overhead was allocated to product lines on the basis of planned production, which often differed significantly from actual production.. Manufacturing overhead was part of nonvariable cost of sales, and corporate overhead was part of administrative expense. Logan thought the effect of allocation policies was to distort the relative financial performance of product lines and make it difficult to interpret year-to-year changes in product line performance. Logan concluded that product line P&Ls did not reflect the true contribution of each product to the corporation as a whole. Furthermore, he felt it was no longer possible to conclude with any accuracy how well each product manager had performed his or her job. When Mr. Logan had occasion to discuss some of his thoughts in a presentation to the management group, he was surprised when the president said right away that he thought it was a good idea and asked for a recommended format for financial reporting.

ECONOMIC PROFIT

Having studied the problem, Logan decided that the time was ripe for revising the method of calculating product-line profitability. All of the changes would be instituted simultaneously so that the resulting figures would measure what Logan would call the product line's "Economic Profit." He recommended that four items be added to the product line P&Ls to arrive at Economic Profit. Trading Profit would be calculated in its present form, but below that changes would be made to reflect the costs of continuing to operate each product line. The specific changes were (1) a deduction to reflect the difference between CRV depreciation and historic cost depreciation, (2) an interest charge for capital employed by a product line, (3) elimination of the new-product development charge, and (4) inclusion of previously unallocated corporate OI&D items. **Exhibit 4** shows the proposed P&L format. Logan thought that Economic Profit would be a measure of the true economic earnings generated by a product. If Economic Profit was positive, then real wealth would have been created for Lipton and for Unilever.

Logan also thought that Economic Profit would provide information that would enable senior managers to make better decisions. He noted that the difference between Economic Profit and Trading Profit could point out particular long-term problems or advantages associated with particular product lines that were not apparent by just looking at Trading Profit. He believed that in the long run Lipton would want to focus its financial resources on those product lines that showed a positive Economic Profit.

Logan believed that Economic Profit would induce product managers to make decisions beneficial to the corporation as a whole. Explicitly charging for working capital would eliminate the incentive to unnecessarily increase working-capital balances. Allocating brand-related OI&D income and expenses would increase product managers' awareness of these items. By evaluating managers on an inflation-adjusted basis, the product managers would be evaluated on the same basis as Unilever judged Lipton. In short, product managers would face the same economic environment as the firm when making decisions.

Logan believed that Economic Profit offered advantages as the basis for measuring product performance. In summary, Economic Profit would

- reflect the existence of inflation and high interest rates;

- create a consistency between Lipton's internal P&Ls and those used by Unilever to evaluate Lipton;

- provide a more accurate allocation of product line expenses;

- force product managers to focus on the strengths and weaknesses of their product lines; and

- indicate to upper management what areas of the business deserved more attention.

Indeed, preliminary analysis showed that the Economic Profit approach would give a far different "snapshot" of product-line performance than historical profit. **Exhibit 5** shows the difference between Trading Profit and Economic Profit for one of the product lines. Although Trading Profits were positive for this line, the Economic Profit was negative.

FINANCIAL ANALYSIS VIEWPOINT

In a presentation to his staff, Robert Sims, manager of Marketing Financial Analysis, stated:

The main thrust of all this change is to communicate to the product managers that business conditions are going to make it tougher. Lipton is smaller than many other food companies and therefore we need to be more efficient, better marketers, and more careful with our capital. It doesn't make sense to disguise the profitability of certain products. We need to eliminate all those distortions to know where our profits are coming from. This will enable us to take strategic actions on some of our "problem" products.

Logan followed by explaining:

> For too long, product managers have proceeded along, thinking our capital costs are free. They only see what they want to see. It has taken me a long time to convince them that there can be a big difference between reported income and "real" income. Finally I think we've come up with a financial performance measure that will work on the brand level. The keys are to build flexibility into the system and find an equitable way to motivate product managers. I view this as an opportunity to mold product managers into well-rounded business people—aware of all aspects of the business, financial as well as marketing.

PRODUCT MANAGER CONCERNS

Management approval for both the new P&L format and the change in performance measurement was quickly secured; soon thereafter Logan and other members of the Marketing Financial Analysis section made presentations to the product managers. Although many product managers agreed that a change was necessary, their immediate reactions were fear and suspicion. Logan inferred from the managers' questions that the underlying financial concepts were not understood. He realized that product managers would have to be taught how Economic Profit was derived and how its components could be managed so that financial goals could be met. Product managers' cooperation was essential if the change was to be successful.

In early September Logan sat at his desk and mulled over the entire situation. He realized that certain details of the system needed to be resolved. He had to decide on a percentage rate for the capital charge and whether different rates should be assessed against fixed assets and working capital. He also knew that an incentive system would have to be designed to motivate the product managers. He wondered what was the best way to educate the product managers and whether there should be different performance standards for each product line. Finally, he was concerned that the new performance measurement system might have some unforeseen consequence, motivating product managers to take actions detrimental to the long-term health of their brands.

Logan's concentration was broken by a knock at the door. Michael Hirst, a product manager, walked in, appearing very troubled.

> Don, do you realize you're making me build inflation into my prices so I can cover these additional costs? I'll be priced right out of the market. It also looks like I'm going to be penalized because my brand is capital-intensive and I'm going to be responsible for fixed manufacturing costs that I have no control over. I won't even know when I've done a good job. How will I be compared to other product managers? If I cut down on my working capital balance, that's going to hurt my service level. What should I target for anyway? I hope you can tell me in a few weeks what I'll be charged for interest. When new brand P&Ls come out, I

hope you can tell me what actions I'll need to take to improve my performance.

Later that afternoon, Logan became involved in a similar discussion with another product manager.

You know, Don . . . I still don't see what's wrong with excluding OI&D from the brand P&L's, and I'm still having trouble grasping this CRV depreciation you've spoken so much about. Why should I start charging now to cover the cost of an asset I will need in 15 years, after I just bought one last year? My Trading Profit shows I made a profit last year, but your figures say a negative Economic Profit resulted. That doesn't make sense to me. If I have negative Economic Profit several years in a row, what does that mean? Am I pricing high enough? If so, will future be diverted away from me? Right now I'm keeping my prices low so I can grab market share. This makes my Economic Profit low, but don't you think I should be compensated for contributing to the growth and diversification of the firm?

The last remark concerned an aspect of performance measurement about which Logan had been thinking for some time. In fact, he had already discussed with several people the need to reflect real growth in some sort of measure. So far he had not found a satisfactory way to put a dollar value on growth, nor did he see how one could distinguish between growth in a rising economy and growth in recessionary times.

Exhibit 1

PERFORMANCE MEASUREMENT AT THOMAS J. LIPTON

Statement of Product Line Profit and Loss

Sales volume
Standard cases - 12/8 oz.

NET SALES

Freight
Public warehousing
Manufacturing - Variable Cost

Total Variable Cost of Sales

VARIABLE PROFIT CONTRIBUTION

Manufacturing nonvariable Cost
Plant warehousing
Other nonvariable Costs

Total nonvariable Cost of Sales

DELIVERED PROFIT

Advertising
Sales promotion
Marketing services - direct
Marketing write-offs
Product group
Selling-direct

Total Direct Marketing Expenses

DIRECT PROFIT CONTRIBUTION

Selling
Marketing services
Technical research
Administrative

Total Indirect Expenses

New product development charge

TRADING PROFIT

Exhibit 2

PERFORMANCE MEASUREMENT AT THOMAS J. LIPTON

Inflation-Adjusted Measure of Financial Performance

	Historical Cost	CRV Cost
Sales	100	100
Cost of goods sold	70	70
Adjustment for CRV depreciation	-	10
Trading Profit before tax	30	20
Taxes	15	15
Profit after tax	15	5
Average gross fixed assets	135	200
Accumulated depreciation	70	125
Average net fixed assets	65	75
Average working capital	15	15
Average gross capital employed	80	90
Sales/average gross capital employed	1.25	1.11
Trading profit before tax/net sales	30/100 = 30%	20/100 =20%
Profit after tax/average gross capital employed	15/80 = 18.85%	5/90 = 5.5%

Exhibit 3

PERFORMANCE MEASUREMENT AT THOMAS J. LIPTON

Corporate OI&D Items Applicable to Product Lines

Benefits to Brands   Costs to Brands

1. Discount on purchase   8. Profit-Sharing Costs
2. T.J.L. media   Sundry Expenses
3. Operations income
4. Inventory revaluations
5. Over absorption of fixed overhead
6. Tax benefit of donations
7. Commodity profits

1. Prompt payment discounts received by central purchasing were to be distributed.

2. T. J. L. Media-A centralized department handled media purchases and the savings of about 6 percent of advertising expense were to be distributed in proportion to advertising.

3. Operations Income was income received from auxiliary operations, such as sales of computer time or billing services.

4. Inventory Revaluations occurred when the standard cost of inventory increased from one accounting period to the next. This was usually small but at times had been a significant amount.

5. Overabsorption of Fixed Overhead occurred if volume was higher than the planned level.

6. The Tax Benefit of Donations resulted from occasional gifts in kind to charitable organizations.

7. Commodity Profits resulted from centralized commodity transactions.

8. Profit-Sharing Costs resulted from a system in which Lipton distributed to employees a part of earnings above a certain level, that level defined in terms of a rate of return on shareholders' equity. The amount each employee received was based on salary level. The amount of profit-sharing to be borne by each brand would be based either on the brand's profitability or on its share of total salaries. It had not been decided which base was most appropriate.

Exhibit 4

PERFORMANCE MEASUREMENT AT THOMAS J. LIPTON

Product Line P&L Format

NET SALES

-     VARIABLE COST OF SALES

=   VARIABLE PROFIT CONTRIBUTION

-     NON-VARIABLE COST OF SALES

=   DELIVERED PROFIT

-     ADVERTISING

-     SALES PROMOTION

-     OTHER DIRECT MARKETING EXPENSES

=   DIRECT PROFIT CONTRIBUTION

-     INDIRECTS

-     NEW PRODUCT DEVELOPMENT CHARGE

=   TRADING PROFIT

-     CRV DEPRECIATION ADJUSTMENT

-     WORKING CAPITAL CHARGES

+   NEW PRODUCT DEVELOPMENT CHARGE

-     OTHER DEDUCTIONS (INCOME) (OI&D ADJUSTMENTS)

=   ECONOMIC PROFIT

Exhibit 5

PERFORMANCE MEASUREMENT AT THOMAS J. LIPTON

XYZ Product Line
Economic P&L
(in thousands of dollars)

Sales	$ 30,274
Historical cost trading profit	4,526
Working capital charge	(2,416)
CRV depreciation adjustment	(547)
Fixed-asset charge[1]	(2,821)
OI&D and other	148
New product development charge	244
Economic profit	$ (866)

---

[1]The fixed-asset charge was computed by multiplying a percentage rate times a value for fixed assets, which was the current replacement cost minus accumulated depreciation based on current replacement cost.

Source: Disguised figures based on a marketing financial analysis presentation.

VALMONT INDUSTRIES, INC.

Forty years ago we made our first center pivot irrigation system. It was essentially a long steel pipe resting upon a set of wheels that would travel in a circle, watering crops. A few years later, we stood that irrigation pipe on its end and made our first light pole. It was our first lesson in leverage. It wouldn't be our last.

—Valmont 1993 Annual Report

After being one of the most successful Fortune 500 companies during the 1980s, Valmont Industries fell on difficult times in the 1990s. For the period 1990-92, Valmont's earnings fell well below the company's peak year of 1989, and Valmont management believed that the company's stock had fallen out of favor with Wall Street (see **Exhibit 1**). Although Valmont management fought back by cutting costs, restructuring, and spinning off segments of its business, by the summer of 1993 there was still no tangible evidence that the tide had been turned.

Earlier in the year, several cross-functional teams had been formed to evaluate the company's performance and recommend a course of action to senior management. Terry McClain, vice president of Finance and Administration–Irrigation Division, had been assigned to a team charged with discovering what drove shareholder value and how best to create it. This team was prepared to recommend that Valmont implement a new management concept known as "economic profit" or "economic value added" (EVA™).[1] With just a few days left before their deadline, McClain and other team members were wondering whether EVA could live up to its promise of motivating managers to act like shareholders and ultimately lead managers toward making value-enhancing decisions that would reverse Valmont's weak earnings and lackluster stock-price performance.

VALMONT'S HISTORY

Valmont Industries was begun in 1946 by an inventor, Sam McCleneghan, and a U.S. marine, Robert B. Daugherty, who had just returned home after World War II. Recognizing the potential of McCleneghan's small farm-machine-manufacturing company, Daugherty invested his life savings of $5,000 in the Valley Manufacturing Company. (The name was changed to Valmont in 1967, although products continued to be sold under the "Valley" registered trademark.) In 1952, when a recession hit the farm industry, Daugherty looked for a way to diversify the business. He came across an inventor of an unusual new machine that pulled a long pipeline, mounted on wheels, across a field; attached to the pipeline was a sprinkler. In 1953, Valley Manufacturing purchased the patent rights to the machine, and Valmont's dominance of the agricultural-irrigation industry began.

Valmont spent the following decade improving that first irrigation machine and developing a marketing organization to sell it. Its gradual success fostered the development of additional business lines. In 1959, the company began manufacturing six-

---

[1]EVA™ is a trademark of Stern Stewart & Co., New York, New York.

inch steel pipe and tubing. During the 1960s, the company developed high-speed resistance welding for tubular products, which led to the manufacture of tapered steel poles to support street lights, traffic signals, and lighting for parking lots and stadiums.

With the issuance of 20 percent of its stock in 1968, Valmont went public but continued to grow "entrepreneurially." During the 1970s, Valmont began to develop overseas markets for its products, through licensing agreements with Saudi Arabia, Brazil, Yugoslavia, and the Soviet Union. In the United States, the company's Industrial Products Division expanded by manufacturing transmission towers for the electrical-utility industry. The company's Irrigation Division developed a computer program called ValCom to help farmers size and price out their irrigation systems. It then saw an opportunity to market PCs to farmers and their accountants, and created a microcomputer-reselling business by the same name.

The 1980s saw a period of growth through acquisition. In 1981, Valmont purchased Gate City Steel, a manufacturer of steel reinforcing bars for use in buildings, bridges, and general construction. In 1987, Valmont purchased a manufacturer of ballasts from General Electric, with the goal of leveraging its electric-utility and commercial-lighting customer bases. (A ballast is a small transformer that converts electrical current to the appropriate frequency for a fluorescent lamp; every fluorescent lamp requires a ballast.) In 1988, it acquired a 50 percent interest in Rudolf Bauer A.G., a financially distressed Austrian manufacturer of irrigation equipment that Valmont hoped to turn around. During the following three years, it purchased interests in European and Canadian manufacturers of light poles, with the intent of further penetrating surrounding markets.

During this growth period, the company enjoyed consistent financial success and frequent recognition for its performance. On sales of $663 million in 1988, its stock returned 129.6 percent to investors, earning it fifth place in *Fortune*'s "Ten Highest" list that year.[2] In October 1989, *Fortune* profiled Valmont as a "company to watch," noting Valmont President William Welsh's prediction that he would "build sales to $2 billion in five years and increase profits an average 15 percent a year."[3] In May 1990, President Bush named Valmont one of 11 companies to receive a Presidential "E Star" Award for excellence in exporting.

Then Valmont suddenly and unexpectedly faltered in 1990. Despite Welsh's forecast that 1990 would be another record year for Valmont, earnings were down for the year and by 1991 the company had recorded an $8 million loss. (See **Exhibits 2** and **3** for a financial summary.) The reversal of fortune was attributable to the impact of the recession in the United States, the end of the drought, and the Persian Gulf War. Rudolf Bauer A.G. lost substantial business in the Middle East, and was liquidated in Austrian bankruptcy proceedings. In a $15- million restructuring, Valmont relocated its ballast-manufacturing operation. Although its microcomputer-reselling subsidiary, ValCom, had performed beyond all expectations, producing almost 50 percent of the company's sales and 26 percent of its operating profit in 1990, Valmont decided to refocus its energies on its core manufacturing competencies by gradually divesting itself of ValCom. For a summary of Valmont's acquisitions and divestitures, see **Exhibit 4**.

[2]Reed Abelson and Rahul Jacob, "The Biggest Blowout Ever," *Fortune* (April 24, 1989): 346.
[3]"Companies to Watch," *Fortune* (October 23, 1989): 134.

In 1993, Valmont's operations were divided into two major business segments: the Irrigation Division and the Industrial Products Division. The Irrigation Division specialized in center-pivot and linear-move irrigation systems, contributing 30 percent of Valmont's revenues and 42 percent of its operating profit. The remaining 70 percent of revenues and 58 percent of operating profits were contributed by Valmont's Industrial Products Division, which had two major units: pole structures for the lighting, electrical-transmission, and wireless- communication industries; and Valmont Electric, the ballast operation it had purchased from General Electric in 1987 for $28 million.

MECHANIZED IRRIGATION INDUSTRY

Irrigation benefits areas with little rainfall, as well as areas where rainfall is undependable or unseasonable. In 1992, 58 million acres, or 15 percent, of U.S. farmland was irrigated. Of that amount, 54 percent was irrigated by a mechanical sprinkler system, 42 percent by a less sophisticated method known as "surface/gravity" (flood) irrigation, and 3 percent by a new technology known as "low flow" (i.e., surface spray). Roughly half the mechanical irrigation systems in use were of the center-pivot or linear-move type that Valmont produced, and of which it was the market leader.

Initially, mechanical systems were used to irrigate unarable land, but by 1993 growth in irrigated acreage in the United States had come to a halt. Domestically, 50 percent of sales now resulted from conversions of surface-method users. Although expensive (a system that lasted 10-15 years and irrigated 132 acres sold for $50,000), mechanical systems were preferable because they gave the farmer precise control of water distribution, increasing crop yields by 10-20 percent. They could also be used to apply fertilizers and pesticides.

Agricultural equipment was a highly cyclical industry: in the mid-1980s, when the U.S. agricultural industry fell into a recession, irrigation-equipment sales fell by almost 50 percent in 1985 and another 30 percent in 1986. Those cash-strapped farmers who purchased equipment at all were likely to purchase it used. The economics of mechanical-irrigation systems, however, improved during the drought of the late 1980s, when water became expensive, because mechanical systems used 50 percent less water than flooding. Environmental concerns also favored mechanized methods.

In the United States, sales were driven primarily by farm income and interest rates. Worldwide, irrigated acreage had increased 10 percent since 1975, almost all the increase overseas. Up to 1993, however, sales by U.S. manufacturers to foreign markets had been volatile because of economic and political changes in those markets, primarily in the Middle East and Eastern Europe. Analysts forecast the long-term growth rate of the international market to be 5-7 percent in unit volume.

The mechanized-irrigation industry had just two major American competitors, both headquartered in Nebraska—Valmont Industries, with 45 percent of the domestic market and 200 dealers, and Lindsay Manufacturing Company, with 30 percent of the domestic market and 270 dealers. Lindsay derived 80 percent of its revenues from irrigation equipment, sold under the Zimmatic trademark. Dealers reported that the two companies offered similar products, although Valmont offered a unique product called C:A:M:S (Computer Aided Management System). Introduced in 1990, C:A:M:S gave farmers the ability to control their irrigation systems from their homes and offices, and had been well received by customers. Although Valmont was both the technological and U.S. market leader, Lindsay had been more successful in the Saudi Arabian market. Lindsay had also taken steps to become the industry's low-cost producer. As one observer stated in a 1991 *Forbes* profile, "In a decade they had reduced the number of man-hours needed to produce a system from 500 to 184."[4] See **Exhibit 5** for Valmont's results by business segment and **Exhibit 6** for selected data on Lindsay.

INDUSTRIAL PRODUCTS DIVISION

At the end of 1992, the Industrial Products Division consisted of three segments: Industrial and Construction Products (poles and tubing), Gate City Steel, and Valmont Electric (the ballast operation and Good-All Electric). By the summer of 1993, Valmont had liquidated the operating assets of Gate City Steel and had sold Good-All Electric (a manufacturer of cathodic protection rectifiers, power supplies, and battery chargers). Industrial Products produced $298 million in revenues in 1992; of that amount, analysts estimated that $200 million came from poles and tubing, with the remaining $98 million from the ballast operation. See **Exhibit 7** for an analysis of the Industrial Products Division.

INDUSTRIAL AND CONSTRUCTION PRODUCTS

This segment consisted of three major product lines: poles for lighting applications, utility poles, and wireless-communication towers. Of the three lines, poles for lighting applications was the largest contributor to revenue. Valmont began manufacturing steel poles to support traffic lights, signals, parking-lot lights, and stadium lights in the early 1960s. With its strengths in product design and manufacturing, Valmont learned to market these products over a period of several years. By 1992, however, Valmont's domestic-market share of steel poles was estimated to be 40 percent. Its closest competitor, with a 25 percent market share, was Union Metal Corporation, with annual sales of $38 million and 300 employees. Valmont had overtaken Union Metal some years earlier to become the market leader. Recognizing the maturity of the domestic market for lighting poles, Valmont began expanding internationally in 1989. By early 1993, Valmont was the second-largest pole manufacturer in Europe.

In the 1970s, Valmont expanded by manufacturing larger poles for use by electrical utilities for transmission, distribution, and substations. Again, this was a difficult market to enter, but through perseverance Valmont learned to market to the utility industry. The market's potential was clear: 3 percent of the nation's wooden distribution poles were being replaced by steel poles each year because of steel's lower life-cycle costs and more pleasing appearance; 60-80 percent of all new transmission structures were made of tubular steel. In 1992, Valmont was the second-largest manufacturer of domestic utility poles, with 25 percent of the market. The leader in the industry was Thomas & Betts, which had a 50 percent market share. The two were the only national competitors in the industry. Valmont was an early competitor in the market for wireless-communication poles; by 1992, analysts estimated its market share to be 50 percent.

The early 1990s had been a difficult time for the Industrial Products Division because of the recession in both the United States and Europe. Sales were heavily dependent on public-infrastructure spending and private commercial-construction spending, which contributed equally to the division's revenues. In 1991, the company

---

[4]James Cook, "Making Every Drop Count," *Forbes* (April 29, 1991): 103.

reported that commercial-construction spending had fallen 25 percent from 1990's already-depressed levels. In December 1991, however, Congress passed the six-year, $151-billion Surface Transportation Act, which increased annual funding to improve the nation's roads, bridges, and transit systems by 40 percent. Valmont was optimistic that its lighting-pole and ballast products would benefit from that spending. *U.S. Industrial Outlook* reported that the value of shipments of noncurrent-carrying wiring devices declined another 1.5 percent in 1992, and forecast growth of just 1.5 percent annually for the period 1993-97. Stock analysts expected double-digit growth in wireless-communication towers, but otherwise believed that Valmont's most promising opportunities were international.

VALMONT ELECTRIC

Valmont Electric was primarily a manufacturer of magnetic and electronic ballasts for fluorescent lights. The less-sophisticated magnetic ballasts were cheaper but less energy-efficient than the newer-generation electronic ballasts, which cost $17 or $18 and saved 40 percent more energy than magnetic ballasts. Because roughly 25 percent of all electricity in the United States was used for lighting, utility companies with demand-side management mandates logically made ballasts the target of their rebate programs in the early 1990s. Ninety-five percent of the nation's 1.5 billion fluorescent-lighting fixtures were considered candidates for retrofitting. Although demand between 1989 and 1991 had declined because of the recession, it picked up dramatically in 1992. By year-end, MagneTek, Valmont Electric's most formidable competitor, reported a $300 million backlog. (**Exhibit 7** presents the outlook for the ballast industry.)

The ballast industry was dominated by MagneTek and Advance Transformer (a subsidiary of North American Phillips), each with a 40-45 percent market share. With 12 percent of the magnetic-ballast market and 7.5 percent of the electronic-ballast market, Valmont was third in the industry. When demand for ballasts fell between 1989 and 1991, prices fell and margins eroded. In 1991, Valmont spent $11.3 million pretax to restructure its ballast operations. The company moved its operations from Illinois to its lower-cost locations in Texas and Mexico, purchased automated manufacturing equipment to increase productivity and capacity, outsourced activities, and redesigned its products to utilize lower-cost components. In 1992, the company formed employee teams to further streamline operations. The teams developed computer links with customers and suppliers so that orders, billing, and deliveries could be communicated on-line. They developed partnerships with vendors that shortened cycle times. Their purchasing manager won *Purchasing* magazine's first Cost Savers' Hall of Fame contest for a previously unknown "fixed-forward-purchase" arrangement he worked out with copper suppliers that saved Valmont $700,000 a year.[5] The outlook was positive: at year-end 1992, Valmont's backlog was $91.6 million, 11 percent higher than the year before, with most of the increase attributable to Valmont Electric. Valmont announced:

> In the lighting-ballast market we are the third-largest producer in North America and have prime positions in niche markets. We have significantly restructured this business to allow us to compete as a low-cost producer of high- quality products. Our strengthened manufacturing and engineering

---

[5]Anne Millen Porter, "Cost Savers' Hall-of-Fame Drafts Valmont's Foley," *Purchasing* (December 10, 1992): 20.

capabilities position us for the future, and we have scaled our operations to support markets that yield profitable growth. Electronic and efficient electromagnetic ballast-lamp combinations are growth areas for the next decade. We have the design technology and production capabilities to continually improve our position in these market areas. (1992 Annual Report)

MagneTek's story paralleled Valmont Electric's. A $1.5-billion manufacturer of electrical equipment, MagneTek employed 18,000 workers and operated 52 manufacturing plants and service centers in the United States and 9 overseas. During the low-demand period of 1989-91, MagneTek, like Valmont, had restructured, expanded capacity, and developed a continuous-improvement program. Results had been encouraging, leading MagneTek in early 1993 to adopt an organizational structure comprising 60 strategic business units. See **Exhibit 8** for business-segment information on MagneTek. **Exhibits 9** and **10** present comparison data for MagneTek and other Valmont competitors.

ECONOMIC VALUE ADDED

In the early 1990s, Economic Value Added was gaining rapid momentum as an integrated financial measurement and incentive-compensation system that could significantly improve a company's bottom line and stock price. According to *Fortune:*

> [EVA is] . . . today's hottest financial idea and getting hotter. Seeing why is easy. . . . Managers who run their businesses according to the precepts of EVA have hugely increased the value of their companies. . . . Little wonder that highly regarded major corporations—Coca-Cola, AT&T, Quaker Oats, Briggs & Stratton, CSX, and many others—are flocking to the concept. . . . Explains Quaker's CEO William Smithburg: "EVA makes managers act like shareholders. It's the true corporate faith for the 1990s."[6]

Economic Value Added (generically known as "economic profit" or "residual income") was not a new concept: the economist Alfred Marshall described it as early as 1890 when he wrote, "What remains of his [the owner's or manager's] profits after deducting interest on his capital at the current rate may be called his earnings of undertaking or management." It was not well understood or applied by corporate management, however, until G. Bennett Stewart and Joel Stern made it the cornerstone of their financial consulting firm, Stern Stewart & Company, in 1982.

As McClain and his team prepared for their presentation, they reflected on the merits of Economic Value Added, principal among them the simplicity of its calculation. The distinct advantage of economic profit was that it treated the cost of capital as a line item rather than as a percentage-hurdle rate. In the words of one author, "Anyone with fourth-grade arithmetic skills can do it; no calculator is needed, let alone a computer."[7] In its most basic form, EVA could be calculated as after-tax operating profit less a cost-

---

[6]Shawn Tully, "The Real Key to Creating Wealth," *Fortune* (September 20, 1993): 38.
[7]Daniel J. McConville, "All about EVA," *Industry Week* (April 18, 1994).

of-capital charge. The capital charge was computed as the firm's weighted average cost of capital (WACC) times the invested capital:

Sales
– Operating Expenses
– Income Taxes
= NOPAT (Net Operating Profit After Tax)
– Cost of Capital (WACC × Invested Capital)
= EVA

Invested Capital could be measured as either the sources of funds (i.e., debt and equity) or as the uses of funds (i.e., assets net of non-interest bearing current liabilities). Because EVA was frequently used to measure divisional and business unit performance, it was normally more convenient to rely upon net assets as the measure of invested capital. This approach allowed EVA to be defined in a shorthand method as the spread of return on net assets (RONA) over the cost of capital (WACC) times Net Assets (which equaled Invested Capital).[8]

$$EVA = (RONA - WACC) \times Net\ Assets$$

McClain knew that he would need to be prepared to explain EVA to the board of directors in simple terms and also answer their detailed questions about its implementation. He continued to research books and articles on EVA, and to probe financial and compensation consultants for information. He learned that operating expenses included depreciation and amortization, but excluded interest expense. Adjustments were sometimes made to the calculation of economic profit to take into account a company's unique operating characteristics. For example, to prevent the calculation from unduly penalizing a line manager for making investments with long-term benefits, but short-term losses, such items as R&D expenses, advertising expenses, and training expenses were sometimes capitalized and included as part of Invested Capital.

McClain took comfort in knowing that the concept of economic profit stood on firm academic ground. In particular, net-present-value (NPV) calculations could be reconciled with economic-profit calculations when both were projected into the future (i.e., NPV equaled the present value of future economic profits). Unlike NPV, however, last year's capital investments would not become this year's "sunk costs" in the minds of line managers. On the contrary, any assets acquired would continue to bear a cost—the cost of capital—for as long as they were held. Over the years, too many enthusiastic managers had taken Valmont down paths that had grown earnings in the short term, but that were strategically unsound for the long term and had ultimately destroyed shareholder value. McClain wondered if EVA might be the tool to prevent decisions on capital from being made on the basis of too much emotion and too little analysis.

By way of preparation for the presentation, McClain and his team condensed their EVA research to a handful of its major benefits, and collected supporting testimonials from the dozen Fortune 500 companies already using EVA. Most important, the team believed, EVA linked employees' rewards with shareholders' rewards, and thereby encouraged managers to think like owners and entrepreneurs. CSX had supplied compelling anecdotal evidence in the business press:

---

[8]Although there was no standard, it was a common practice to use the beginning-of-the-year balance for net assets to simplify the calculation.

"EVA is anything but theoretical," says CEO John Snow, who introduced the concept at his company in 1988. . . . On the route from New Orleans to Jacksonville, Florida, four locomotives used to power trains at 28 mph. But the trains arrived at midnight, long before they were unloaded onto trucks or freighters. Spurred by the EVA imperative, CSX decided to run the trains at 25 mph with only three locomotives and arrive three hours later, still in plenty of time to be unloaded at 4 or 5 a.m. The three locomotives also use some 25 percent less fuel than four. Intermodal's EVA was $10 million last year and is on track to triple in 1993. Wall Street has noticed: CSX stock was at $28 when Snow introduced the EVA program and was recently at $75.[9]

The team observed that companies that adopted EVA generally believed that economic profit was the single best predictor of stock performance:

We believe that the best financial proxy for shareholder-value creation is a measure that we call Controllable Earnings [i.e., EVA]. Our analysis, and that of Stern Stewart & Co., the consulting firm that introduced us to EVA, shows a very close correlation between the trend in EVA and shareholder value. (William Smithburg, Chairman, Quaker Oats)[10]

Many of the EVA companies quoted in the business press emphasized EVA's value in focusing management attention on balance-sheet management, where before it had tended to focus excessively on earnings. That is, EVA helped managers up and down the line to distinguish projects and activities with positive NPVs from those with positive earnings but negative NPVs. As James Meenan, AT&T's chief financial officer, observed, "'Good' is no longer positive operating earnings. It's only when you beat the cost of capital."[11]

The ease with which EVA could be calculated and understood, when linked to incentive compensation, gave it the power to harness the good ideas of a company's employees at all levels:

Not only do we agree intellectually with the EVA concept, but we find it easy to use within the context of existing information and simple to explain. We have operating people explaining EVA to other operating people.[12]

In effect, EVA converts the balance sheet into another expense ("capital costs") that may be compared directly with and managed in the same way as normal operating expenses. For this reason, companies that have a tradition

---

[9]Tully, "Real Key to Creating Wealth," 38.

[10]*Enterprise* (April 1993).

[11]Tully, "Real Key to Creating Wealth," 38.

[12]Basil Anderson, chief financial officer of Scott Paper Company, quoted in Stern Stewart & Co. brochure.

of managing for earnings find it relatively simple in practice to switch the focus of their managers to EVA.[13]

Some companies also liked EVA because it helped avoid disputes over budget and capital expenditures; it focused management efforts on profits rather than politics:

> Most companies determine bonuses by how an executive performs against a budget; the most common target is a percentage rise in operating earnings. But the budget benchmark has a glaring flaw: managers have an incentive to negotiate a target that's easy to beat. "The negotiation process is long and difficult," says Derek Smith, executive vice president of Atlanta's Equifax, an information-services company that now bases compensation on EVA. "Instead of reaching for the stars, managers have an incentive to aim low."[14]

Finally, the team considered it a good sign that Wall Street seemed to hold EVA in high regard, and that some investment managers even made a practice of inquiring whether target companies used value-based management systems:

> Investors understandably favor companies committed to increasing EVA. Eugene Vesell, senior vice president of Oppenheimer Capital, which manages $26 billion, says, "We like to invest in companies that use EVA and similar measures. Making higher returns than the cost of capital is how we look at the world."[15]

As Joel Stern noted, "Just announcing that a company will go to EVA increases its market value by 12 percent on average."[16]

EVA seemed to offer a number of substantial benefits. But the team understood that EVA must be adopted, rather than simply calculated, to make a difference. They also knew that there were a number of implementation issues to iron out along the way. In particular, the team wondered whether Valmont should implement a compensation system that would chasten poor performance as well as reward superior. Given Valmont's particular culture and the industries in which it competed, exactly how should the link to compensation be accomplished? Using Valmont's WACC of 10 percent for the business segments seemed fair, but how should Valmont treat items such as "corporate overhead" in the EVA calculation for a divisional manager? Was EVA a sustainable concept, or was it the "flavor-of-the-month program"? Would some other means of motivating management and raising the company's stock price work better than EVA?

---

[13]G. Bennett Stewart, "EVA™: Fact and Fantasy," *Journal of Applied Corporate Finance* (Summer 1994): 77.

[14]Tully, "Real Key to Creating Wealth," 38.

[15]Ibid.

[16]Gerard A. Achstatter, "EVA: Performance Gauge for the 1990s?" *Investors Business Daily* (June 21, 1995).

Exhibit 1

VALMONT INDUSTRIES, INC.

Stock-Price Performance: Valmont versus S&P 500[1]

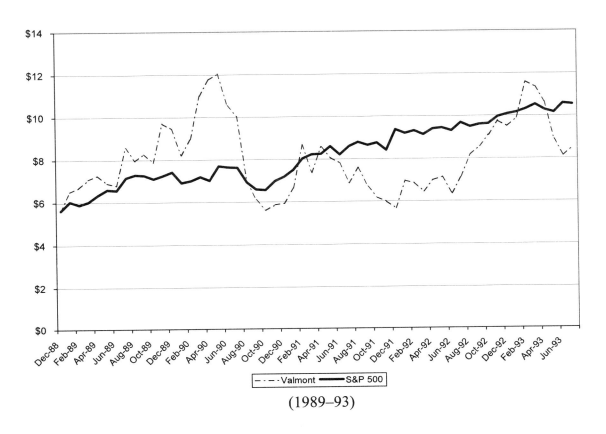

(1989–93)

Exhibit 2

VALMONT INDUSTRIES, INC.

Consolidated Statement of Operations
($000)

	1988	1989	1990	1991	1992	1Q 93E	2Q 93E	3Q 93E	4Q 93E
Net sales	$427,818	$430,721	$446,536	$429,718	$424,685	$106,909	$113,000	$97,000	$108,000
Cost of goods sold	331,736	324,764	340,630	340,178	327,359	81,567	85,600	73,500	80,200
S G & A	72,462	74,153	80,525	80,560	76,336	19,624	20,000	18,500	20,000
Restructuring charge	-	-	-	15,005	-	-	-	-	-
Operating profit	23,620	31,804	25,381	(6,025)	20,990	5,718	7,400	5,000	7,800
Interest expense	6,490	5,602	8,636	7,813	6,847	1,558	1,100	1,000	1,000
Other income (loss)	4,746	2,080	1,313	275	618	100	229	300	300
Pretax profit	21,876	28,282	18,058	(13,563)	14,761	4,260	6,529	4,300	7,100
Taxes	6,679	11,235	6,279	(4,713)	5,134	1,459	2,479	1,122	2,240
Income before equity in affiliates	15,197	17,047	11,779	(8,850)	9,627	2,801	4,050	3,178	4,860
Equity in earnings of affiliates	107	3,611	3,770	840	3,585	687	300	-	-
Net income	$15,304	$20,658	$15,549	$(8,010)	$13,212	$3,488	$4,350	$3,178	$4,860
Earnings per share	**$1.38**	**$1.78**	**$1.34**	**$(0.69)**	**$1.14**	**$0.30**	**$0.37**	**$0.27**	**$0.41**
Dividends per share	$0.17	$0.22	$0.26	$0.26	$0.26	$0.065	$0.065	$0.065	$0.065
Average shares outstanding	11,120	11,604	11,635	11,527	11,583	11,751	11,700	11,750	11,780
Common stock-market prices									
High	$11.25	$20.00	$25.00	$18.50	$18.75				
Low	$4.38	$11.00	$9.25	$9.50	$10.38				

Note: Estimate does not include FASB 109 charge to earnings of $4.9 million ($0.42 per share) in the first quarter of 1993 or an estimated $4-million gain ($0.37 per share) in second-quarter 1993 from the sale of a subsidiary.

Source: Dain Bosworth Incorporated, Research Update, "Valmont Industries, Inc." (June 14, 1993); and Valmont Industries, Inc., 1992 Annual Report.

Exhibit 3

VALMONT INDUSTRIES, INC.

Consolidated Balance Sheets
(fiscal year-end December 31; $000)

Assets	1988	1989	1990	1991	1992
Current assets:					
Cash and cash equivalents	$5,299	$13,826	$10,859	$7,283	$12,747
Receivables, net	60,578	67,491	79,803	65,968	65,630
Inventories	70,390	76,746	71,783	67,954	60,560
Other current assets	7,023	4,161	7,607	18,188	14,406
Total current assets	143,291	162,224	170,052	159,393	153,343
Other assets	24,190	29,080	33,571	39,302	44,135
Property, plant, and equipment, net	51,600	70,286	79,610	82,164	75,740
Total assets	$219,081	$261,590	$283,233	$280,859	$273,218
Liabilities					
Current liabilities:					
Current long-term debt and notes payable	$17,592	$7,940	$35,432	$14,362	$15,161
Accounts payable	35,180	50,436	29,615	34,086	32,326
Other accrued liabilities	34,930	34,130	41,482	45,360	41,989
Total current liabilities	87,702	92,506	106,529	93,808	89,476
Long-term debt	45,550	60,726	54,463	70,428	60,357
Other long-term liabilities	6,726	9,421	10,852	15,542	12,067
	52,276	70,147	65,315	85,970	72,424
Shareholders' equity:					
Common stock ($1 par) and paid-in capital	8,000	12,000	12,792	12,421	12,000
Retained earnings	75,856	85,918	98,951	87,997	98,224
Currency-translation adjustment	548	1,065	1,972	2,029	1,439
	84,404	98,983	113,715	102,447	111,663
Less:					
Cost of common shares in treasury	5,301	46	1,768	969	145
Unearned restricted stock	-	-	558	397	200
Total shareholders' equity	79,103	98,937	111,389	101,081	111,318
Total liabilities and shareholders' equity	$219,081	$261,590	$283,233	$280,859	$273,218

Exhibit 4

VALMONT INDUSTRIES, INC.

Summary of Acquisitions and Divestitures

1981   Purchased 50 percent of Gate City Steel (steel service center and reinforcing-bars company).

1985   Purchased remaining 50 percent of Gate City Steel.

1987   Purchased ballast operation from General Electric for $28 million.
ValCom, Valmont's microcomputer-reselling subsidiary, taken public.

1988   Purchased 50 percent interest in Rudolf Bauer A.G., an Austrian manufacturer of irrigation equipment.

1989   Acquired majority position in Sermeto, a French manufacturer of steel light poles.

1990   Acquired Dutch company, Nolte Mastenfabriek B.V., a manufacturer of steel poles
    sold in the Netherlands and neighboring countries.
Acquired an 80 percent interest in Lampadaires Feralux, Inc., a Canadian manufacturer of
    aluminum lighting and traffic-signal poles.
Merger of ValCom and Inacomp Computer Centers; renamed InaCom Corp. Valmont reduced its
    ownership from 78 percent to 38 percent.
Rudolf Bauer A.G. liquidated in Austrian bankruptcy proceedings.

1992   Restructured ballast business; moved facilities from Illinois to Texas and Mexico.
Downsized Gate City Steel; closed two locations.
Increased ownership in Sermeto to 99.5 percent.

1993   Sold 38 percent stake in InaCom; proceeds of $48 million pretax.

Decision made to sell operating assets of Gate City Steel and exit the steel-reinforcing business
    (sales of Gate City Steel estimated at $30 million).
Decision made to divest interest in Good-All Electric (sales estimated at $10 million).

Exhibit 5

VALMONT INDUSTRIES, INC.

Summary of Business Segments
($000)

	1989	1990	1991	1992	1993E
Revenues					
Industrial Products	$273,411	$306,082	$301,677	$297,907	$295,100
Irrigation Products	158,167	140,653	128,210	126,965	129,909
Intersegment Sales	(857)	(199)	(169)	(187)	(100)
Total	$430,721	$446,536	$429,718	$424,685	$424,909
Operating profit (loss)	1989	1990	1991	1992	1993E
Industrial Products	$24,647	$19,092	$(4,305)	$15,545	$19,518
Irrigation Products	20,482	14,229	8,721	11,472	12,400
Corporate	(13,325)	(7,940)	(10,441)	(6,027)	(6,000)
Total	$31,804	$25,381	$(6,025)	$20,990	$25,918
Net assets	1989	1990	1991	1992	
Industrial Products	$102,148	$126,127	$115,508	$112,167	
Industrial/Construction	63,405	79,430	77,548	76,020	
Valmont Electric	38,743	46,697	37,960	36,147	
Irrigation Products	31,717	29,431	27,647	23,647	
Corporate	43,159	56,578	58,258	63,089	
Total	$177,024	$212,136	$201,413	$198,903	

Sources: Valmont Industries Annual Reports and casewriter estimates.

Exhibit 6

VALMONT INDUSTRIES, INC.

Selected Financial Data on Lindsay Manufacturing Company
(fiscal year-end August 31; $000, except per-share data)

	1988	1989	1990	1991	1992
Net sales	$76,120	$92,630	$102,710	$98,660	$108,930
Cost of goods sold	64,330	74,060	82,700	77,180	85,130
S G & A	7,000	8,240	9,630	10,480	10,930
Operating income	4,790	10,330	10,380	11,000	12,860
Interest expense	-	-	-	-	-
Other income (loss)	170	810	2,520	1,600	2,880
Pretax profit	4,960	11,140	12,900	12,600	15,740
Taxes	1,180	3,780	4,510	3,700	4,720
Net income	$3,770	$7,370	$8,390	$8,900	$11,020
Earnings per share	$0.36	$0.69	$0.81	$0.85	$1.01
Average shares outstanding	10,480	10,700	10,570	10,460	10,870

	1988	1989	1990	1991	1992
Assets					
Cash and equivalents	$3,140	$12,770	$16,850	$18,670	$18,270
Receivables	6,210	6,540	8,500	7,330	8,210
Inventories	9,170	6,930	9,790	9,060	4,280
Other current assets	640	1,100	3,530	4,220	4,990
Current assets	**19,160**	**27,340**	**38,680**	**39,280**	**35,760**
Gross fixed assets	19,350	19,340	20,380	21,070	21,690
Accumulated depreciation	14,710	14,950	15,700	15,680	15,740
Net fixed assets	4,650	4,390	4,680	5,390	5,950
Long-term investments and other	160	-	3,590	15,750	29,650
Total assets	$23,970	$31,730	$46,940	$60,420	$71,360
Liabilities and equity					
Accounts payable	$7,070	$4,260	$7,710	$5,320	$5,570
Short-term debt	960	-	-	-	-
Other accrued liabilities	7,410	10,900	14,480	21,560	20,610
Current liabilities	**15,440**	**15,160**	**22,190**	**26,880**	**26,180**
Long-term debt	-	-	-	-	-
Other long-term liabilities	530	580	710	740	750
Total liabilities	**15,970**	**15,740**	**22,900**	**27,620**	**26,930**
Shareholders' equity	8,000	15,990	24,040	32,800	44,430
Total liabilities and equity	$23,970	$31,730	$46,940	$60,420	$71,360

Source: Bloomberg Financial Analysis.

Exhibit 7

VALMONT INDUSTRIES, INC.

Analysis of Industrial Products Division
(in millions of dollars)

Revenues	1990	1991	1992	1993E
Industrial/construction	$190.0	$190.0	$200.0	$200.0
Valmont Electric	116.1	111.7	97.9	95.1
Total	$306.1	$301.7	$297.9	$295.1

Operating profit (loss)	1990	1991	1992	1993E
Industrial/construction	$17.0	$13.0	$19.0	$19.0
Valmont Electric	2.1	(6.0)	(3.5)	0.5
Restructuring	0.0	(11.3)	0.0	0.0
Total	$19.1	$(4.3)	$15.5	$19.5

Operating-profit margins	1990	1991	1992	1993E
Industrial/construction	8.9%	6.8%	9.5%	9.5%
Valmont Electric	1.8%	-5.4%	-3.6%	0.5%
Total	6.2%	-1.4%	5.2%	6.6%

Fluorescent-ballast industry **Estimated unit volume, in millions**	1990	1991	1992	1993E
Magnetic ballasts	62.3	61.0	70.0	65.0
Electronic ballasts	5.5	10.0	13.0	25.0
Total	67.8	71.0	83.0	90.0

Exhibit 8

VALMONT INDUSTRIES, INC.

MagneTek Business-Segment Analysis
(fiscal year-end June 30; in millions of dollars)

Revenues	**1991**	**1992**	**1993**
Ballasts and transformers	$521.3	$654.6	$828.5
Motors and controls	613.0	575.2	683.7
Total	$1,134.3	$1,229.8	$1,512.2

Operating profit (loss)	**1991**	**1992**	**1993**
Ballasts and transformers	$63.3	$71.9	$63.7
Motors and controls	52.3	33.9	39.7
Total	$115.6	$105.8	$103.4

Operating-profit margins	**1991**	**1992**	**1993**
Ballasts and transformers	12.1%	11.0%	7.7%
Motors and controls	8.5%	5.9%	5.8%
Total	10.2%	8.6%	6.8%

Net assets	**1991**	**1992**	**1993**
Ballasts and transformers	$234.8	$396.8	$470.3
Motors and controls	298.8	367.1	384.3
Total	$533.7	$763.9	$854.6

Sources: MagneTek Annual Report (June 30, 1993), and casewriter estimates.

Exhibit 9

VALMONT INDUSTRIES, INC.

Estimated Market-Share Data

Irrigation Systems		Wireless-Communication Poles	
Valmont	45%	Valmont	50%
Lindsay Manufacturing	30%	Others	50%
Others	25%		

Domestic Lighting Poles		Domestic Utility Poles	
Valmont	40%	Thomas & Betts	50%
Union Metal	25%	Valmont	25%
Others	30%	Others	25%

Magnetic Ballasts		Electronic Ballasts	
Advance Transformer	45%	MagneTek	50%
MagneTek	40%	Advance Transformer	37%
Valmont	12%	Valmont	8%
Others	3%	Others	6%

Source: Lehman Brothers Report (August 19, 1993).

Exhibit 10

VALMONT INDUSTRIES, INC.

Comparisons of 1992 Financial Statements

	Long-Term Debt/ Total Capital	Return on Assets	Operating Margin	Net Fixed Asset Turnover
Lindsay Manufacturing	0.0%	15.4%	11.8%	18.31
MagneTek	69.9%	2.7%	6.8%	6.35
Thomas & Betts	47.4%	8.1%	2.3%	3.55
Valmont Industries	32.2%	4.8%	4.9%	5.61

Sources: Lehman Brothers Report (August 19, 1993), and Bloomberg Data Service.

MAVERICK LODGING

In early January 2000, Cindy Baum was reviewing the 1999 balanced scorecard results for Maverick Lodging. As the vice president of Asset Management, Baum had developed and implemented the balanced scorecard throughout 1998. Thus, 1999 represented the first full year of results using the balanced scorecard approach. She was anxious to see if the scorecard she had created was accomplishing its primary objective of aligning the company's strategy, structure, measurements, and incentives.

Developing a balanced scorecard had been a considerable challenge because of the complicated nature of the hotel industry. Baum's employer, Maverick Lodging, managed hotels on behalf of third-party owners who had franchise agreements with the Marriott Corporation. Maverick Lodging concentrated on managing three specific types of Marriott properties: Fairfield Inns, Courtyards by Marriott, and Marriott Residence Inns. Fairfield Inns and Courtyards by Marriott offered the typical variety of hotel rooms, whereas Residence Inns offered "suite arrangements" that included a kitchen, sitting room, and one or two bedrooms. The Courtyards typically had a restaurant, whereas the Fairfield Inns and Residence Inns did not. Instead, they had a "gatehouse" area that served complimentary breakfast.

Because third-party owners had many choices among hotel-management companies, including the Marriott Corporation, Maverick Lodging believed that adopting a balanced scorecard framework might help differentiate its services. In addition, Baum believed that a good balanced scorecard would be particularly useful to her because, as the vice president of Asset Management, she was the principal liaison between the hotel owners and Maverick Lodging. Therefore, she had primary responsibility for ensuring that the contract terms and both parties' objectives were met. Maverick Lodging was one of the earliest hotel-management companies to implement a balanced scorecard management system.

As Baum reviewed the results for 1999 (see **Exhibit 7**), she wanted to understand how the business had performed, assess the overall effectiveness of her balanced scorecard, and look for ways in which it might be improved. She was to report her findings and recommendations to Robert Sandlin, Maverick Lodging's president and CEO, the following week.

Baum felt that her meeting with Robert Sandlin would decide the fate of her career with the company. Maverick Lodging had brought Baum in to be a change agent, including the development and implementation of the balanced scorecard. This first year was crucial for the success of the scorecard and her role in the organization. Successful results from the balanced scorecard could help Maverick Lodging attract more hotels to manage, which would increase Baum's responsibilities. In addition, the hotel managers were counting on the scorecard to work properly, as it was their performance assessment and compensation that would be affected by the results. For instance, although the hotel

---

managers had some influence over their hotel rates, prices were largely determined by local market conditions and the market segment being served.

HOTEL INDUSTRY

The hotel industry was characterized by complexity and competition, and both of these features influenced Baum's decision to join Maverick Lodging after she completed her joint master's degree in Business and Hotel Management. One of her first assignments was to lead the development and implementation of a balanced scorecard management system. Baum felt that implementing a balanced scorecard in a hotel-management company was particularly challenging owing to the multiple parties involved in the hotel industry. Incorporating the perspectives and balancing the various economic benefits of each of the three parties (see **Table A**) would be necessary in order for the balanced scorecard approach to be successful.

Table A
Structure of the Hotel Industry

Party	Description	Economic Benefits
Franchiser (Marriott Corporation)	"Licenses" name and concept to franchisee/owner.	Receives from franchisee/owner an initial franchise fee and royalties based on a specified percentage of revenues.
Franchisee/Owner (Various third parties)	Enters into a contract with the franchiser and actually owns the hotel. Has the responsibility for capital expenditures and for operating the hotel. Frequently hires a hotel-management company.	Retains all the net profit from the hotel.
Manager (Maverick Lodging)	Manages (operates) the hotel in compliance with franchiser's policies and under the direction and supervision of the franchisee/owner.	Receives from the franchisee/owner a base management fee and an incentive management fee based on a percentage of house profit. ("House profit" is a common hotel term for the hotel's net profit.)

MAVERICK LODGING

At the end of 1999, Maverick Lodging managed 38 hotels with total revenues of $140 million. The hotels ranged in size from 50 rooms to 347 rooms, with the majority ranging between 75 and 140 rooms. The hotels were primarily located in and around relatively large cities in the states of Florida, Illinois, Indiana, and Texas. In comparison with Marriott International, Maverick was quite small. At the end of 1999, Marriott International owned, managed, or franchised 1,880 hotels with 355,900 rooms and had plans to double the number of rooms over the next five years. The company's 2001 target was to manage 65 properties with $225 million in sales. Maverick Lodging had two types of stated objectives: (1) objectives concerning Maverick Lodging and (2) objectives concerning each managed hotel.

Objectives concerning Maverick Lodging

1. 15 percent annual compound growth in managed revenues

2. $300 million in managed revenues by 2004

3. Achieve annual budgets

4. Deliver a 15 percent ROI to franchisees/owners

5. Retain management employees by achieving less than 20 percent turnover

6. Retain 100 percent of franchisees/owners

Objectives concerning each managed hotel[1]

1. Exceed brand average yield. (Yield was the ratio of the hotel's revenue per available room [RevPAR] to its local competitors' revenue per available room. RevPAR was the hotel's room revenue divided by the number of available rooms. Brand average yield was the average yield for all Marriott hotels of a comparable brand [e.g., Courtyard by Marriott].)

2. Grow RevPAR at a specified rate greater than local competitors (i.e., grow yield at a specified rate)

3. Exceed the profitability levels of Marriott-branded hotels owned and managed by Marriott

4. Be in the top 20 percent of brand in guest-satisfaction scores

5. Retain nonmanagement employees (i.e., associates) by achieving less than 60 percent turnover

At the time the balanced scorecard was developed, the typical hotel managed by Maverick Lodging was four years old. In general, properties older than five years

---

[1]The external information relating to specific hotel performance was collected on a monthly basis from two sources. Information regarding local competitor performance was purchased from an independent data clearinghouse. Information regarding Marriott-branded hotels (e.g., Courtyard by Marriott, Fairfield Inn, Marriott Residence Inn) was provided by Marriott Corporation and, except for information regarding profitability, included both Marriott-managed and -franchised hotels. Profitability information pertained only to Marriott-managed hotels.

experienced a decline in guest-satisfaction scores owing to their overall condition and appearance. Robert Sandlin recognized this undesirable tendency and felt that the balanced scorecard might help remedy the situation.

Maverick's organizational structure (see **Table B**) added another level of complexity to the balanced scorecard implementation. The balanced scorecard was implemented at the hotel level, and was used as a management-control/performance measurement system for each hotel's general manager, who was typically 25 to 35 years old with a college degree but little management experience. As a result, Baum felt that the balanced scorecard needed to be comprehensive but not overly complex.

Table B
Maverick Lodging's Organizational Structure

DESIGNING MAVERICK'S BALANCED SCORECARD

Baum involved the four other vice presidents and the three regional managers in the balanced scorecard design process. Not surprisingly, there was considerable disagreement about what the balanced scorecard should look like. The entire team finally agreed to create a scorecard with the following attributes:

1. It tracks financial performance.
2. It tracks nonfinancial measures that are important for long-term growth and value creation.
3. It communicates franchisees'/owners' objectives for growth, profitability, and physical maintenance.
4. It is understandable and acceptable to hotel general managers, and it provides them with useful and relevant information.
5. It is understandable, useful, and relevant to Maverick Lodging's management.

Exhibit 1 illustrates how Maverick's nonfinancial and financial measures were linked in achieving the company's objectives. **Exhibit 2** details the actual balanced scorecard.

BALANCED SCORECARD AS A PERFORMANCE MEASUREMENT SYSTEM

Prior to the introduction of the balanced scorecard, the regional managers had a great deal of discretion in determining the amount of each hotel manager's bonus. The average bonus generally ranged between 20 percent and 40 percent of the hotel manager's $40,000–$50,000 salary. The bonus depended on the size of the bonus pool, hotel profitability, and the regional manager's assessment of the hotel manager's overall performance. Consequently, most hotel managers felt that their bonuses were somewhat arbitrary. Nevertheless, they paid close attention to whatever they believed their regional managers deemed important.

In order to rate each hotel manager's performance through the use of the balanced scorecard, Maverick implemented a numerical point system and five-color rating scheme (see **Table C**), with concrete targets (see **Exhibit 3**) for each scorecard measure.

Table C
Point System and Color Rating Scheme

Performance	Color Ranking	Points
Superior	Platinum	10
Above Expectations	Gold	7.5
At Expectations	Green	5
Below Expectations	Yellow	2.5
Unacceptable	Red	0

In determining a hotel manager's bonus, each measure on the balanced scorecard was assigned a color ranking based on performance relative to the target. This color ranking was translated into a point score based on a predetermined scale from 0 to 10 (see **Table C**). Then, an overall point score for the hotel manager was derived by calculating a weighted average score using the point scores for the five measures. Each measure was weighted 20 percent. This overall point score was then translated into a performance factor (see **Table D**).

Table D
Overall Point Score and Performance Factor

Performance	Color Ranking	Weighted Average Overall Point Score	Performance Factor
Superior	Platinum	9.0–10.0	200%
Above Expectations	Gold	7.5–8.9	150%
At Expectations	Green	5.0–7.4	100%
Below Expectations	Yellow	2.5–4.9	50%
Unacceptable	Red	0–2.4	0%

The performance factor was multiplied by 40 percent of the hotel manager's salary to determine the bonus. Thus, each hotel manager would receive a bonus ranging from 0 percent to 80 percent of salary.

The corporate executives and the regional managers were not compensated based on the balanced scorecard. The scorecard was initially devised to be applicable only at the hotel-general-manager level.

BALANCED SCORECARD DESIGN

Baum realized that the measures and targets selected for the scorecard (**Exhibits 2** and **3**), plus its roll-out, would affect its ultimate success or failure. She knew there were many possible measures from which to choose, but that those selected must be consistent with corporate objectives. In addition, she wanted to make sure that the measures (1) supported Maverick's strategy and structure, (2) could be understood and used by the hotel managers, and (3) could be controlled or reasonably influenced by the hotel managers.

Financial—top-line yield: The objectives for this measure were for the hotel to exceed brand average yield and to grow revenue per available room at a specified rate greater than local competitors. The key driver in this metric was the hotel's yield, which was defined as the hotel's revenue per available room relative to the local competitors' revenue per available room. (Revenue per available room [RevPAR] was a standard revenue measure in the hotel industry. RevPAR = [# of rooms sold × rate per room]/[# of available hotel rooms × # of days in period].)

As seen in **Exhibit 3**, more aggressive targets were applied to hotels that were underperforming brand averages in an effort to drive improved performance at those hotels.

Financial—controllable profit relative to flexible budget (flowthrough flexible budget): The objectives for this measure were to (1) achieve budget targets, (2) obtain superior financial management of hotels, (3) outperform brand average profitability, and (4) deliver high investment returns to owners. Because the flowthrough model (see **Exhibit 4**) entailed the use of a flexible budget, it considered only the costs and expenses that could be influenced or controlled by hotel managers and simultaneously adjusted expected performance to account for variances in top-line room-revenue achievement. The hotel's owner and Maverick Lodging's top management worked together in establishing the annual budgets. The hotel managers had limited influence on setting their budgets.

The flowthrough flexible budget allowed hotel owners and managers to concentrate on costs and expenses that were under the hotel manager's influence or control. As seen in **Exhibit 3**, more aggressive performance thresholds were applied to hotels that were underperforming expected profitability levels to encourage improved performance at those hotels.

Customer—guest-satisfaction survey: The objectives for this measure were to ensure (1) the most satisfied guests across the brand and (2) internal consistency (no property scoring below brand average guest satisfaction). Maverick Lodging executives knew that guest scores correlated with investment returns; thus, they reinforced the desire for high guest-satisfaction scores.

As shown in **Exhibit 5**, the guest-satisfaction survey was quite comprehensive and detailed. The balanced scorecard, however, incorporated only the overall score as shown in the first line of survey question 5.

Internal business—process audit: The objective of the consolidated process audit (see **Exhibit 6**) was to ensure that hotel management addressed "the basics" of running a property. The audit was conducted by a manager of Internal Audit and had a maximum possible score of 100 points.

Learning and growth—turnover of associates: The learning and growth section was intended to identify initiatives needed to provide the infrastructure for the organization's future growth. The objective was to ensure that turnover of associates was minimized, as hotels with lower turnover generally performed better.

Communication of the balanced scorecard: Baum felt that the communication associated with the implementation of the balanced scorecard had been successful. Because the regional managers were part of the design and implementation team, they understood the scorecard and supported its measures and targets. In addition, throughout the design process, the regional managers had communicated with the hotel managers regarding the development of the scorecard and how it would affect them.

Baum explained the balanced scorecard to all the hotel managers at the company's annual retreat in June 1998. She also gave them a report showing how their hotel would have performed in 1997 and what their approximate bonus would have been had the scorecard been used the previous year. Thus, the hotel managers had an expectation of what their bonus would be if they had a similar year of performance. None of the measures on the balanced scorecard was completely new to the hotel managers, but the balanced scorecard formalized how their bonuses would be determined and how management would be reviewing their results. The balanced scorecard, with its linked measures, was intended to help the hotel managers understand better what they needed to concentrate on to achieve strong performance results at their hotels. Jane Ellmann, general manager of the Courtyard Hotel in Bloomington, Indiana, stated: "Our balanced scorecard provides us with tremendous focus. It lets our entire leadership team know where we are going, and our priorities guide us on how to get there."

CONCLUSION

Baum reviewed the 1999 results (see **Exhibit 7**) and began to assess the major conclusions based on the scorecard data. She thought back to when she developed the balanced scorecard and remembered the discussions she had with the design team regarding its desire to balance substance and simplicity. The vice president of Operations had been adamant about the scorecard's being understandable and useful to the hotel managers.

Initially, Baum was pleased that the major issues of balanced scorecard design and implementation had been anticipated. She had not, however, anticipated the need for hotel managers to have the scorecard modified for individual circumstances. For example, the general manager of the Fairfield Inn in Orlando, Florida, felt that certain aspects of the balanced scorecard did not apply to his hotel because his room rates were around $150 a night, which was extremely high for a Fairfield Inn but in line with room rates in Orlando. Thus, the guest-satisfaction results from his hotel were low because guests did not feel they received $150 worth of value. Baum was happy that the system was flexible enough that it could be modified on a hotel-by-hotel basis for special situations like this one. Nevertheless, she planned to make sure that these exceptions did not become the rule.

In preparation for her meeting with the CEO, she focused her analysis on four important aspects:

1. What happened in 1999? Was it a good year for the company?

2. What exactly is the company's value-added proposition? Just what competitive advantage is the company trying to build, and do the balanced scorecard system and its related bonus plan support that objective?

3. Is the flowthrough flexible budget a useful management tool? Is it too complex and confusing? Is it being used properly?

4. What changes, if any, should be made to the balanced scorecard?

Exhibit 1

MAVERICK LODGING

Relationship of Nonfinancial and Financial Measures

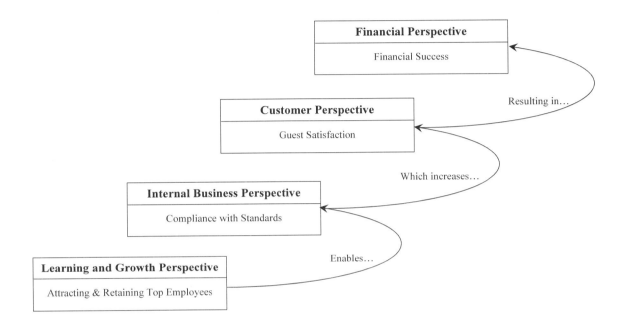

Exhibit 2

MAVERICK LODGING

Balanced Scorecard Measures

Perspective	Indicator	Performance Measure	Target
Financial	Top-line yield	Yield = $$\frac{\text{Hotel's RevPAR}}{\text{Local competitors' average RevPAR}}$$ Where RevPAR = $$\frac{\text{Total room revenue}}{\text{(Room Rate} \times \text{\# of rooms sold)}}$$ # of available rooms for period (this is # of rooms in the hotel less rooms out-of-service)	See **Exhibit 3**
Financial	Controllable profit relative to flexible budget (flowthrough flexible budget)	A flexible budget that reforecasts profitability based on actual top-line achievement (see **Exhibit 4**) • Breaks costs and expenses into two components: controllable and uncontrollable • Variable controllable costs and expenses are reforecast based on the appropriate driver • Fixed controllable costs and expenses are not reforecast • Uncontrollable costs and expenses are not reforecast	See **Exhibit 3**
Customer	Guest-satisfaction survey	Overall score from a guest-satisfaction survey (see **Exhibit 5**)	See **Exhibit 3**
Internal Business	Process audit	Score from a comprehensive process audit (see **Exhibit 6**) conducted by an internal-audit manager	See **Exhibit 3**
Learning and Growth	Turnover of associates (non-management employees)	Associate turnover = $$\frac{\text{\# of hotel associates who left during year}}{\text{Average \# of associates}}$$	See **Exhibit 3**

Exhibit 3
MAVERICK LODGING
Balanced Scorecard Targets

Metric	Platinum	Gold	Green	Yellow	Red
			Color Ranking		
Top-line yield—2 classifications of hotel performance:					
(a) **Top-line** yield above brand average[1]	6% increase in yield or 110% of brand average yield	4% increase in yield or 105% of brand average yield	0.1% increase in yield or 100% of brand average yield	2.5% decline in yield	> 2.5% decline in yield
(b) **Top-line** yield below brand average[1]	12% increase in yield	8% increase in yield	4% increase in yield	1.5% increase in yield	<1.5% increase in yield
Flowthrough-flexible-budget ratings—3 classifications of hotel performance:					
(a) Low performers (house profit under 90% of budget)[2]	106.0% of flexible budget controllable profit	104.0% of flexible budget controllable profit	102.0% of flexible budget controllable profit	99.0% of flexible budget controllable profit	<99.0% of flexible budget controllable profit
(b) Base performers (house profit at 90–105% of budget)[2]	104.0% of flexible budget controllable profit	102.0% of flexible budget controllable profit	99.0% of flexible budget controllable profit	97.5% of flexible budget controllable profit	<97.5% of flexible budget controllable profit
(c) High performers (house profit >105% of budget)[2]	102.0% of flexible budget controllable profit	100.0% of flexible budget controllable profit	97.5% of flexible budget controllable profit	95.0% of flexible budget controllable profit	<95.0% of flexible budget controllable profit
Customer satisfaction					
Guest-satisfaction score	Increase by 80% or top 10% of brand	Increase by 60% or top 20% of brand	Increase by 40% or top 30% of brand	Increase by 20% or top 40% of brand	Increase by <20% or below top 40% of brand
Comprehensive process audit					
Internal-process-audit score	At least 97.5	At least 95	At least 92.5	At least 90	Below 90
Employee retention					
Annual associate turnover	30% or below or reduce by 75%	40% or below or reduce by 50%	50% or below or reduce by 40%	60% or below or reduce by 30%	>60% or reduce by <30%

[1]The hotel's yield is compared with the brand average yield, which determines whether the hotel's performance is assessed in classification a or b.
[2]The hotel's actual house profit/budgeted house profit determines whether the hotel's performance is assessed in classification a, b, or c. See Exhibit 4 for the calculation of house profit.

Exhibit 4

MAVERICK LODGING

Flowthrough Flexible Budget for Courtyard

	1999 Budget	Reforecast Target	1999 Actual	Drivers
Rooms available	72,270	72,270	72,270	
Rooms occupied	57,809	57,994	57,994	
Average rate	$82.79	$86.98	$86.98	
Revenue				
Room	$4,786,251	$5,044,032	$5,044,032	$86.98 per room occupied
Food	204,132	204,785	266,507	$3.53 per room occupied
Beverage	34,135	34,244	29,319	$0.59 per room occupied
Phone	193,253	193,871	157,963	$3.34 per room occupied
Other	92,312	92,607	107,371	$1.60 per room occupied
Total revenue	$5,310,083	$5,569,540	$5,605,192	
Controllable expenses:				
Cost of goods sold				
Phone	$28,171	$23,027	$12,179	14.58% of actual phone revenue
Phone equipment	15,262	15,262	7,840	Fixed
Other	207,334	252,879	260,127	62.72% of actual food, beverage and other revenue
Total cost of goods sold	250,767	291,168	280,146	
Payroll				
Housekeeping	310,981	311,976	300,677	$5.38 per room occupied
				$.62 per room occupied up to budgeted rooms; $.31 per room occupied over budgeted rooms
Laundry	35,931	35,988	38,038	$1.41 per room occupied up to budgeted rooms
Front desk	81,700	81,700	81,549	Fixed
Administration	57,415	57,415	62,510	Fixed
Sales	18,016	18,016	15,359	$27,429 plus $.47 per room occupied up to budgeted rooms
Maintenance	54,857	54,857	50,358	34.0% of food & beverage revenue up to budgeted rooms
Other	80,970	80,970	89,741	

Exhibit 4 (continued)

MAVERICK LODGING

	1999 Budget	Reforecast Target	1999 Actual	Drivers
Mgmt (salary)	186,223	186,223	174,624	Fixed
Employee relations	17,113	17,949	25,790	0.32% or total revenue
Total payroll	843,206	845,095	838,646	
Other controllable expenses				
Linen	31,217	31,317	29,947	$0.54 per room occupied
Guest supplies	47,322	47,473	53,975	$0.82 per room occupied
Cleaning expense	29,911	30,007	30,966	$0.52 per room occupied
Rooms, other	61,348	61,348	71,629	Fixed
Postage	6,500	6,500	5,477	Fixed
Office supplies	13,832	13,832	11,676	Fixed
Administration phone	12,688	12,688	12,975	Fixed
Travel	10,306	10,306	13,841	Fixed
Cash over/short	-	-	(806)	0.0% of total revenue
Bad debt	5,310	5,570	1,998	0.1% of total revenue
Administration, other	23,516	23,591	31,357	$0.41 per room occupied
Advertising	14,560	14,560	11,743	Fixed
Main supplies	6,110	6,110	10,548	Fixed
Main. trash, grounds	19,535	19,535	18,231	Fixed
Maintenance	66,326	66,326	70,330	Fixed
Utilities	183,573	183,867	176,824	$91,787 plus $1.59 per room occupied
House charges, other	33,124	33,124	32,673	Fixed
Total other expenses	565,178	566,154	583,384	
Total controllable expenses	1,659,151	1,702,416	1,702,176	
Controllable profit	$3,650,932	$3,867,124	$3,903,016	
Actual vs. flexible budget controllable profit			100.93%	Actual controllable profit/ reforecast controllable profit
Uncontrollable expenses	1,060,261		1,127,929	Given
House profit	$2,590,671		$2,775,087	Controllable profit − uncontrollable expenses
Actual vs. budget house profit			107.12%	Actual house profit/budget house profit

Exhibit 5

MAVERICK LODGING

Guest-Satisfaction Survey for Residence Inn

Please indicate your answers with an ⊠ in the boxes or on the lines provided.

1. What <u>one</u> hotel or motel chain have you stayed at most often in the past year, while traveling on business? *(Please select one hotel chain only.)*

Courtyard by Marriott .... ☐   Marriott Hotels .... ☐

Hampton Inn .... ☐   Residence Inn .... ☐

Holiday Inn .... ☐   Other (please specify below) ☐

_____

2. Was this your first visit ever to any Residence Inn?

Yes .... ☐   No .... ☐

3. On your next rip to this area, how likely will you be to stay in this Residence Inn again? Would you say you:

Definitely Will .... ☐ ⎤
Probably Will .... ☐ ⎬ *Skip to Q. 5*
May or May Not .... ☐ ⎦

Probably Will Not .... ☐ ⎤
Definitely Not .... ☐ ⎦ *Continue*

4. Why do you say you probably or definitely will not stay at this Residence Inn again?
(Please check all that apply.)

Poor cleanliness/upkeep .... ☐

Hotel in poor physical condition .... ☐

Problems with suite features/amenities .... ☐

Unfriendly/unresponsive/poor service .... ☐

Reservation problem/mistake .... ☐

Noise .... ☐

Price .... ☐

Location/other hotels more convenient .... ☐

Layout/configuration of suite .... ☐

Lack of service (e.g., restaurant) .... ☐

Prefer another hotel in this area .... ☐

Not returning to this area .... ☐

Other (please specify below) .... ☐

_____

5. Please rate this Residence Inn on each of the features listed below, using a scale of 1-10, where 10 is "excellent" and 1 is "poor". *(If not applicable, leave blank.)*

	Excellent 10	9	8	7	6	5	4	3	2	*Poor* 1
Residence Inn hotel overall	☐	☐	☐	☐	☐	☐	☐	☐	☐	☐
Overall service	☐	☐	☐	☐	☐	☐	☐	☐	☐	☐
Overall value for the money	☐	☐	☐	☐	☐	☐	☐	☐	☐	☐
Overall maintenance and upkeep	☐	☐	☐	☐	☐	☐	☐	☐	☐	☐
Price	☐	☐	☐	☐	☐	☐	☐	☐	☐	☐
Speed/efficiency of check-in	☐	☐	☐	☐	☐	☐	☐	☐	☐	☐
Speed/efficiency of check-out	☐	☐	☐	☐	☐	☐	☐	☐	☐	☐
Ease of making reservation	☐	☐	☐	☐	☐	☐	☐	☐	☐	☐
Suite reservation in order at check in	☐	☐	☐	☐	☐	☐	☐	☐	☐	☐
Suite quality	☐	☐	☐	☐	☐	☐	☐	☐	☐	☐
Comfortable place to stay	☐	☐	☐	☐	☐	☐	☐	☐	☐	☐
Friendliness of staff	☐	☐	☐	☐	☐	☐	☐	☐	☐	☐
Attentiveness of staff	☐	☐	☐	☐	☐	☐	☐	☐	☐	☐
Responsiveness to special requests	☐	☐	☐	☐	☐	☐	☐	☐	☐	☐
Friendliness of Front Desk staff	☐	☐	☐	☐	☐	☐	☐	☐	☐	☐
Physical condition of the hotel	☐	☐	☐	☐	☐	☐	☐	☐	☐	☐
Physical condition of the suite	☐	☐	☐	☐	☐	☐	☐	☐	☐	☐
Cleanliness of suite upon entering	☐	☐	☐	☐	☐	☐	☐	☐	☐	☐
Cleanliness and upkeep of suite during stay	☐	☐	☐	☐	☐	☐	☐	☐	☐	☐
Weekend housekeeping	☐	☐	☐	☐	☐	☐	☐	☐	☐	☐
Suite odor	☐	☐	☐	☐	☐	☐	☐	☐	☐	☐
Suite lighting	☐	☐	☐	☐	☐	☐	☐	☐	☐	☐
Ability to work in suite	☐	☐	☐	☐	☐	☐	☐	☐	☐	☐
Feeling of safety	☐	☐	☐	☐	☐	☐	☐	☐	☐	☐
Overall breakfast	☐	☐	☐	☐	☐	☐	☐	☐	☐	☐
Breakfast staff attentiveness	☐	☐	☐	☐	☐	☐	☐	☐	☐	☐
Breakfast staff friendliness	☐	☐	☐	☐	☐	☐	☐	☐	☐	☐
Variety of food at breakfast	☐	☐	☐	☐	☐	☐	☐	☐	☐	☐
Food quality at breakfast	☐	☐	☐	☐	☐	☐	☐	☐	☐	☐
Weekday hospitality hour	☐	☐	☐	☐	☐	☐	☐	☐	☐	☐

Exhibit 5 (continued)

MAVERICK LODGING

Only answer the following question if you've been to the area more than once in the past year. Otherwise, skip to Q. 7.

6. Please think about this Residence Inn in comparison to other hotels in the area. Is **this** Residence Inn better, the same, or worse on the following features?

	Better	Same	Worse
Hotel overall	☐	☐	☐
Value	☐	☐	☐
Location	☐	☐	☐
Overall service	☐	☐	☐
Physical condition of the hotel	☐	☐	☐
Physical condition of the suite	☐	☐	☐

7. Did you experience any hotel related problems during your stay?

Yes .... ☐ *Continue*

No .... ☐ *Skip to Q.9*

8. If you experienced problems, please indicate below what the problems were and how they were resolved.

	Resolved promptly	Resolved but took too long	Not resolved	Experienced problem, but did not report to staff
Bathroom cleanliness	☐	☐	☐	☐
Bathroom supplies	☐	☐	☐	☐
Bedding cleanliness	☐	☐	☐	☐
Billing	☐	☐	☐	☐
Broken items	☐	☐	☐	☐
Carpet cleanliness	☐	☐	☐	☐
Heat/air-conditioning	☐	☐	☐	☐
Hot tub/pool/sports court/ exercise room	☐	☐	☐	☐
Insects/pests	☐	☐	☐	☐
Kitchen appliances	☐	☐	☐	☐
Kitchen cleanliness	☐	☐	☐	☐
Light bulb not working	☐	☐	☐	☐
Message not delivered/ incorrect	☐	☐	☐	☐
No water/hot water	☐	☐	☐	☐
Noise	☐	☐	☐	☐
Plumbing	☐	☐	☐	☐
Reservations	☐	☐	☐	☐
Suite cleanliness	☐	☐	☐	☐
Suite type/location unavailable	☐	☐	☐	☐
Smoking preference unavailable	☐	☐	☐	☐
Staff contact/service	☐	☐	☐	☐
Telephone	☐	☐	☐	☐
TV/remote not working	☐	☐	☐	☐
Wake-up call	☐	☐	☐	☐
Other *(please specify below)*	☐	☐	☐	☐

_____

9. Which one of the following best describes the primary purpose of your trip to **this** Residence Inn?

Project assignment .... ☐   Relocation/Interim housing ... ☐

Training .... ☐   Visiting friends/Relatives ...... ☐

Sales call .... ☐   Other leisure activities .... ☐

Business meeting .... ☐   Other *(please specify below)* ☐

Convention/Conference ..... ☐   _____

10. Overall, would you say your stay at **this** Residence Inn:

Exceeded your expectations .... ☐

Met your expectations .... ☐

Did not meet your expectations .... ☐

11. In the last **twelve months**, how many overnight business trips did you take? *(Please write one number.)*

_____ Trips

12. How many of these trips lasted **5 or more consecutive nights** in the same accommodation?

_____ Trips

13. How many of the trips that last **5 or more consecutive nights** were to any Residence Inn?

_____ Trips

14. In the last **twelve months**, how many overnight leisure trips did you take? *(Please write one number.)*

_____ Trips

15. Was this your first visit ever to **this** Residence Inn?

Yes .... ☐   No .... ☐

16. Was Residence Inn your **first choice** for this trip?

Yes .... ☐   No .... ☐

17. Based on your stay at this Residence Inn, how likely would you be to stay at other Residence Inns?

Definitely Will	Probably Will	May or May Not	Probably Will Not	Definitely Will Not
☐	☐	☐	☐	☐

18. What is your age, please?

Under 18	18 – 34	35 – 44	45 – 54	55 – 64	65 or Over
☐	☐	☐	☐	☐	☐

19. Are you: Female .... ☐   Male .... ☐

20. Daytime phone?

(☐ ☐ ☐) ☐ ☐ ☐ - ☐ ☐ ☐ ☐

21. E-mail address?

☐ ☐ ☐ ☐ ☐ ☐ ☐ ☐ ☐ ☐

☐ ☐ ☐ ☐ ☐ ☐ ☐ ☐ ☐ ☐

☐ ☐ ☐ ☐ ☐ ☐ ☐ ☐ ☐ ☐

Please provide us with any additional comments you may have about your stay. Feel free to include an additional piece of paper if necessary.

_____

_____

_____

_____

Thank you for taking the time to give us your opinions. Please return this questionnaire in the enclosed postage-paid envelope as soon as possible.

Exhibit 6

MAVERICK LODGING

Comprehensive Process Audit

Human Resources Best Practices

1. Personnel files (e.g., reviews, discipline, tax forms) are properly maintained.
2. Associates adhere to training schedules.
3. Uniforms are worn per policy.
4. Hotel complies with human-resources regulations (e.g., OSHA, ADA, Workers' Compensation).

Hotel Improvement Best Practices

1. Associates are aware of mission statement, critical success factors.
2. Guest rooms and public areas are properly cleaned and inspected.
3. Defects and guest complaints are properly recorded and resolved.
4. Sales and marketing goals are posted and results tracked properly.
5. Hotel adheres to accounting and internal-control processes.

Maintenance Best Practices

1. Guest rooms and public areas are refreshed with quarterly preventive maintenance.
2. Major equipment items are maintained according to schedule.
3. Inspections (e.g., fire, elevator, health) are kept current.
4. Pool readings are conducted and logged correctly.
5. Capital expenditure file is maintained correctly.

Exhibit 7

MAVERICK LODGING

Comprehensive Scorecard Results

Section 1: Balanced Scorecard Results

	1997	**1998**	**1999**

Top-Line Yield

Maverick Lodging yield vs. brand average yield = percentage of brand average yield; growth in Maverick Lodging yield			
Maverick Courtyard vs. Average Courtyard	114.3% vs. 112.2% = 101.87%	116.7% vs. 113.3% = 103.00%; 2.10% growth	121.1% vs. 116.5% = 103.95%; 3.77% growth
Maverick Fairfield Inn vs. Average Fairfield Inn	110.1% vs. 111.3% = 98.92%	112.6% vs. 111.9% = 100.63%; 2.27% growth	115.1% vs. 111.0% = 103.69%; 2.22% growth
Maverick Residence Inn vs. Average Residence Inn	119.3% vs. 123.9% = 96.29%	122.7% vs. 123.5% = 99.35%; 2.85% growth	127.0% vs. 124.3% = 102.17%; 3.50% growth

Flowthrough Flexible Budget

Actual house profit as a percentage of budget house profit; actual controllable profit as a percentage of flexible-budget controllable profit			
Maverick Courtyard	N/C (not calculated)	N/C	107.1%; 100.9%
Maverick Fairfield Inn	N/C	N/C	88.5%; 101.1%
Maverick Residence Inn	N/C	N/C	100.7%; 101.1%

Guest-Satisfaction Score

Maverick Lodging overall guest score vs. brand average guest score; change in Maverick Lodging guest score			
Maverick Courtyard vs. Average Courtyard	82.1 vs. 83.0 (bottom 50%)	85.9 vs. 83.0 (top 30%) 4.63% increase	85.1 vs. 82.6 (top 40%) -0.93% decrease
Maverick Fairfield Inn vs. Average Fairfield Inn	94.0 vs. 91.5 (top 30%)	89.2 vs. 86.2 (top 40%) -5.11% decrease	86.3 vs. 85.3 (top 50%) -3.25% decrease
Maverick Residence Inn vs. Average Residence Inn	90.2 vs. 84.6 (top 20%)	89.7 vs. 83.5 (top 20%) -0.55% decrease	87.0 vs. 82.8 (top 30%) -3.01% decrease

Comprehensive Audit Performance

Internal-process-audit score	N/C	88.3	95.3

Maverick Lodging's Turnover

Associate turnover; change in turnover	85.4%	69.9%; 18.15% reduction	61.3%; 12.3% reduction

Exhibit 7 (continued)

MAVERICK LODGING

Section 2: Other Results

	1997	1998	1999

Revenue Performance

RevPAR:			
Consolidated RevPAR	$54.05	$58.88	$62.74
Growth in RevPAR	Not available	8.94% growth	6.56% growth
Yield:			
Consolidated yield index	115.5%	118.8%	120.4%
Growth in yield	Not available	2.86% growth	1.35% growth

Profitability Performance

House-profit percentage[1] compared with Marriott averages			
Maverick Courtyard vs. Average Courtyard	48.3% vs. 53.6%	52.2% vs. 54.3%	54.1% vs. 54.0%
Maverick Fairfield Inn vs. Average Fairfield Inn	54.9% vs. 51.9%	54.9% vs. 48.9%	54.6% vs. 45.8%
Maverick Residence Inn vs. Average Residence Inn	53.8% vs. 53.5%	57.0% vs. 54.3%	56.8% vs. 53.6%

Maverick Lodging's Turnover

Manager turnover; change in turnover	32.6%	20.9%; 35.89% reduction	24.3%; 16.27% increase

Note: The balanced scorecard was implemented during 1998, but managers were not evaluated on the balanced scorecard results until 1999. Maverick Lodging tracked the majority of these performance measures for 1997 and 1998 for comparative purposes.

---

[1]House-profit percentage is house profit/total revenue.

LYNCHBURG FOUNDRY: THE DUCTILE DILEMMA

Martin Peterson, the materials manager for Lynchburg Foundry, was faced with the controversial decision of whether it was economically desirable to ship ductile iron return[1] from the castings plants at Lynchburg and Archer Creek to the pipe-making plant in Radford, Virginia. If so, he needed to figure out the best way to implement his decision, including the establishment of an appropriate transfer price or prices.

Founded in 1896 as the Lynchburg Plow Company, manufacturing gray iron plows and plow replacement parts, it represented one of the oldest manufacturing companies in the Commonwealth of Virginia. The company grew quickly and soon began to diversify. With the addition of cast iron pipe production in the early 1900s, the company changed its name to the Lynchburg Foundry Company. In 1948, with the discovery of ductile iron, a new form of cast iron with properties similar to steel, the company became a major producer of gray and ductile iron precision castings and pipe. The precision castings were produced for cars, trucks, construction equipment, and farm equipment. The pipe was produced for municipal water systems and home construction. The company had over 4,000 employees at its three manufacturing facilities in Virginia.

LYNCHBURG AND ARCHER CREEK CASTINGS PLANTS

The Casting Process

A casting was made by pouring molten metal into a sand mold of the desired shape. Once the metal cooled and solidified, the sand mold was shaken and knocked away from the metal, leaving a casting. There were four steps in making a casting: melting and alloying the metal, making molds and cores, pouring iron into the molds, and finishing or cleaning the casting.

Melting and Alloying

Most of the raw materials were received by rail cars in the iron yard behind the plants. These materials included coke for melting fuel, limestone to promote coagulation of slag or impurities, pig iron for carbon and silicon, and steel scrap for the iron content. A mixture of these raw materials and ductile iron return, a process by-product, was prepared in the required proportions, making a "charge" to be melted. **Exhibits 1 and 2** illustrate typical charges for the Lynchburg and Archer Creek plants.

---

[1]*Ductile iron return* was a by-product of the iron castings process due to the low yield (approximately 50 percent to 60 percent) of good finished castings that resulted when molten iron was poured into a sand mold. Its chemical composition was the same as the finished castings, and thus it could be "returned" to the melting facility and remelted to produce more good castings.

The molten iron was received in refractory lined ladles at approximately 2800°F. The slag, or impurities, was removed, and various alloys were added to produce the different types of iron. Samples of the iron for laboratory analysis were taken, and other quality control checks were made. The iron was then ready to be poured into the sand molds.

Cores and Mold-Making

The mold was formed by packing a moist mixture of sand and certain hardening ingredients around the desired pattern. The pattern was then drawn away, leaving the two mold halves that formed the casting cavity.

The final step in mold-making was mold assembly. Cores were placed into recesses in the mold, and the halves of the mold were joined and clamped, making a complete casting cavity ready to receive the molten iron.

Pouring the Iron

The metal entered the top of the mold through a pouring basis. This basin was only part of a carefully designed network of internal channels called the gating system, which was a system of openings, or gates, that were shaped and located to control the rate and direction of molten metal as it entered the casting cavity.

As the metal cooled and changed from a liquid to a solid, there was an accompanying decrease in volume that would cause voids and make the casting defective. This problem was avoided through the use of a molten metal reservoir or "riser" in the gating system that supplied additional metal to the casting as contraction occurred. **Figure 1** illustrates a typical cross-section of a mold with a casting activity and grating system. Both the gating system and riser were filled and remained full of metal, thus making a good casting. The amount of metal required to fill the system exceeded the amount of metal in the casting. After solidification of the casting, the gating system became excess material that, along with some scrap castings, was the source for the "ductile iron return." The ductile iron return was available for remelting in the cupola.

Finishing or Cleaning

After the iron in the mold solidified, the mold was shaken off and the sand reclaimed. The gating system, which also solidified while attached to the casting, was removed and returned to the iron yard area. The remaining sand was blasted off the casting, and the rough edges were ground, yielding a smooth clean casting. **Figure 2** contains a diagram of the steps in the total casting process.

THE RADFORD PIPE PLANT

The Pipe-Making Process

Pipe was produced in a somewhat different manner than iron castings. The iron melting and alloying was done in the same manner as castings. However, the raw materials charge was not the same for pipe-making. A typical pipe charge is shown in

Exhibit 3. Pipe charges were different from castings charges for two basic reasons. The chemical composition of ductile iron pipe was different from ductile iron castings, and the pipe-making process had a higher yield (over 80 percent vs. 50 percent to 60 percent) than the castings process, thus leaving less ductile iron return available for remelting.

Figure 1
Lynchburg Foundry: The Ductile Dilemma
Cross-Section of a Sand Mold

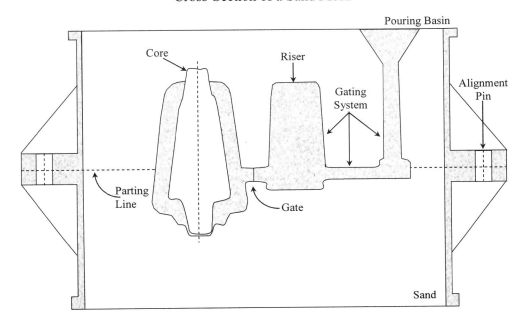

Figure 2
Lynchburg Foundry: The Ductile Dilemma
Production Flow Diagram

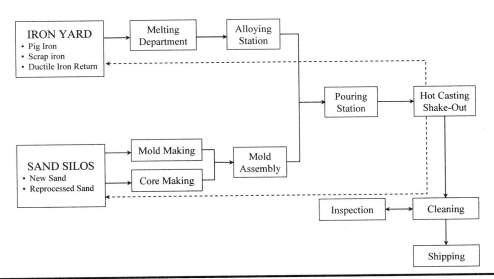

Permanent Mold Pipe-Making

A permanent mold for pipe-making was made of special high alloy steel that allowed for high temperature performance and long life. The mold was a long cylindrical tube with its interior surface the desired shape and dimensions of the exterior of the desired ductile iron pipe size. The mold was completely enclosed in a large mold spinning machine with a water jacket that covered the length of the mold. The entire machine sat on a slightly inclined track that allowed the molten metal to flow down the length of the mold. With the mold spinning rapidly, a measured amount of molten iron was injected at one end of the mold. The spinning caused centrifugal force on the molten iron to form the walls of the pipe with a uniform thickness. The water jacket surrounding the mold quickly absorbed the heat from the molten iron through the mold wall and solidified the pipe.

The ductile iron return from the pipe-making process came from scrap pipe, excess metal in the permanent mold injection system, and spillage and excess during ladle transfers. This process typically yielded 80 percent to 90 percent good pipe, and the rest became ductile iron return.

USES OF DUCTILE IRON RETURN

As part of the deliberations regarding whether or not to transfer ductile iron return from the Lynchburg and Archer Creek castings plants to the Radford pipe-making plant, Mr. Peterson reviewed how the ductile iron return was typically used. Because the Lynchburg and Archer Creek plants' yield was in the 50 percent to 60 percent range, there was 40 percent to 50 percent return available to use in subsequent charges. If it were available, these plants could have used a charge containing as much as 60 percent ductile iron return, but because not enough ductile iron return was produced internally, and it was seldom available on the metals market, additional amounts of pig iron and steel scrap had to be purchased. As ductile iron return was removed from the castings charge, it had to be replaced by a combination of steel scrap and pig iron.[2] The disadvantages of adding pig iron and steel scrap were that pig iron was the most expensive raw material, and steel scrap required more heat to melt. Based on extensive testing of different castings charges, the melting supervisors at the Lynchburg and Archer Creek castings plants had determined that 40 percent ductile iron return was the minimum amount that castings charges should have to meet the demand for molten iron. Thus, the plant managers attempted to work within this constraint when considering any materials transfers.

Historically, company policy had been for each plant to consume its own ductile iron return, except for some very large scrap castings produced at the Lynchburg plant. These castings were shipped to the Radford plant because the melting facilities at Radford could accommodate these larger pieces of ductile iron return. Otherwise, the large scrap castings would require a very costly cutting process to enable them to be used

---

[2] The ratio of steel scrap to pig iron in a castings charge had to remain the same, regardless of the percentage of ductile iron return in the charge.

at the Lynchburg plant.[3]   This type of ductile casting scrap amounted to approximately 3,500 tons per year and allowed the Radford plant enough material for about 200 pounds, or 4 percent, of each 5,000 pound charge. This 4 percent was added to the 12 percent (600 pounds per charge) of ductile iron return generated by the pipe-making process. The result was 16 percent ductile iron return available per pipe-making charge as compared to 40 percent to 50 percent ductile iron return available per castings charge. Because of the high required melt rate in pipe-making, the charges could not contain more than the present 38 percent of steel scrap. The remaining 62 percent must be either pig iron or ductile iron return. According to the metallurgist at the pipe-making plant, each additional pound of ductile iron return from the castings plants could be substituted for pig iron on a one for one basis.

In order to reach a decision, Mr. Peterson gathered data on the cost of producing ductile iron return.   As shown in **Exhibit 4**, he arrived at $195 per ton as the cost of ductile iron return. In calculating the cost of ductile iron return, Mr. Peterson included only the weighted average cost of the original raw materials. This cost was somewhat less than the true cost of making the ductile iron return because it did not include freight costs for material, the fuel cost, the variable cost of labor and other supplies, the cost of facilities and equipment, or the cost of supervisory personnel.

Mr. Peterson consulted with the Vice-President of Production and the Vice-President of Sales to determine the maximum amount of ductile iron return that would be available for shipment to the Radford plant. This amount was based on historic castings and pipe production. The results of their calculations are shown in **Exhibit 5**. Mr. Peterson had explicitly assumed, as he had been told, that the Lynchburg and Archer Creek plants could cut their consumption of ductile iron return to 40 percent of the charge mix. Freight costs between the two castings plants and the Radford plant were assumed to remain at $25 per ton. There was no cost charged for loading and unloading the material from the rail cars because the workers and equipment were already available at each plant.

THE RECOMMENDATION

There seemed to be at least three possible methods for valuing the ductile iron return. One method would treat it as a free by-product with no cost except for freight. Another method would use the market price of $175 a ton. A third method would use estimated production cost, either the approach used by Mr. Peterson or some variation thereof.

In the absence of a clear directive regarding the use of the excess ductile iron return and its transfer price, Mr. Peterson was concerned about the plant managers' motivations, as well as the effect on individual plant performances. The individual plants were cost centers, and the plant managers were evaluated on their ability to meet good ton shipment requirements efficiently and at minimum cost. If a transfer program for

---

[3]Although no attempt had ever been made to sell these large pieces of ductile iron return, buyers could be found through the metals market. The net price per ton was estimated to be in the range of $175. Freight costs of $25 per ton were charged to the Radford plant, and this represented the only cost the Radford plant incurred for the large scrap castings.

ductile iron return were adopted, a transfer pricing system would need to credit the Lynchburg and Archer Creek plants with the internal transfer price of the ductile iron return transferred to Radford. The Radford plant would then be charged the same amount, or some other amount, in addition to the actual freight costs.

Mr. Peterson was also aware of the long-term trends in the product markets and the age of the individual facilities. The castings market was growing at a good rate, and many parts that were formerly made with steel were being switched to ductile iron castings. Lynchburg Foundry was a leader in ductile iron castings and was one of the most respected independent foundries in the United States.

The pipe market was not as strong as the market for ductile castings, as it was more closely linked to the general economy, particularly housing construction. There was also strong competition from numerous substitute materials for pipe, such as plastic. Lynchburg Foundry was among the smaller pipe producers, and most of its equipment was old. Growth, or even continuation of present operations, would eventually require significant amounts of capital. Mr. Peterson was concerned about how the transfer of ductile iron return to Radford would affect the profitability of that operation, as changes in profitability might be significant enough to affect future investment decisions. Mr. Peterson was scheduled to make a comprehensive presentation, including plans for implementation, to the company's chief operating officer within a week.

Exhibit 1

LYNCHBURG FOUNDRY: THE DUCTILE DILEMMA

Typical Raw Materials Charge and
Ductile Iron Casting Cost

Lynchburg Plant (2000 lb. charge)

Material	Percent of Charge	Weight per Charge(lbs.)	Material Cost per Ton	Cost per Charge
Ductile Iron Return	45	900	$195	$ 87.75
Pig Iron	21	420	300	63.00
Steel Scrap:				
Shredded	17	340	120	20.40
Structural	17	340	140	23.80
	100	2,000		$194.95

Calculation of good casting cost:

Average casting yield = 55 percent
Good castings per charge = 1,100 pounds
Ductile iron return generated = 900 pounds

Charge cost	$194.95
less credit for ductile iron return (900 pounds @ $195/ton)	87.75
Cost of 1,100 pounds good castings	$ 107.20

Convert to castings cost per ton:

$$\frac{2,000 \, pounds}{1,100 \, pounds} \quad X \quad \$107.20 = \$194.91/ton$$

Exhibit 2

LYNCHBURG FOUNDRY: THE DUCTILE DILEMMA

Typical Raw Materials Charge and
Ductile Iron Casting Cost

Archer Creek Plant (4000 lb. charge)

Material	Percent of Charge	Weight per Charge(lbs.)	Material Cost per Ton	Cost per Charge
Ductile Iron Return	46	1840	$195	$ 179.40
Pig Iron	19	760	300	114.00
Steel Scrap:				
Shredded	19	760	120	45.60
Structural	16	640	140	44.80
	100	4,000		$383.80

Calculation of good casting cost:

Average casting yield = 54 percent
Good castings per charge = 2,160 pounds
Ductile iron return generated = 1,840 pounds

Charge cost	$ 383.80
less credit for ductile iron return (1,840 pounds @ $195/ton)	179.40
Cost of 2,160 pounds good castings	$ 204.40

Convert to castings cost per ton:

$$\frac{2,000 \text{ pounds}}{2,160 \text{ pounds}} \quad X \quad \$204.40 = \$189.25/\text{ton}$$

Exhibit 3

LYNCHBURG FOUNDRY: THE DUCTILE DILEMMA

Typical Raw Materials Charge and
Ductile Iron Casting Cost

Radford Plant (5,000 lb. charge)

Material	Percent of Charge	Weight per Charge(lbs.)	Material Cost per Ton	Cost per Charge
Ductile Iron Return:				
Scrap Pipe	12	600	$ 195	$ 58.50
Scrap Castings	4	200	195[1]	19.50
Pig Iron	46	2300	300	345.00
Steel Scrap:				
Shredded	18	900	120	54.00
Structural	20	1,000	140	70.00
	100	5,000		$547.00

Calculation of good pipe cost:

Average pipe yield = 88 percent
Good pipe per charge = 4,400 pounds
Ductile iron return (pipe) generated = 600 pounds

Charge cost	$547.00
less credit for ductile iron return (600 pounds @ $195/ton)	58.50
Cost of 4,400 pounds good castings	$ 488.50

Convert to castings cost per ton:

$$\frac{2,000 \text{ pounds}}{4,400 \text{ pounds}} \quad X \quad \$488.50 = \$219.82/\text{ton}$$

---

[1]This $195 transfer cost does not include the $25 per ton freight charge.

Exhibit 4

LYNCHBURG FOUNDRY: THE DUCTILE DILEMMA

Materials Manager's Valuation of Ductile Iron Return

Calculation of the cost of the raw material without ductile iron return (based on Lynchburg plant charge shown in **Exhibit 1**).

Material	Weight per Charge (lbs.)	Material Cost per Ton	Cost per Charge
Pig Iron	420	$ 300	$ 63.00
Steel Scrap:			
Shredded	340	120	20.40
Structural	340	140	23.80
	1,100		$107.20

If 1,100 pounds cost $107.20, then 2,000 pounds cost:

$$\frac{2,000}{1,100} \quad X \quad \$107.20 = \$194.91/ton$$

Use $195/ton to recognize variations in charge mix and variations in raw materials prices.

Exhibit 5

LYNCHBURG FOUNDRY: THE DUCTILE DILEMMA

Projection of Maximum Available Ductile
Iron Return (tons)

Plant	Estimated Pouring Weight	Number of Charges	Yield	Good Castings	Ductile Iron Return
Lynchburg	84,000	84,000	55 %	46,200	37,800
Archer Creek	30,000	15,000	54 %	16,200	13,800
Radford	87,500	35,000	88 %	77,000	10,500
Total Available					62,100 tons

Lynchburg and Archer Creek ductile iron return requirements at 40 percent per charge:

Plant	Tons Available	Required for 40 percent of charge	Excess available for Radford Plant
Lynchburg	37,800	33,600	4,200[1]
Archer Creek	13,800	12,000	1,800
Total			6,000 tons

Affect on individual Radford pipe charge:

Number of charges required per year = 35,000 charges
Pounds of Ductile Iron Return available per pipe charge:

From Lynchburg
4,200 tons ÷ 35,000 charges = .120 ton (240 lbs/charge)

From Archer Creek
1,800 tons ÷ 35,000 charges = .051 ton (103 lbs/charge)

Total = 343 lbs/charge

---

[1]This includes the 3,500 tons of large scrap castings already being shipped to the Radford plant.

XYBERSPACE CONSULTING, INC.

Laura Barnes finished her chicken fajita and looked out upon Town Lake, shimmering under the fierce Texas sun. She had recently relocated to Austin from Silicon Valley to head up the Accounting Department for Xyberspace, a rapidly growing technology-consulting firm. Only two weeks on the job, she was being asked to resolve a controversy within the company. The controversy centered on the allocation of the costs associated with the company's Training and Educational Service Group to each of the company's profit centers that used those services. Opinions on the issue were heated, and she had come to the lakeshore with her notes to calmly sort out the facts and consider the relevant issues. Her manager and Xyberspace's CFO, Martin Henry, had made it clear he expected a quick resolution of the controversy, which he felt was hurting company morale and had large strategic implications for Xyberspace.

BACKGROUND

Xyberspace was a successful Internet consulting firm located in Austin, Texas. The company's Consulting Group provided e-strategy solutions to corporate and non-profit clients, while the Customer Care Group performed IT implementation and provided telephone, e-mail, and on-site client support. As Austin became home to an increasing number of Internet start-ups as well as established high tech firms, Xyberspace had grown rapidly. In May of 2000, the company employed 800 people, 500 of who were consultants and 250 of who were Customer Care Technicians. The remaining 50 were either corporate officers or performed corporate functions such as accounting, marketing, training, and public relations. The company owned its own building in downtown Austin.

Training was an integral part of the company's strategy, and Xyberspace was wholeheartedly committed to training and continuing education. According to Richard Malinovich, the company's founder and CEO, "Our goal is to have absolutely the best-educated consultants in the marketplace. We think this will set us apart from many firms, who no doubt have bright people, but who don't invest anywhere near what we do in education. And I am absolutely convinced that training our consultants in-house is critical to achieving this goal."

All employees of the Consulting and Customer Care Groups were required to receive one full week of computer training twice a year on Internet-related languages such as html, xml, perl, and cgi scripting, and Java as well as tutorials on software packages from Oracle, Vignette, Siebel, and other firm partners. The actual content of the classes depended on the newest software developments as well as the Consulting and Customer Care Groups' strategic focus areas. For example, the health care practice of the Consulting Group had recently received customized training in the latest hospital automation software. The Training and Educational Services Group spent much effort and resources to design courses for its consultants built around Xyberspace's client needs.

Classes generally lasted one week and could cover a number of different topics. The normal class size was ten people, and three classes were typically going on at any one time. The Training and Educational Services Group had found that trainees generally preferred smaller class sizes, which tended to work better because courses were often designed around specific needs the trainees had in serving their clients.

Company policy stated that all employees received two weeks of training, but experience had shown that, on average, 75 percent of employees actually were able to complete the training, and this was the figure used in budgeting for the Training and Educational Services Group. Employee turnover played a part in determining the participation rate, as did the fact that some employees on long-term assignments simply could not find the time to undergo training. Others were able to complete one week of training, but not two.

Regina Rosenthal, director of the Xyberspace's Training and Educational Services Group, summed up her department's mission:

> We are here to make the consultants better at their jobs and to do so in an efficient manner. We hire the best trainers, all people with extensive software experience, to tailor training programs and materials to the particular needs of the company. By developing our own programs, we can make sure the consultants are getting exactly what they need in a focused and concise fashion.

THE 1999 TRAINING AND EDUCATIONAL
SERVICES GROUP BUDGET

The total Training and Educational Services Group budget for 1999 was $497,700 (see **Exhibit 1**). The budget was based on the company's estimate that the Training and Educational Services Group would conduct training sessions for 450 employees during the course of the year. It was estimated that 300 consultants (75 percent of the projected annual average employment total of 400) and 150 Customer Care employees (75 percent of the projected annual average employment total of 200) would receive two weeks of training each during the year, for a total of 900 training sessions. During the balance of the year, trainers prepared course materials and devoted time to learning new software, languages, and systems. The budget consisted of the following items:

- Salary ($250,000): One Group manager made $75,000/year, an office assistant made $25,000, and three full-time trainers made $47,000, $48,000, and $55,000, respectively. The office assistant scheduled the trainings for the company's employees and handled administrative functions for the group. The Group manager oversaw the other four employees, set training priorities and teaching schedules, and acted as a trainer herself as needed.

- Benefits ($50,000): Employee benefits such as health insurance, etc. were 20 percent of salary.

- Software Licenses ($20,000): Generally, half of the software licenses were negotiated in advance. However, since Xyberspace liked to make sure that its employees stayed up to date on the latest releases, an additional $10,000 was budgeted to cover additional software that may need to be purchased during the year. The software licenses covered Training and Educational Services Group computers only.

- Depreciation ($28,000): 35 computers were purchased at $4,000 each and were depreciated on a straight-line basis for five years.

- Maintenance Contract ($2,000): This annual fee paid to the computer vendor covered all of the computer equipment and provided for repair or replacement of defective hardware within 24 hours.

- Course Development ($12,500): Since the Training and Educational Services Group developed many of its own training materials specifically for company use, trainers worked with outside editors, graphic artists, and print shops to develop course materials.

- Professional Development ($10,000): This included membership in professional associations and fees to attend conferences and training sessions to facilitate their staying current with software developments and enhancements and to learn new software programs and languages as needed.

- Travel ($8,800): This included travel expenses for travel to attend conferences and/or workshops.

- Phone/Fax ($2,600)

- Office Supplies ($800)

- Training Supplies ($67,500): It cost the Training and Educational Services Group $75 per trainee to print and distribute new manuals and workbooks.

- Lunch ($45,000): Catered lunches were $10 per person or $50 per trainee, for each 5-day training session. Since the training was intensive and many participants preferred to work through lunch, catered meals were much appreciated. In addition, past experience had shown that allowing class participants to go off-site for lunch often resulted in participants being late for afternoon sessions.

- Other ($500): This amount covered miscellaneous expenses not covered elsewhere.

Based on the Training and Educational Services Group's budget of $497,700 and expectations about training usage of 900 sessions, the expected allocation rate per training session was $553 (**Exhibit 1**).

ALLOCATING COSTS ASSOCIATED WITH TRAINING
AND EDUCATIONAL SERVICES GROUP

While the Training and Educational Services Group prepared a budget at the beginning of each year, actual costs were allocated at the end of the year based on the Training Group's actual expenses and the user departments' actual usage of training services. **Exhibit 2** reports that actual expenses for the Training Group for 1999 totaled $548,625. In addition, the Consulting Group received 600 training sessions, and the Customer Care Group received 225 training sessions during 1999. As a result, the actual allocation rate charged to the user departments was $665 per training session.

THE CONTROVERSY

Laura Barnes recalled the meeting she and Martin Henry had yesterday with Regina Rosenthal, David Anderson, director of Xyberspace's Consulting Group, and Rajit Gupta, director of Xyberspace's Customer Care Group. Neither Barnes nor Henry had anticipated the objections raised by David Anderson to the costs of Training and Educational Services that had been allocated to his Group for 1999:

> First of all, I was charged $665 per training session last year when I had budgeted $553 per session…. I don't get it. I used 600 training sessions, just like I had planned to. And not only that, I can get outside training for $500 per session, which is even less than we budgeted to start with. I was willing to swallow the additional cost because I think the trainers do a good job. And I like the extent to which they can customize the training to the needs of my consultants. However, it does hurt to pay above market rates, especially when you're running a profit center like I am. I can't keep training my people here when I can go somewhere else for only $500 per session.

Rosenthal, however, didn't think the cost was too high:

> I have a lot of fixed costs that I work hard to control, but they are going to occur whether we train 50 people or 500 people. Granted, our costs may be higher at this point than some outside companies, but with the growth in our company I think the fixed portion of our costs will be allocated across more training sessions, and the rate should go down. And besides, there are huge benefits to training inside.

Barnes thought that Rosenthal was onto something with her distinction between fixed and variable costs. In her experience, many companies separated these costs, allocating fixed costs from support to user departments as a lump sum and charging the user groups based on the variable costs of each incremental service. She was determined to take a close look at this particular situation and recommend a cost allocation system that would be fair to all sides.

While Rosenthal said she didn't think that her department would again exceed its budget by 10 percent, she did believe that the increases in last year's spending had been necessary to maintain the quality and quantity of training demanded by her clients.

> It's true we did have to hire a new assistant last year and that cost us more than we expected.... In addition, we had to increase the salaries of our trainers more than expected to remain competitive. With software licenses, we try to be conservative in our budgeting but sometimes we are simply told by the Consulting and Customer Care Groups, "You need to buy this software and train our people in it." It is very much a function of what is hot at the moment and we have no control over that.

> Professional development and travel expenses were higher last year, but again that was because of new software products that we had to get up to speed on. In order to deliver the best possible training, we need to get trained ourselves and stay up to date on the newest releases.

> Regarding the telephone expenses and the increased price of the catered lunches, these are things we will try to control better this year. Our food vendor foisted a price increase on us during the middle of last year, and we didn't have time to shop around for a new vendor because we were too busy.

While Rosenthal admitted that some expenses were controllable, she believed the groups should be allocated actual training costs. "If the group managers are going to demand we do certain things, then they need to bear those costs," she reasoned. "Of course I can stick strictly to the budget, but then my clients won't get the services they want and will be disappointed."

Anderson disagreed, saying that allocating actual training costs gave the Training and Educational Services Group no incentive to control costs.

> Part of the reason their costs are so high is that they can simply pass them off to other groups.... I'm not saying they are not telling the truth when they say that they need to spend money to do a good job, but if they have to bear the brunt of budget variances, they may think twice before going to another conference or paying extra for meals.

Barnes could see both points of view. Anderson didn't want to put himself at the mercy of the Training Group's spending, especially since he was compensated based on the profitability of his group. Rosenthal also didn't want to be hamstrung by a provisional budget, especially if her spending depended on the sometimes rapidly changing needs of the user groups. Using budgeted rates would force the Training Group to stick to its budget, but would limit its flexibility to respond to client demands.

Anderson continued:

Our having to cover the Training Group's cost overruns is bad enough.... But we also get penalized if the Customer Care Group doesn't use as much training as they say they're going to. Last year, we used 600 training sessions, just like we had originally budgeted. The Customer Care Group, though, only used 225 sessions, so we ended up paying quite a bit more per session. It isn't fair that we have to cover more of Training's costs just because the Customer Care Group used less of their services this year. Again, this is something over which I have no control. I used exactly the amount of services that I said I would, and I'm being penalized for that. Maybe next year I'll just wildly overestimate the amount of training we'll need, so that I can use less and make the Customer Care Group pay the difference.

The Customer Care Group's Manager, Rajit Gupta, argued that the Consulting Group should bear a higher portion of the Training Group's costs. "Granted, we had trouble sending people to training last year," he admitted. "But we should not be charged for services we didn't use."

On this point, Rosenthal made no argument. In previous years, both groups had come very close to their budgeted usage amounts, so it hadn't been an issue. The Customer Care Group, however, had been going through significant turmoil in 1999 due to a high amount of employee turnover and had not managed to send a sufficient number of employees to training.

QUESTIONS

Prior to leaving for the lakeshore for the weekend, Barnes had collected data on the 1999 actual costs incurred by the Training and Educational Services Group and summarized several statistics regarding actual training sessions attended by the Consulting and Customer Care Groups (see **Exhibit 2**). She was sure she would find this information helpful as she reflected on the issues.

It seemed to Barnes that there were key allocation questions involved in the controversy at Xyberspace. First of all, did the Training and Educational Services Group's use of a single rate cause its services to look too expensive to the Consulting and Customer Care Groups? Would a dual rate, which separated fixed from variable costs, better capture the true costs of the training? Second, should budgeted or actual rates be used to allocate training costs to the user groups? Finally, should the user groups be allocated training costs based on their budgeted or actual usage of services? Just how should the costs of the Training and Educational Services Group be allocated?

Exhibit 1

XYBERSPACE CONSULTING, INC.

1999 Training and Educational Services Group Budget

Salaries:

Rosenthal – Manager	$ 75,000
Jones – Trainer	47,000
Chen – Trainer	48,000
Ivanov – Trainer	55,000
Hickery – Assistant	25,000
Total Salaries	$ 250,000
Benefits	50,000
Software Licenses	20,000
Depreciation	28,000
Maintenance Contract	2,000
Course Development	12,500
Professional development	10,000
Travel	8,800
Phone/Fax	2,600
Office Supplies	800
Training Supplies	67,500
Trainee Lunches	45,000
Other	500
Total	$ 497,700

Number of Training Sessions:

Consulting Group	600
Customer Care Group	300
Total	900

Allocation rate per training session	$553

Budgeted allocation of Training Group costs to:

Consulting Group	$ 331,800
Customer Care Group	$ 165,900

Exhibit 2

XYBERSPACE CONSULTING, INC.

1999 Training and Educational Services Group Actual Expenses

Salaries:

Rosenthal – Manager	$ 75,000
Jones – Trainer	50,000
Chen – Trainer	51,000
Ivanov – Trainer	57,000
Hauser – Assistant	32,000
Total Salaries	$ 265,000

Benefits	53,000
Software Licenses	27,500
Depreciation	28,000
Maintenance Contract	2,000
Course Development	12,500
Professional development	22,500
Travel	12,000
Phone/Fax	3,800
Office Supplies	800
Training Supplies	64,775
Trainee Lunches	56,250
Other	500
Total	$ 548,625

Number of Training Sessions:

Consulting Group	600
Customer Care Group	225
Total	825

Allocation rate per training session	$665

Actual allocation of Training Group costs to:

Consulting Group	$ 399,000
Customer Care Group	$ 149,625

BAY INDUSTRIES

As he listened in January 2002 to a presentation by Ben Robinson, one of his three division managers, Jim Quick, president of Bay Industries, was beginning to draw some conclusions. Within a week, he would have to guide a series of decisions on divisional and corporate strategy and determine each division manager's bonus. About half the bonus was fairly automatically computed from profits and performance to budget, but the other half would depend on his evaluation. He was glad of the opportunity to apply his own judgment, for he had never quite trusted the numbers to give a reliable reading on a manager's performance. On the other hand, he knew that his unsupported judgments could be perceived as being arbitrary.

CONTROL DEVICES DIVISION

Robinson had managed the Control Devices Division for three years and had done reasonably well, although profit in 2001 was down a bit from the previous year. At the moment, he was talking about some guy in the South Pacific named Ona, a mystic Robinson called him, who he said had made life difficult for his division. Robinson said Ona had caused Papua New Guinea's Bougainville copper mine, one of the world's largest mines, to shut down in mid-2001, thereby pushing up the price of copper just when he needed to buy. Quick remembered an article about it in the *Wall Street Journal* a few days before, with the headline "An Audacious Rebel in Papua New Guinea Shakes Copper Market."

The Control Devices Division made machine controllers for large specialized installations, as well as numerous smaller installations, in the chemical, paper, and petroleum industries. In the middle 1970s, the division had developed and patented an electro-mechanical thrust transmission device that had allowed the division to achieve a large market share. In the last two decades, electronic components had been added to maintain the company's competitive position.

Earlier in his presentation, Robinson had noted that competition came from unexpected sources. Two months earlier, the division had lost a large customer in Denmark. His European representative said the division's price should have been low enough to get the business and hinted darkly at some under-the-table deal by the winning German company. Because about one-third of the division's sales were in Europe, Quick wondered what the implications of this event might be. Robinson had said little about it except that it had clobbered his bottom line.

COOKWARE DIVISION

Colin Wood's report on the Cookware Division had shown remarkably consistent profits and a high return on investment during his two years as manager. The division made ceramic cookware that could go in the oven and on the table. Most sales were through mass merchandisers like K Mart. The item was not branded and depended on good design and wide distribution to maintain sales volume. The business was competitive, but Wood had shown a good sense of what would sell in each distribution channel and geographical area. He previously was division director of marketing and had been promoted when his predecessor left to head a larger operation in another company.

While listening to Wood, Quick remembered that the division's Christmas sales had benefited when a major competitor was shut down for two months to work on compliance with environmental-protection standards. Quick was glad that Bay Industries had installed the necessary screening devices three years earlier.

Wood noted in his report that two of the division's three melting tanks and most of the forming machines were ten years old and in need of replacement. In his long-term capital forecast, submitted in both 2000 and 2001, he had estimated that $60 to $80 million would be needed to provide the new equipment.

ELECTRONICS DIVISION

Martha Hadley's report on the Electronics Division showed a disturbingly consistent low rate of profit. Hadley had taken over the moderately profitable division three years earlier. The division's main product had been an automatic-frequency-control (AFC) component that went into many radios and television sets. After joining the division, Hadley had designed a similar component that could be effectively used in cordless and cellular telephones. Sometimes it was built into the telephone, and sometimes it was part of the installation. The division's competition was mostly from larger companies, but Hadley had been able to break into the phone market by having a six-month lead with a superior product.

Hadley said that the only way to succeed in the business was to keep a jump ahead of everyone else. An example of that, she said, was when she had recognized earlier in the year that fast delivery was key to getting the order in about a third of the phone-component business. Not only was speed important in some orders, but precise delivery time was required by almost all customers to keep their inventory down; many customers used just-in-time manufacturing systems. Hadley's competition had regional warehouses, which allowed them to deliver overnight to most places. So she had arranged with an express-service firm to deliver fast and reliably, usually by air. Sometimes, when delivery was a week or more away, air freight was not used, but the carrier=s delivery could still be timed to within three hours. Hadley believed the key was reliability and that the higher direct cost per shipment would be less than the cost of warehousing. Her volume was rising, but her costs had not gone up as much.

Hadley estimated that her share of the radio AFC market was about 10 percent, and that her share of the newer telephone-frequency-control market was nearly 25 percent and holding steady as the market continued to grow. She had invested in new equipment in 2001 to be able to service the growing phone market and capture economies of scale.

BONUS

Jim Quick reviewed the financial results of each division (see **Exhibits 1, 2, and 3**) to see how the division managers' bonuses would come out. The 2001 bonus pool for these three managers amounted to $100,000, which was based on overall corporate profit.

The bonus plan currently in force said that half of the pool would be distributed on the basis of points and half on the basis of the president's judgment.

Points were awarded in two ways, both based on the percentage return on capital employed (ROCE). The first way gave one point for each percentage point that actual ROCE was above planned ROCE minus 5 percent. This method allowed a manager to receive a bonus even if the division did not quite achieve the planned results. (The plan figure was the result of a budgeting process that started in the divisions and ended with a discussion or negotiation between Quick and each division manager.) The second way in which points were awarded gave one point for each 1 percent that actual ROCE was above the average of the previous two years. Following those rules Quick computed these bonuses:

	First Method	Second Method	Total Points	Bonus
Ben Robinson, Control Devices	1	0	1	$ 2,040
Colin Wood, Cookware	12	7	19	38,760
Martha Hadley, Electronics	2	2.5	4.5	9,180
				$49,980

As he pondered these results, Quick wondered whether they represented proper rewards for the results achieved. He also wondered whether the form of this part of the bonus system was as good as it could be.

Because Quick was to use his own judgment in the second part of the bonus system, if he did not like the way the first $50,000 was divided, he could remedy the situation -- at least partially -- dividing up the remaining $50,000.

INVESTMENT PROPOSALS

Each division had submitted a proposal for capital expenditures in 2002 and after, brief summaries of which follow.

Control Devices Division

In submitting his proposal, Robinson noted that he had unused capacity. Normally, using that capacity would not require new investment, but in this case, he said he had an opportunity to pursue a special contract, which would be worth about $10 million in sales in 2002, if he could purchase two pieces of automatic equipment for a total $2 million. Although the machines would require some unique programming, he was intrigued because one of the machines used a control device produced by the division. They were, of course, accustomed to programming their own devices, but they had not worked with this application and he hoped to learn from it.

Noting that the investment would produce a high rate of return, Robinson submitted the following pro forma for the contract:

Revenue		$10,000,000
Costs:	Material	5,200,000
	Labor	1,600,000
	Overhead	1,400,000 (includes only variable overhead)
	Distribution	200,000
Total cost		8,400,000
Profit		$ 1,600,000

Cookware Division

Wood submitted a proposal for replacement of the two aging melting tanks and the forming equipment. The tanks had been installed ten years before at a cost of about $14 million; replacement would cost about $30 million. The repair cycle for the tanks had started at 18 months but had shortened to 10 months. He noted that, although the technology had not changed much, the new tanks would be more flexible and somewhat more efficient in the use of energy. He also noted some concern about the safety of the aging tanks.

The forming machines were also about 10-years old and were requiring increasing amounts of maintenance. New forming machines would cost about $30-$40 million. Again, the technology had not altered, but the new machines could be changed over faster, accommodated a greater variety of molds, and included a quick replacement system for molds that wore out with regularity. Quality would be more consistent with the new machines, and overall capacity would increase about 20 percent, half from the expected decline in rejects.

Wood advised replacing the tanks within a year and the forming machines within two years. If the two replacements were done together, however, about $10 million could be saved.

Electronics Division

Hadley's investment proposal was for additional capacity to enable an increase in output of 25 percent. She expected to continue serving the expanding telephone market, with its continual demand to refine product designs. She requested $16 million for equipment and facilities and $4 million for net working capital, for a total of $20 million. She submitted the following pro forma showing projected increases in revenue and expenses:

	($ millions)
Revenue	$40.0
Material	21.0
Labor	5.0
Other conversion	4.2
Total	30.2
Margin	9.8
New-product development	2.8
Marketing	1.4
Distribution	2.0
Administration	0.4
Corporate	
Total, other costs	6.6
Net profit	$ 3.2

Exhibit 1

BAY INDUSTRIES

Control Devices Division
($000,000)

	1999		2000		2001	
Income Statement	Plan	Actual	Plan	Actual	Plan	Actual
Sales	$154.0	$154.4	$160.0	$163.6	$166.0	$152.0
Manufacturing cost						
Material cost		80.0		84.4		77.4
Conversion cost:						
Labor		20.2		19.6		17.6
Overhead		23.2		27.6		27.6
Total cost		123.4		131.6		122.6
Margin		31.0		32.0		29.4
Other costs						
New-product development		4.2		4.6		3.8
Marketing		4.4		4.6		4.0
Packing and distribution		2.6		3.0		3.0
Administration		1.8		2.2		2.8
Corp. for divisions		1.2		1.4		1.8
Total other		14.2		15.8		15.4
Net division profit	$16.0	$16.8	$16.4	$16.2	$16.8	$14.0
Balance Sheet						
Accounts receivable		$25.8		$27.4		$25.4
Inventory		20.0		21.0		23.8
Plant and equipment cost		72.8		76.6		84.0
Accumulated depreciation		38.2		44.2		51.2
Net plant and equipment		34.6		32.4		32.8
Total assets		80.4		80.8		82.0
Current liabilities		22.4		23.0		24.4
Capital employed	$60.0	$58.0	$60.0	$57.8	$60.0	$47.6
Return on capital employed	27%	29%	27%	28%	28%	24%

Exhibit 1 (continued)

BAY INDUSTRIES

Notes on the divisional financial statements

1. The expense labeled "Corp. for divisions" represented an allocation of corporate expenses that were believed to benefit the divisions directly. Other corporate expenses, totaling about $10 million, were not allocated to the divisions. The three divisions represented substantially the whole of Bay Industries' business.
2. The division balance sheets were somewhat abbreviated. Cash was not allocated to divisions. Also, other corporate assets, amounting to about $14 million, were not represented on the divisional balance sheets.
3. Divisional current liabilities were mostly trade payables.
4. Corporate income taxes were not allocated to the divisions.

Exhibit 2

BAY INDUSTRIES

Cookware Division
($000,000)

	1999		2000		2001	
	Plan	Actual	Plan	Actual	Plan	Actual
Income Statement						
Sales	$110.0	$110.2	$116.0	$120.4	$126.0	$140.6
Manufacturing cost						
Material cost		20.0		22.6		28.8
Conversion cost:						
Labor		28.2		31.8		39.4
Overhead		36.0		37.2		37.8
Total cost		84.2		91.6		106.0
Margin		26.0		28.8		34.6
Other costs						
New-product development		1.0		1.2		1.2
Marketing		6.2		6.6		7.2
Packing and distribution		7.8		8.2		9.8
Administration		1.0		1.4		1.6
Corp. for divisions		0.8		1.0		1.6
Total other		16.8		18.4		21.4
Net division profit	$8.0	$9.2	$9.8	$10.4	$11.0	$13.2
Balance Sheet						
Accounts receivable		$13.2		$15.0		$17.0
Inventory		1.6		1.8		2.4
Plant and equipment cost		39.4		43.6		48.0
Accumulated depreciation		28.6		32.4		36.6
Net plant and equipment		10.8		11.2		11.4
Total assets		25.6		28.0		30.8
Current liabilities		2.2		2.4		3.0
Capital employed	$22.8	$23.4	$25.8	$25.6	$27.4	$27.8
Return on capital employed	35%	39%	38%	41%	40%	47%

Exhibit 3

BAY INDUSTRIES

Electronics Division
($000,000)

Income Statement	1999 Plan	1999 Actual	2000 Plan	2000 Actual	2001 Plan	2001 Actual
Sales	$86.0	$90.4	$116.0	$111.8	$140.0	$146.6
Manufacturing cost						
Material cost		52.2		61.0		75.4
Conversion cost:						
Labor		10.8		14.8		18.8
Overhead		9.0		14.4		17.2
Total cost		72.0		90.2		111.4
Margin		18.4		21.6		35.2
Other costs						
New-product development		6.0		6.4		9.8
Marketing		2.4		3.0		4.6
Packing and distribution		3.0		4.0		8.2
Administration		1.6		1.6		2.2
Corp. for divisions		0.8		1.0		1.8
Total other		13.8		16.0		26.6
Net division profit	$4.0	$4.6	$6.0	$5.6	$8.0	$8.6
Balance Sheet						
Accounts receivable		$12.6		$15.2		$19.8
Inventory		10.6		12.2		14.2
Plant and equipment cost		45.8		52.2		68.6
Accumulated depreciation		19.6		24.4		29.6
Net plant and equipment		26.2		27.8		39.0
Total assets		49.4		55.2		73.0
Current liabilities		14.4		19.4		22.4
Capital employed	$26.6	$35.0	$35.2	$35.8	$40.0	$50.6
Return on capital employed	15%	13%	17%	16%	20%	17%

MOUNTAIN LUMBER COMPANY

"A new incentive plan," thought Willie Drake, the owner and president of Mountain Lumber Company. "Yes, I'm sure of it. That's what we need, a renewed sense of motivation for all of our employees."

At his next meeting with John Peterson, the company's controller, Willie told him of his idea. "John, I've been thinking. We've talked a lot about growth around here lately. And I see it happening. You can look at our revenues and see that we're growing right on target. But look at our margins. In 1998, they're down a bit from 1997. We've got to keep growing like this, but we've got to keep our margins up while doing it. We've got to keep volume and yield up as well. I'd like us to think about a new incentive plan for our employees. I want to make sure we maintain this rate of growth that is our main objective. And, I want to make sure we increase margins. I think we should use an incentive plan to make sure everyone knows how he or she can contribute to achieving these goals, and I want everyone to be rewarded when we do it."

INDUSTRY DESCRIPTION

In 1998, the size of the U.S. antique (reclaimed) flooring industry was estimated to be around $50 million. The industry was very fragmented, with many small competitors. Mountain Lumber Company was one of the largest competitors in the industry, holding just under a 10 percent market share. The primary use for antique flooring was in individual homes. Other uses included historical restoration projects, museums, restaurants, and other commercial businesses searching for an environmentally friendly rustic look.

The manufacturers in the industry obtained their raw materials from various sources, including demolition sites of old mills, factories, and warehouses; river bottoms; and old barns. The raw material was shipped to the manufacturer's lumber mills where the wood was resawn, molded, graded, and sold as antique, or reclaimed, flooring. Manufacturers typically specialized in a source and type of wood. For companies obtaining raw material from demolition sites, purchasing the raw material required knowledge of demolition activity. Prices were negotiated prior to demolition, based on a walk-through by the floor manufacturer's purchasing agent. Since quality and usability of material was somewhat uncertain at the time of purchase, the manufacturer assumed much of the risk of material yield loss, which could be substantial, during the manufacturing process. In addition, because sources of supply were limited and uncontrollable by the manufacturers, manufacturers had to purchase the material in large quantities whenever it came on the market. For these reasons, when resources permitted, manufacturers typically carried large amounts of inventory to ensure they could meet market demand for the flooring.

Product quality was determined by several characteristics of the flooring. Higher quality was associated with lower defects in the wood (e.g., knots and nail holes) and a tight or dense grain pattern. All companies in the industry graded their flooring to indicate product quality; however, there was no grading standard in the industry, so the quality within grades could vary substantially from manufacturer to manufacturer. Higher product quality (as indicated by defects and grain pattern), wider width, and longer length flooring commanded higher prices.

COMPANY DESCRIPTION

Mountain Lumber Company, located in Ruckersville, Virginia, saw its mission as one of producing reclaimed wood flooring of the highest quality. Mountain Lumber management felt that the company differentiated its product from that of other antique flooring manufacturers based on superior quality, consistency, and customer service. The company was founded in 1974 by Willie Drake, the current majority owner and president of the company, when he spent his summer reclaiming antique lumber from an old barn, contracted with a local saw mill operator to refurbish it, and sold it to a local architect down the road in Charlottesville, Virginia. The company grew from a one-man shop in 1974 to a company employing 50 people in 1998.

Revenues totaled $3.6 million in 1998, reflecting revenue growth of 22 percent over 1997. Gross margin for 1998 was 42 percent, down from 50 percent in 1997 and 45 percent in 1996. The company expected revenue growth of 23 percent in 1999 to yield revenues of $4.5 million. Gross margin was expected to increase to 44 percent in 1999 (see **Exhibit 1** for financial and operating data).

The company's revenues were derived primarily from wood flooring. However, it also sold molding (e.g., baseboards, crown molding, door frames), and rough-sawn lumber, and it occasionally resold raw timber to other manufacturers of wood products. Rough-sawn lumber had been through some processing in the saw mill, but was not finished flooring. Raw timber was as purchased from the supplier. In 1997, wood flooring accounted for 71 percent of revenues; molding accounted for 3 percent of revenues; rough-sawn lumber accounted for 13 percent of revenues; and the resale of raw timber accounted for 11 percent of revenues. This mix was fairly representative of a typical year. In 1998, however, flooring accounted for only 64 percent of revenues, lower than its typical share. The company sold a large amount of raw timber after a large inventory purchase, so raw timber sales represented 16 percent of sales in 1998. This shift in mix was a primary cause of the lower gross margin in 1998.

Of its flooring sales, heart pine typically represented around 80 percent.[1] Oak and chestnut flooring typically accounted for 20 percent of flooring sales. Approximately 70 percent of the company's flooring was sold directly to the end customer for high-end homes, historical restoration projects, or commercial use; the remaining 30 percent was sold through local dealers that sold and installed the product for the end customer. Mountain Lumber offered consultation services on product installation as needed.

---

[1]Most of the pine forests located on the East Coast of the United States in the eighteenth and nineteenth centuries were cut to build early American industry or were exported to other countries. Often only the hard center of the wood, called the heartwood, was used because the wood was so abundant. The outer few inches, which was soft wood, was often discarded. The heartwood became known as *heart pine*. It was sometimes referred to as old growth pine.

Materials costs represented just over 70 percent of the cost of the flooring. Labor represented approximately 20 percent, and manufacturing overhead accounted for the remainder. Manufacturing overhead costs were primarily fixed in nature. Labor varied only to the extent that overtime was used to meet periods of excessive demand. Mountain Lumber took pride in its low turnover rate among its workforce.

Inventory represented between 40 percent and 45 percent of total assets. Because it was necessary to purchase inventory in large quantities whenever it came on the market, the company financed its inventory purchases with short-term debt, at a rate of 1 percent over prime.[2] In keeping with its strategic emphasis on growth and profitability, Mountain Lumber's total assets increased 60 percent in 1998 over 1997. This increase was due to: (1) an increase in inventory; (2) the purchase of new molding equipment to accommodate an increase in volume and to improve product quality; and (3) the purchase of the land and facility the company previously leased. These purchases were financed with an additional equity infusion from a large shareholder, and an increase in debt.

The company's organization chart is presented in **Exhibit 2**. Reporting to Willie Drake were the following individuals: (1) vice president for Engineering, (2) vice president for Operations, (3) vice president and controller, and (4) vice president for Purchasing and Sales. The vice president for Engineering was primarily responsible for special projects and for maintaining equipment to ensure optimum performance. The vice president for Operations managed the manufacturing process, from the time the lumber arrived at the lumber mill until it was shipped to the customer. The operations area consisted of four departments. The lumberyard stored timber and removed nails and other metal from the timber. The saw mill sawed raw timber into floor-sized boards. The mill shop molded the boards into finished wood flooring. The shipping department shipped the finished product to the customer. The vice president and controller managed the accounting and control, finance, production planning, and other administrative areas. The vice president for Purchasing and Sales was responsible for locating and purchasing raw material and for sale of the product to the customer. In support of the purchasing function, there were three purchasing representatives to assist in the location and purchase of raw material. In support of the sales function, there was one sales manager and one sales representative.

THE PURCHASING PROCESS

Mountain Lumber purchased three types of timber: (1) old growth pine, (2) oak, and (3) chestnut. Mountain Lumber obtained pine primarily from demolition sites on the East Coast of the United States, especially in industrial areas and mill towns that were tearing down old mills and manufacturing plants. Mountain Lumber obtained large beams and columns, joists, and decking. Large beams and columns were typically 12 to18 inches square by 12 to 20 feet long. Beams, columns, and joists were the most desirable wood because they resulted in the greatest usable material. Decking had been used as flooring in the site being demolished. Decking was the least desirable wood because the quality of wood was low, the widths were narrow, and the wood contained a large number of defects. It resulted in the least usable material, and Mountain Lumber

---

[2] In 1998, the prime rate fluctuated between 7.75 percent and 8.5 percent, according to Standard & Poor's *Current Statistics*, McGraw-Hill Companies, August 1999.

sometimes resold it as is, if buyers could be located. Purchasing only the beams, columns, and joists, however, was often not an option. Sellers often required that manufacturers purchase all the timber and decking from the site.

The company learned of demolition sites from word-of-mouth and from purchasing agents knowledgeable of local area demolition activity on the East Coast. Because the lumber was obtained from demolition sites containing antique wood, there was a limited supply. In addition, supply was very "lumpy", because timber from an entire demolition site was typically purchased all at once, and demolition sites were not always available. As a result, the company had to purchase lumber whenever it came on the market. There was a large amount of purchasing risk, because the purchase decision was typically made based on a walk-through of a demolition site by one of Mountain Lumber's purchasing agents. During the walk-through, the purchasing agent tried to assess wood type, size of lumber and overall wood quality. In addition, the agent examined the timber for possible environmental hazards, such as lead-based paint and spilled oils, and for nails and fasteners that would be difficult to remove, because these features increased the cost of production. However, during a walk-through, type and quality of wood were not always known with certainty. In addition to a walk-through by the purchasing agent, Mountain Lumber's vice president of Sales and Purchasing conducted a walk-through for larger sites.

As of 1998, several import/export firms had begun to purchase timber for resale outside the United States. The presence of these firms had begun to increase the price manufacturers had to pay for the timber, and further reduced the supply of antique lumber available to the manufacturers.

THE MANUFACTURING PROCESS

Once Mountain Lumber purchased the timber, the demolition company removed it from the demolition site and placed it on trucks of independent trucking company with which Mountain Lumber contracted to deliver the timber to Mountain Lumber's location. Once the timber was on the truck, Mountain Lumber took ownership and paid freight charges. When the shipment arrived at Mountain Lumber's location, timber volume was determined and payment was made to the supplier. Large purchases could generate enough inventory to keep production up and running for four to six months, so inventory levels and inventory carrying costs could be very high.

Once the timber arrived at Mountain Lumber, it was graded and stacked by wood type (pine, oak, and chestnut) in proper storage locations. High-grade timbers were stored inside to minimize damage from extreme temperature and moisture. Lower grade timbers were stored outside on the lumberyard. In general, from this point, timber moved through the production process by wood type, but the production process was similar for all wood types. **Exhibit 3** presents a plant layout, which shows the lumberyard, nail shed, saw mill, and mill shop areas, all of which were involved in the manufacturing of the flooring.

Lumberyard laborers pulled timber from stacks in storage locations based on the production plan and moved it by forklift trucks to the nail shed. Two-man crews removed all nails and metal from the timber, using hand tools and metal detectors. Any nails or metal left in the timber created serious production problems down the line because they dulled or damaged production equipment and created a safety hazard for those individuals operating the equipment. If nails or other metal objects were inadvertently left in the timber, the production line would likely be shut down for extended periods of time.

After all metal objects were removed from the timber, forklift trucks moved the timber to the sawmill area and place the timber onto a conveyor. One of the sawmill operators guided the timbers into the saw. Various stages in the saw mill were designed to cut the timber into one-inch thick boards (or alternative thickness for special orders such as counter tops) of the greatest width and length possible after considering the elimination of sections of the board with defects. Defects included nail holes, bolt holes, cracks, knots, rot, and stains. Saw mill operators made decisions regarding the width *and* length of the boards based on their observation of defect locations and the need to maximize board feet of flooring.[3] **Exhibit 4** provides an example of the decision to be made by saw mill operators in response to defects. All defects were not removed from the wood because some number of defects was thought to give the wood a certain "character". However, Mountain Lumber management felt it was less forgiving of defects in this respect than were many of its competitors. Management felt that the company's wood contained less defects than competitors' products, and this was one dimension that it used to differentiate the quality of its products from that of other competitors.

After the timber passed through the saw mill area, it was stacked on the lumber yard and stored until the production plan indicated that it was required for further processing. The saw mill was thought to be the bottleneck in the production process. Through this stage in the process, total material yield loss averaged about 50 percent. At current production levels, it was estimated that a one-point decrease in material yield resulted in a decrease in gross margin of almost $100,000 annually.

When the timber was required for further processing, forklift trucks loaded the timber into kilns for drying. The timber remained in the kiln for 3–5 days, depending on moisture content and insect infestation. After the timber was dried, it was placed in queue for processing. At this point, the product could be sold to other mill shops as rough-sawn timber, or remain in process for production of wood flooring or molding.

The timber that remained in production was moved to the mill shop area, where the rough-sawn lumber was molded into tongue and groove flooring (see **Exhibit 5** for an illustration of tongue and groove flooring). One of the molder operators set up the molder to meet specifications. He examined the timber to determine which side of the board would become the flooring surface and which side would be the underside of the floor.[4] He then placed the timber into the molder accordingly. Linear feet were the primary measure of output from the mill shop for several reasons. First, the time required for the molder to process a board was independent of board width. Second, the width of the board was determined in the sawmill area. The mill shop influenced only the length of the board. Third, effort expended by the molder operator to examine the length of a board for defects was the same regardless of the width of the board.

---

[3]Larger width and longer length boards commanded higher prices. A *board foot* was a volume unit of measure intended to capture the combined effect of width and length. One board foot equals 1 inch x 12 inches x 12 inches, or the equivalent. For example, 1-inch x 3-inch x 48-inch and 1-inch x 4-inch x 36-inch boards are also equivalent to one board foot.

[4]Many minor defects were allowed on the under side that were not allowed on the flooring surface.

As the flooring exited the molder, a second operator monitored the quality of the flooring by continuous visual checks and regular measurement audits. Conveyor belts moved the flooring from the molder to the trim saw, also in the mill shop, where any remaining undesired defects were eliminated from the flooring by trimming the length of the board. Remaining defects included any loose knots or cracks not previously cut out in the process, or any defects created in the production process itself. There were four trim saw operators, each operating a trim saw. Through this stage in the process, total yield loss averaged about 60 percent.

Once the flooring passed through the trim saw, it was graded. Five boards of the same grade and length were banded together, total linear footage, and board footage were calculated, and the boards were labeled. The banded boards were then moved to the shipping warehouse. The boards were shipped according to customer orders.

THE SALES PROCESS

Seventy percent of Mountain Lumber's revenues were generated from retail sales directly to the end customer, typically a homeowner or a builder. Retail prices for Mountain Lumber products were similar to competitors' prices for flooring of similar quality. However, Mountain Lumber's flooring was typically of higher quality, and therefore priced higher, than that of competitors. The remaining 30 percent of revenues were generated through dealers, who purchased the flooring from Mountain Lumber, then resold it at a markup to the end customer. These dealers also provided installation services to the customer.

Mountain Lumber sales personnel were typically involved in all sales. In general, for retail sales, it was an inquiry by a potential customer that started the sales process. Initial inquiries by customers generally could be attributed to one of four sources: (1) advertisements in fine homebuilding magazines and other trade publications; (2) the company's Web site; (3) referrals, or "word-of-mouth"; and (4) published editorials regarding the company. These inquiries were primarily by phone or email, although the company also received some walk-in inquiries by customers interested in seeing the product in the company's showroom at its Ruckersville headquarters. Upon receipt of an inquiry by a potential customer, the company sent to the customer, at no charge, a brochure describing the product, a grade sheet picturing the product in different grades, and a retail price list. Upon request, the company also provided the potential customer a sample kit, which included small samples of flooring, and for which the company charged $25. (This $25 was refunded if the customer placed an order.)

A sales representative (either the sales representative, sales manager, or vice president of sales) followed up with the potential customer by phone in an attempt to make the sale. The representative had the authority to discount the product up to 10 percent off retail price without approval. Discounts greater than 10 percent required the approval of the vice president of Sales or the president.

In general, for sales to dealers, sales personnel responded to dealer inquiries with price and availability, and had the ability to influence the dealer's purchase decision. Dealers typically purchased the flooring at a 20 to 25 percent discount off of the retail price. Sales personnel had some flexibility in discounting to dealers. Relationships with dealers and the availability of the product at the dealer's request were key factors in the purchasing decision.

MOUNTAIN LUMBER COMPANY'S INCENTIVE PLAN

Several months after their initial conversations regarding an incentive plan for Mountain Lumber employees, Willie and John finalized the incentive plan. A copy of the incentive plan is included in **Exhibit 6**. The plan was implemented in April of 1999 and was designed so that the lowest reward level was based on budgeted performance, with successively higher reward levels for successively higher levels of performance. Payouts from the incentive plan were expected to amount to an average of 3–4 percent of salary and wage expenses, and the plan was implemented in lieu of a previously contemplated across-the-board increase in salaries and wage rates of a comparable amount.[5]

---

[5]For more information on Mountain Lumber, see the company's Web site at <http://www.mountainlumber.com.

Exhibit 1

MOUNTAIN LUMBER COMPANY

Financial and Operating Data

	1998	**1997**	**1996**
Revenues	$ 3,666,699	$ 3,001,022	$ 2,582,199
Cost of Goods Sold	2,110,313	1,489,622	1,412,382
Gross Margin %	42%	50%	45%
Product Mix:			
Flooring	64%	71%	71%
Molding	6%	3%	4%
Rough-sawn lumber	14%	13%	13%
Raw timber	16%	11%	10%
Balance Sheet Data:			
Inventory	$1,444,293	$943,516	$977,570
Other current assets	501,862	266,173	266,400
Total current assets	1,946,155	1,209,689	1,243,970
PP&E	1,593,741	974,588	945,702
Total assets	3,543,089	2,184,737	2,217,255
Total liabilities	2,227,907	1,288,001	1,350,219
Stockholder's equity	1,315,182	896,737	867,036
Total liabs + equity	$3,543,089	$2,184,738	$2,217,255
Debt / Total assets	63%	59%	61%

Exhibit 2

MOUNTAIN LUMBER COMPANY

Organizational Chart

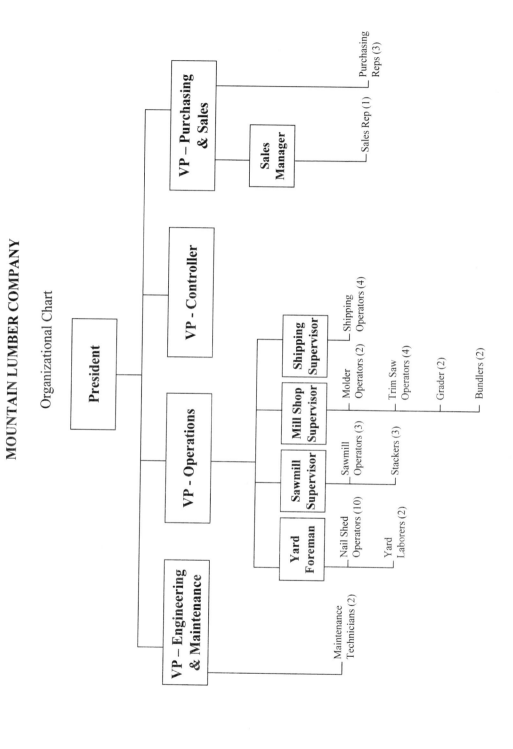

Exhibit 3

MOUNTAIN LUMBER COMPANY

Facility Layout

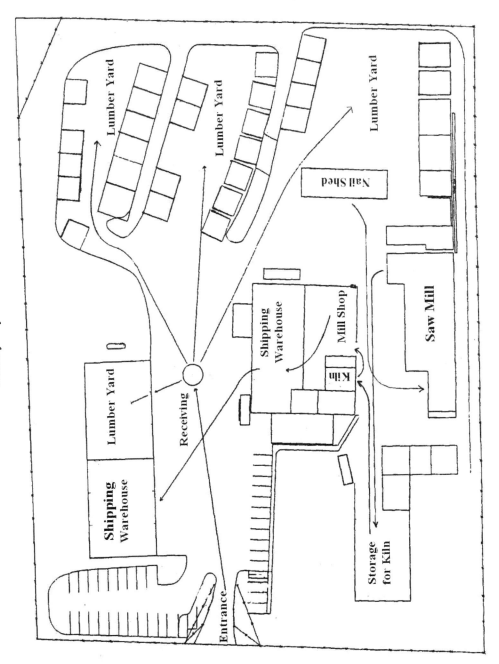

Exhibit 4

MOUNTAIN LUMBER COMPANY

Example of Decision to Be Made by Sawmill Operator Regarding Defects

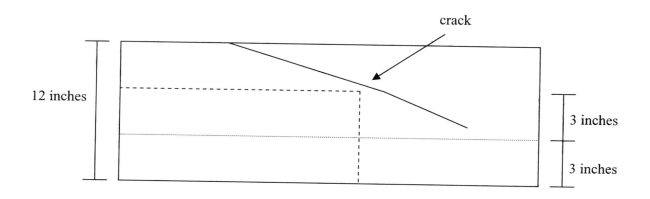

Suppose the sawmill operator encounters a 12-inch wide board with a crack as depicted above. In removing the defect, he has several alternatives. He can cut one 3-inch wide board of the same length of the original board. Alternatively, he can cut one 6-inch wide board of considerably shorter length than the original board. He makes the decision, based on visual inspection, and some measuring as needed, as to which alternative is preferred. Since both wider boards and longer boards command a higher price, the decision he makes trades off the higher value of a wider (longer) board for the higher value of the longer (wider) board. In general, to make this tradeoff, he opts for the alternative that yields the greatest usable board feet.

Exhibit 5

MOUNTAIN LUMBER COMPANY

Cross-Section of Hardwood Flooring

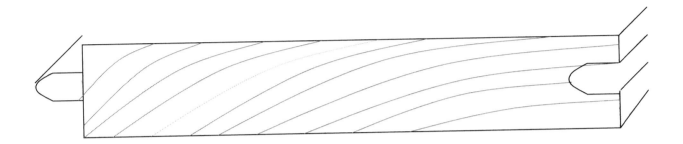

Tongue   **Groove**

CASE: MOUNTAIN LUMBER COMPANY

Exhibit 6
MOUNTAIN LUMBER COMPANY

Mountain Lumber Incentive Program
(This program will be reviewed quarterly, and may be changed)

VP – Purchasing and Sales

Objective:

The objective of this program is to improve profitability of Mountain Lumber Company (MLC) by creating incentives to achieve MLC sales objectives, reduce the purchase price of timber, and control the type of timber on the yard.

Programs:

Sales

The following bonus will be paid for achieving the total monthly sales, excluding raw timber sales. (See Attachment 7)

- 0.2% of the monthly net sales for achieving 100% of monthly sales budget
- If the total year-end sales are achieved, this bonus will be paid for all months after March/99 (because of April/99 implementation date) where the sales budget was not achieved.

Procurement

1. MLC will pay 50% of any revenue generated from the resale of decking which is in excess of 1.3 x MLC cost in that timber.

   Ex. (Decking cost $0.40/BF + Hauling $0.10 + Labor $0.10) x 1.3 = $0.78/BF. If the sale of this Decking generates $0.90/BF, the incentive would be 50% of $0.12/BF or $0.06/BF. Labor cost is determined based on order requirements. This bonus will be split between VP of Sales and any other salesperson involved with the transaction.

   Note: BF = board feet

2. For any purchase of timber, the following incentive will be paid if the total cost (timber, hauling, commissions, other) meets these conditions:

   High Grade Pine Timber
   - If total cost ≤ $1.10/BF, incentive = $0.02/BF
   - If total cost is ≤ $0.90, incentive = $0.02 + ($0.90 - Total Cost) x 50%

   Note: In determining cost of high-grade pine flooring, low-grade pine timber will be valued at a maximum of $0.65/BF.

   Oak
   - If total cost ≤ $0.70/BF, incentive = ($0.70 - Total Cost) x 50%

   Chestnut
   - If total cost ≤ $2.00/BF, incentive = ($2.00 - Total Cost) x 50%

   Note: This incentive will not be paid if Willie purchases the timber.

Exhibit 6 (continued)
MOUNTAIN LUMBER COMPANY

Mountain Lumber Incentive Program
(This program will be reviewed quarterly, and may be changed)

Sales Manager

Objective:

The objective of this program is to improve profitability of Mountain Lumber Company (MLC) by creating incentives for sales force to achieve the sales targets, increase retail sales, and sell slow moving inventory.

Programs:

Total Sales

The following bonus will be paid for achieving the total monthly sales, excluding non-retail timber sales. (See Attachment 7)

- $1,000/ month for achieving 100% of the monthly sales budget
- If the total year-end sales are achieved, this bonus will be paid for all months after March/99 (because of April/99 implementation date), where the sales budget was not achieved.

Non-Discounted Retail Sales

- The salesman will receive a 0.5% commission for all sales made at full retail price.
- If the MLC achieves the sales budget shown in Attachment 7, a 0.6% commission on all sales made at full retail at year-end.

Other Sales Incentives

Sales incentive will be offered only for slow moving inventory, which is sold at a discount.

Decking Sales

If a sales person is involved in the sale of decking, a bonus of 50% will be split with VP of Sales on any revenue generated from the resale of decking which is in excess of 1.3 x MLC cost in that timber.

Exhibit 6 (continued)
MOUNTAIN LUMBER COMPANY

Mountain Lumber Incentive Program
(This program will be reviewed quarterly, and may be changed)

Sales Representative

Objective:

The objective of this program is to improve profitability of Mountain Lumber Company (MLC) by creating incentives for sales force to achieve the sales targets, increase retail sales, and sell slow moving inventory.

Programs:

Total Sales

The following bonus will be paid for achieving the total monthly sales, excluding non-retail timber sales. (See Attachment 7)

- $250/ month for achieving 100% of the monthly sales budget
- If the total year-end sales are achieved, this bonus will be paid for all months after March/99 (because of April/99 implementation date), where the sales budget was not achieved.

Non-Discounted Retail Sales

- The salesman will receive a 0.5% commission for all sales made at full retail price.
- If the MLC achieves the sales budget shown in Attachment 7, a 0.4% commission on all sales made at full retail will be split among the sales representatives at year-end.

Sales Incentive

Sales incentive will be offered only for slow moving inventory, which is sold at a discount.

Decking Sales

If a sales person is involved in the sale of decking, a bonus of 50% will be split with VP of Sales on any revenue generated from the resale of decking which is in excess of 1.3 x MLC cost in that timber.

Exhibit 6 (continued)
MOUNTAIN LUMBER COMPANY

Mountain Lumber Incentive Program
(This program will be reviewed quarterly, and may be changed)

VP -- Operations

Objective:

The objective of this program is to improve profitability of Mountain Lumber Company (MLC) by creating incentives for employees to increase production, improve material yields and productivity, and reduce cost.

Programs:

Saw Mill Output

The value of the saw mill output will be determined by Attachment 1

- Averaging 3300 to 3550 $/day for the month = $200
- Averaging 3551 to 3750 $/day for the month = $300
- Averaging > 3751 $/day for the month = $400

If the total year-end sales target is achieved, a $200 bonus will be paid for each month after March/99 (because of April/99 implementation date) where the sawmill output target of 3300 was not achieved.

Mill Shop Output

The value of the Mill Shop output will be determined by Attachment 2

- Averaging 6000 to 6500 LF/day for the month = $75
- Averaging 6501 to 7000 LF/day for the month = $100
- Averaging > 7001 LF/day for the month = $200

Saw Mill Yield

A quarterly incentive will be paid for achieving the yield targets for heart pine and all hard woods. The yield targets and incentive for each type of timber is shown in the table below. A minimum of 25k BF must be output during the quarter in order to receive a yield bonus for that type of timber. The yield will be determined per Attachment 3.

Heart Pine		Hard Woods	
Bonus $	Yield Loss	Bonus $	Yield Loss
$750	56% to 54%	$250	36% to 34%
$1200	53.9% to 53%	$400	33.9% to 33%
$1800	< 52.9%	$600	< 32.9%

Labor Efficiency (Output/Man Hour)

A monthly incentive for achieving targets for Saw Mill + Nail Shed labor efficiency, which will be determined per Attachment 5

- Achieve $21 /Man Hour = $100/month
- Achieve $22 /Man Hour = $200/month
- Achieve $23/Man Hour = $300/month
- Achieve $24/Man Hour = $400/month

Exhibit 6 (continued)
MOUNTAIN LUMBER COMPANY

Mountain Lumber Incentive Program
(This program will be reviewed quarterly, and may be changed)

Departmental Supervisor – Saw Mill

Objective:

The objective of this program is to improve profitability of Mountain Lumber Company (MLC) by creating incentives for employees to increase production, improve material yields and productivity, and reduce cost.

Programs:

Saw Mill Output

The value of the saw mill output will be determined by Attachment 1

- Averaging 3300 to 3550 $/day for the month = $80
- Averaging 3551 to 3750 $/day for the month = $100
- Averaging > 3751 $/day for the month = $150

If the total year-end sales target is achieved, an $80 bonus will be paid for each month after March/99 (because of April/99 implementation date) where the sawmill output target of 3300 was not achieved.

Saw Mill Yield

A quarterly incentive will be paid for achieving the yield targets for heart pine and all hard woods. The yield targets and incentive for each type of timber is shown in the table below. A minimum of 25k BF must be output during the quarter in order to receive a yield bonus for that type of timber. The yield will be determined per Attachment 3.

Heart Pine		Hard Woods	
Bonus $	Yield Loss	Bonus $	Yield Loss
$240	56% to 54%	$80	36% to 34%
$400	53.9% to 53%	$160	33.9% to 33%
$750	< 52.9%	$250	< 32.9%

Saw Mill Labor Efficiency (Output/Man Hour)

A monthly incentive for achieving targets for Saw Mill labor efficiency, which will be determined per Attachment 5.
- Achieve $41/Man Hour = $50/month
- Achieve $44/Man Hour = $100/month
- Achieve $47/Man Hour = $200/month
- Achieve $49/Man Hour = $300/month

Exhibit 6 (continued)
MOUNTAIN LUMBER COMPANY

Mountain Lumber Incentive Program
(This program will be reviewed quarterly, and may be changed)

<u>Departmental Supervisor – Lumber Yard</u>

Objective:

The objective of this program is to improve profitability of Mountain Lumber Company (MLC) by creating incentives for employees to increase production, improve material yields and productivity, and reduce cost.

Programs:

Nail Shed Quality and Output

A monthly incentive is based on the value of the Saw Mill output. The value of the Saw Mill output will be determined by Attachment 1:

- Averaging 3300 to 3550 $/day for the month = $120
- Averaging 3551 to 3750 $/day for the month = $160
- Averaging > 3751 $/day for the month = $330

This monthly incentive is contingent upon the Saw Mill and Mill Shop processing the whole month without finding nails in the timber. Nails in the timber represent both a safety hazard and a large tooling cost.

If nails are found which cannot be traced to a crew, all crews are eligible for 50% of that month's bonus. If two nails are found and not traced to a crew, the all crews are ineligible for a bonus.

If the total year end sales target is achieved, a $120 bonus will be paid for each month after March/99 (because of April/99 implementation date) where the saw mill output target of 3300 was not achieved, subject to the above conditions on nail shed quality.

Nail Shed Labor Efficiency (Output/Man Hour)

A monthly incentive for achieving targets for Nail Shed Labor efficiency, which will be determined per Attachment 5.

- Achieve $37/Man Hour = $50/month
- Achieve $40/Man Hour = $100/month
- Achieve $43/Man Hour = $200/month
- Achieve $45/Man Hour = $300/month

Exhibit 6 (continued)
MOUNTAIN LUMBER COMPANY

Mountain Lumber Incentive Program
(This program will be reviewed quarterly, and may be changed)

Departmental Supervisor – Mill Shop

Objective:

The objective of this program is to improve profitability of Mountain Lumber Company (MLC) by creating incentives for employees to increase production, improve material yields and productivity, and reduce cost.

Programs:

Mill Shop Output

The value of the Mill Shop output will be determined by Attachment 2

- Averaging 6000 to 6500 LF/day = $150
- Averaging 6501 to 7000 LF/day = $200
- Averaging > 7001 LF/day = $250

If the total year-end sales target is achieved, a $150 bonus will be paid for each month after March/99 (because of April/99 implementation date) where the mill shop output target of 6000 was not achieved.

Trim Saw Yield

If there are no customer complaints, a quarterly incentive for achieving trim saw yield loss targets (yield is determined by Attachment 4):

Minimum yield loss: 15% $240/quarter
Target yield loss: 10% $360/quarter

Mill Shop Labor Efficiency (Output/Man Hour)

A monthly incentive for achieving targets for Mill Shop Labor efficiency, which will be determined per Attachment 5.

- Achieve 80 LF/Man Hour = $50/month
- Achieve 88 LF/Man Hour = $100/month
- Achieve 95 LF/Man Hour = $200/month
- Achieve 100 LF/Man Hour = $300/month

Exhibit 6 (continued)
MOUNTAIN LUMBER COMPANY

Mountain Lumber Incentive Program
(This program will be reviewed quarterly, and may be changed)

Lumber Yard & Nail Shed Department

Objective:

The objective of this program is to improve profitability of Mountain Lumber Company (MLC) by creating incentives for employees to increase production, improve material yields and productivity, and reduce cost.

Programs:

Nail Shed Quality and Output

A monthly incentive is based on the value of the Saw Mill output. The value of the Saw Mill output will be determined by Attachment 1:

- Averaging 3300 to 3550 $/day for the month = $80
- Averaging 3551 to 3750 $/day for the month = $120
- Averaging > 3751 $/day for the month = $220

This monthly incentive is contingent upon the Saw Mill and Mill Shop processing the whole month without finding nails in the timber. Nails in the timber represent both a safety hazard and a large tooling cost.

If nails are found which cannot be traced to a crew, all crews are eligible for 50% of that month's bonus. If two nails are found and not traced to a crew, the all crews are ineligible for a bonus.

If the total year end sales target is achieved, an $80 bonus will be paid for each month after March/99 (because of April/99 implementation date) where the saw mill output target of 3300 was not achieved, subject to the above conditions on nail shed quality.

Exhibit 6 (continued)
MOUNTAIN LUMBER COMPANY

Mountain Lumber Incentive Program
(This program will be reviewed quarterly, and may be changed)

Saw Mill Department

Objective:

The objective of this program is to improve profitability of Mountain Lumber Company (MLC) by creating incentives for employees to increase production, improve material yields and productivity, and reduce cost.

Programs:

Saw Mill Output

The value of the saw mill output will be determined by Attachment 1

- Averaging 3300 to 3550 $/day for the month = $40
- Averaging 3551 to 3750 $/day for the month = $50
- Averaging > 3751 $/day for the month = $75

If the total year-end sales target is achieved, a $40 bonus will be paid for each month after March/99 (because of April/99 implementation date) where the sawmill output target of 3300 was not achieved.

Saw Mill Yield

A quarterly incentive will be paid for achieving the yield targets for heart pine and all hard woods. The yield targets and incentive for each type of timber is shown in the table below. A minimum of 25k BF must be output during the quarter in order to receive a yield bonus for that type of timber. The yield will be determined per Attachment 3.

Heart Pine		Hard Woods	
Bonus $	Yield Loss	Bonus $	Yield Loss
$120	56% to 54%	$40	36% to 34%
$200	53.9% to 53%	$80	33.9% to 33%
$375	< 52.9%	$125	< 32.9%

Exhibit 6 (continued)
MOUNTAIN LUMBER COMPANY

Mountain Lumber Incentive Program
(This program will be reviewed quarterly, and may be changed)

Mill Shop Department

Objective:

The objectives of this program are to improve profitability of Mountain Lumber Company (MLC) by creating incentives for employees to increase production, improve material yields and productivity, and reduce cost.

Programs:

Mill Shop Output

The value of the Mill Shop output will be determined by Attachment 2

- Averaging 6000 to 6500 LF/day = $50
- Averaging 6501 to 7000 LF/day = $75
- Averaging > 7001 LF/day = $100

If the total year-end sales target is achieved, a $50 bonus will be paid for each month after March/99 (because of April/99 implementation date) where the mill shop output target of 6000 was not achieved.

Trim Saw Yield (Trim Saw/Bundling Operator Only)

If there are no customer complaints, a quarterly incentive for achieving trim saw yield loss targets (yield is determined by Attachment 4):

Minimum yield loss: 15% $110/quarter
Target yield loss: 10% $240/quarter

Exhibit 6 (continued)
MOUNTAIN LUMBER COMPANY

Mountain Lumber Incentive Program
(This program will be reviewed quarterly, and may be changed)

Attachment 1

Saw Mill Avg. Value per Day

Avg. Value/Day = $\sum$(BF x Value) / (Scheduled hours/8 hrs/day) where:

Information	Descriptions
BF	BF output by category reported by the manager
Scheduled hours	Scheduled Saw Mill hours for which the BF output is calculated. (Excludes only hours lost due to weather, company holidays, work in other departments, and downtime due to major projects. Production hours lost due to equipment breakage, staffing issues, etc., will be included in the scheduled Saw Mill hours.)

Value determined as follows: (a)

Board Category (b)	Value
3"	$ 1.00
4"	$ 1.00
5"	$ 1.10
6"	$ 1.10
7"	$ 1.20
8"	$ 1.20
9"	$ 1.20
10"	$ 1.20
11"	$ 1.20
12"	$ 1.20

(a) "Value" is intended to represent relative importance across board categories, and is not cost or sales   value.

(b) There are several other categories of low volume with varying assigned values not included in the table above.

Exhibit 6 (continued)
MOUNTAIN LUMBER COMPANY

Mountain Lumber Incentive Program
(This program will be reviewed quarterly, and may be changed)

Attachment 2

Mill Shop Output

Avg. LF/Day = (Total flooring LF) / (Scheduled hours/8 hrs/day) where:

Information	Descriptions
Total flooring LF	Total LF of flooring transferred to the warehouse (excludes subcontracted work)
Scheduled hours	Scheduled Mill Shop hours for which the BF output is calculated. (excludes only hours lost due to weather, company holidays, work in other departments, and downtime due to major projects. Production hours lost due to equipment breakage, staffing issues, etc., will be included in the scheduled Mill Shop hours.)

Attachment 3

Saw Mill Yields

Saw Mill Yield = BF Output / (Beg. Inv. + Purchases – Sales – Ending Inv.) where:

Information	Descriptions
Beg. Inv.	Timber on the yard physically counted at the Start of each quarter
Ending. Inv.	Timber on the yard physically counted at the End of each quarter
Purchases	Timber purchased during the quarter
Sales	Timber sold off the yard
BF Output	Saw Mill output in BF

Exhibit 6 (continued)
MOUNTAIN LUMBER COMPANY

Mountain Lumber Incentive Program
(This program will be reviewed quarterly, and may be changed)

Attachment 4

Mill Shop Yields

Mill Shop Yields = (Mill Shop LF Output) / (Mill Shop LF Input)

Attachment 5

Labor Efficiency (Output/Man Hour)

Labor Efficiency = Total output /Total man hours paid, where:

Information	Descriptions
Total Output:	
For Saw Mill	Value output calculated in Attachment 1
For Mill Shop	LF output calculated in Attachment 2
Total Man Hours Paid	Total man hours used in the following departments to produce the above output:
For Nail Shed	Nail Shed
For Saw Mill	Yard + Saw Mill +Maintenance– Export Shipping Labor
For Mill Shop	Molder + Trim Saw + Mill Work
	Notes: • overtime hours counted a 1.5 actual hours • includes Supervisor hours • excludes vacation hours & holiday hours

Exhibit 6 (continued)
MOUNTAIN LUMBER COMPANY

Mountain Lumber Incentive Program
(This program will be reviewed quarterly, and may be changed)

Attachment 6

Preconditions of Receiving Monthly Incentives:
- No unexcused absences during the month
- Not late for work during the month
- No written or verbal warnings during the month
- A full time MLC employee
- Eligible the 1st full month worked after being employed at MCL for 60 days, except where otherwise noted.

Applies to **all employees**. If department qualifies for a quarterly incentive, the incentive will be paid to the employee based on the number of months they meet the preconditions

Attachment 7

Sales Target:

Excludes export sales, and other non-retail timber sales. Shaded portion is prior to the incentive program and excluded from this incentive program.

Month	Amount
Dec-98	$ 244,000
Jan-99	$ 220,000
Feb-99	$ 287,000
Mar-99	$ 324,000
Apr-99	$ 362,000
May-99	$ 361,000
Jun-99	$ 373,000
Jul-99	$ 374,000
Aug-99	$ 374,000
Sep-99	$ 374,000
Oct-99	$ 374,000
Nov-99	$ 399,000
Year Total	$4,066,000
Apr-Nov/99 Total	$2,991,000

Exhibit 6 (continued)
MOUNTAIN LUMBER COMPANY
Mountain Lumber Incentive Program
(This program will be reviewed quarterly, and may be changed)

VP -- Engineering

Objective:

The objective of this program is to improve profitability of Mountain Lumber Company (MLC) by creating incentives for employees to increase production, improve material yields and productivity, reduce cost, improve safety programs, and complete capital projects on time and within budget.

Programs:

Saw Mill Output

The value of the saw mill output will be determined by Attachment 1
- Averaging 3300 to 3550 $/day for the month = $75
- Averaging 3551 to 3750 $/day for the month = $100
- Averaging > 3751 $/day for the month = $200

If the total year-end sales target is achieved, a $75 bonus will be paid for each month after March/99 (because of April/99 implementation date) where the sawmill output target of 3300 was not achieved.

Mill Shop Output

The value of the Mill Shop output will be determined by Attachment 2
- Averaging 6000 to 6500 LF/day for the month = $75
- Averaging 6501 to 7000 LF/day for the month = $100
- Averaging > 7001 LF/day for the month = $200

Saw Mill Yield

A quarterly incentive will be paid for achieving the yield targets for heart pine and all hard woods. The yield targets and incentive for each type of timber is shown in the table below. A minimum of 25k BF must be output during the quarter in order to receive a yield bonus for that type of timber. The yield will be determined per Attachment 3.

Heart Pine		Hard Woods	
Bonus $	Yield Loss	Bonus $	Yield Loss
$375	56% to 54%	$125	36% to 34%
$600	53.9% to 53%	$200	33.9% to 33%
$900	< 52.9%	$300	< 32.9%

Safety

- Monthly incentive for each company safety meeting: $50/month
- Quarterly safety audits $100/qtr
- No lost time accidents $2,000/year

Projects

The following incentives will be paid for completing the following projects on time and within budget.
- Mill Shop upgrade $500
- Alternative for saw dust disposal $1,500
- Each yield improvement projects $500+ (based on yield increase)

Exhibit 6 (continued)
MOUNTAIN LUMBER COMPANY

Mountain Lumber Incentive Program
(This program will be reviewed quarterly, and may be changed)

Departmental Supervisor -- Shipping

Objective:

The objective of this program is to improve profitability of Mountain Lumber Company (MLC) by creating incentives for the shipping department to achieve the sales targets, improve quality of our shipments, and improve efficiency of the warehouse operations.

Programs:

Sales

The sales incentive is for making the total $ sales for sawn product. This excludes raw timber sales. (See Attachment 7)

- $100/month if Sales Department achieves 100% of monthly sales budget
- If the total year-end sales are achieved, this bonus will be paid for all months after March/99 (because of April/99 implementation date), where the sales budget was not achieved.

Shipping Quality

The shipping quality incentive is paid monthly for maintaining shipping accuracy. To qualify for this incentive no shipping errors, miss-shipped, short shipped or valid customer complaints can occur in the month.

- $200/month

Exhibit 6 (continued)
MOUNTAIN LUMBER COMPANY

Mountain Lumber Incentive Program
(This program will be reviewed quarterly, and may be changed)

Departmental Supervisor -- Maintenance

Objective:

The objective of this program is to improve profitability of Mountain Lumber Company (MLC) by creating incentives for employees to increase production, improve material yields and productivity, and reduce cost.

Programs:

Saw Mill Output

The value of the saw mill output will be determined by Attachment 1

- Averaging 3300 to 3550 $/day for the month = $80
- Averaging 3551 to 3750 $/day for the month = $100
- Averaging > 3751 $/day for the month = $150

If the total year-end sales target is achieved, an $80 bonus will be paid for each month after March/99 (because of April/99 implementation date) where the sawmill output target of 3300 was not achieved.

Saw Mill Yield

A quarterly incentive will be paid for achieving the yield targets for heart pine and all hard woods. The yield targets and incentive for each type of timber is shown in the table below. A minimum of 25k BF must be output during the quarter in order to receive a yield bonus for that type of timber. The yield will be determined per Attachment 3.

Heart Pine		Hard Woods	
Bonus $	Yield Loss	Bonus $	Yield Loss
$120	56% to 54%	$40	36% to 34%
$200	53.9% to 53%	$80	33.9% to 33%
$375	< 52.9%	$125	< 32.9%

Exhibit 6 (continued)
MOUNTAIN LUMBER COMPANY

Mountain Lumber Incentive Program
(This program will be reviewed quarterly, and may be changed)

Shipping Department

Objective:

The objective of this program is to improve profitability of Mountain Lumber Company (MLC) by creating incentives for employees work with Sales Department to achieve sales goals while maintaining accuracy of shipments.

Programs:

Sales

The sales incentive is for making the total $ sales for sawn product. This excludes non-retail timber sales. (See Attachment 7)

- $50/month if sale department achieves 100% of monthly sales budget
- If the total year-end sales are achieved, this bonus will be paid for all months after March/99 (because of April/99 implementation date), where the sales budget was not achieved.

Shipping Quality

The shipping quality incentive is paid monthly for maintaining shipping accuracy. To qualify for this incentive no shipping errors, miss-shipped, short shipped or valid customer complaints can occur in the month. No problems found during the checklist review of each shipment.

- $75/month